The Problem of Evil

The *Problem* of *Evil*

ERIC GREENLEAF, PH.D.

ZEIG, TUCKER & THEISEN, INC.
PHOENIX, ARIZONA

Note: The names and other identifying characteristics have been changed to protect the anonymity of the persons mentioned.

Published by

ZEIG, TUCKER & THEISEN, INC.
3618 North 24th Street
Phoenix, AZ 85016

Book design by Kathleen Lake, Neuwirth & Associates, Inc.

Manufactured in the United States of America

10   9   8   7   6   5   4   3   2   1

In loving memory of Don Wood
Il miglior fabbro

Contents

Acknowledgments

This book has been a long time brewing. It, and I, have been nurtured, fed, loved, and supported by my wife, Lori, whose artistry transforms all that she touches.

My father, Peter, first showed me hypnosis, stretching a volunteer rigid between two chairs at summer camp. He taught me Shakespeare, and Gilbert and Sullivan songs, and the value of hard work. He encouraged my writing. I'm sad that he is not here to read this, my first book. My mother, Anne, has been fiercely loyal and caring and is the source of my strongest sentiments. In our household, my parents, my sister Tema, Grandma Bessie, and our extended family taught me, by demonstration, how tasty a stew humor, irony, passion, and theater can make.

My son, Tatian, has, from birth, shown me the virtues of calm focus, patient concentration, and thoroughgoing thinking. His fine ethical sense and strong friendships make me proud, and, in that pride, sustain my own efforts. And he can write.

My friends, some of 40 years, have been my rudder in the churning waters of adolescence, romance and losses, and the catastrophes of emotion, and they have loved and tolerated me beyond reason and in just the right amount. Their words have become my words; their hearts are within my heart.

Those I have treated, patient while I learned, have made my days rich with their stories and emotions. Each morning, starting very early, they allow me to share their lives. I could not wish for a better living in all its meanings: being alive, a means of earning, a manner of life.

As an author, claiming error and disclaiming praise for my work, I want to thank those of my teachers who educated both mind and spirit: Hannah Arendt, Norman O. Brown, Milton H. Erickson, Lawrence Kohlberg, Dora Venit, and Herbert Zucker.

Jeff Zeig, one of my first students of hypnotherapy, asked me to write a book for his new publishing house. I didn't know, but have been pleased to discover, that that house comes furnished with Suzi Tucker, an excellent editor who has had my pulse in hand from the first. I hope everyone enjoys reading what I have enjoyed writing.

Introduction

A few years ago, I was teaching hypnotherapy in Poland. On a rainy, cold summer day I went with my friend Krzysztof to see Auschwitz. With a young, English-speaking woman as a guide, we began at the iron gate of entry, formed in the words, "*Arbeit Macht Frei.*" We walked slowly behind our guide's measured steps, among clusters of schoolchildren on classroom trips, just as they visit Poland's castles, gardens, and churches. We followed the muddy way between the brick barracks that echoed the lives—and deaths—of the prisoners: workplaces, sleeping straw, toilets, punishment cells, gas chamber, crematorium. Each room offered some display: a glass wall revealed hundreds of suitcases, with the owners' names and cities marked in chalk; prostheses in piles; childrens' clothing; fabric woven from human hair; cans of poison gas. The artwork of prisoners depicted daily life.

Along tall narrow hallways, photographs of prisoners from the death camps and the earlier political prison hung in long rows. Our guide would stop to point toward a photo and tell us: "This man was a priest. This one was a schoolteacher. This woman was an engineer." She paused at the large maps in one room and, as she did at each pause in this slow, cold walk, looked directly at us and recited, with feeling, the text she had repeated so many times. She spoke of the numbers of men, women, and children murdered there, the nations from which they had come, and the cultures that had given them life.

I remember the harsh, low concrete of the gas chamber with ceiling holes to give the gas entry and the narrow cells for standing punishment and the barbed wire and the ghosts of screams and my own tears and anger. And I also remember Krzysztof's courage in coming again to that place as my companion. His uncle, a Catholic activist, had been brought there to die. I remember the face of our guide, her direct regard and her sadness as she told what had been done there, what had been suffered. It was that gaze that led to this writing, that resolve to do what can be done in the aftermath of the sweep of evil into lives: to feel compassion and to show it, to share emotion, to forestall or prevent, where that is possible, the acts of harm and violence. In her work as a translator, our guide helped us to understand, to feel, and to witness. In my work as a therapist, I hope to do for others what she did for me, as we walked along the muddy path.

In writing this book, I wanted to show how dealing with the problem of evil in people's lives affects the conduct and practices of psychotherapy, and influences the ways in which we think and talk about both psychotherapy and lives. The psychotherapy practices I describe have ancient roots and employ modern conventions. Throughout the world dream images and healing trances are used to deal with human pain and distress. Modern psychotherapy was born in Freud's work with hypnosis and dreams, and flowers in the work of Erickson, using trance and story to heal pain.

Like most of its practitioners, I was taught psychotherapy as a practice of empathy and compassion, its effect resting on an understanding of the patterns of lives, unjudging but authoritative. With the addition of Erickson's active, pragmatic, and allusive styles of communication and relationship, this became a starting point for treatment rather than its means. The stories of lives lived became points of intersection for effectively relating to those lives. These practices inform a narrative hypnotherapy: pragmatic, interpersonal, metaphorical, and story-filled.

This book begins with a dream of evil, the treatment of that dream—and an elucidation of that treatment. In this and other therapies, the limits of empathy and the complexity of influences on lives are limned. Other encounters with the influence of evil marked the development of the ideas and practices that inform treatment. In all these instances, I came up to my limits of expertise, reflection, and empathy. I was forced by pursuit of the goals set by caring to compose a "therapy of ignorance," guided by my connection with the other person.

Most of the troubles spoken of in this book are consequences of evil in the lives of those forced to experience pain, humiliation, and confusion at the hands of more powerful persons. Usually—and poignantly—these victims have been children hurt by their parents, sometimes on purpose and for the pleasure of the parents. But sometimes they have been adults and their tormentors torturers. And sometimes the victims of torture or fearful pain have tormented others. For individuals, evil may exist in the form of enacted imagery, as with sexual sadists; of the misuse of trance, heard in the negative voices that remind, direct, and afflict us; and of the betrayal of relationship and trust. This book is organized around cases dealing with the resolution of the consequences of evil.

Psychotherapy—treatment of the spirit—uses those same means of image, trance, and relationship that have been misused to do evil. We may use images to heal the nightmares of the injured, the sufferings of those left with the words, feelings, motives, and acts of their abusers ground into their persons like gravel embedded in wounds. We may utilize trance to help persons act on their own behalf, to focus and compose the self. Trance helps us to recollect the shards of self, hidden or splintered by evil, and to reach our goals of growth and experience. We may employ relationship to communicate, soothe, influence. The therapeutic relationship can separate and heal the painful adhesions brought about by empathy with the agents of torment, or complicity with their acts.

The goal of this book is to approach solutions to difficult human problems through modern psychotherapeutic practices. The problems and troubles are age-old and defy solution, and yet, in particular lives, there can be resolutions to these problems. Chapter 1, "Dreaming and Healing," shows how the ancient healing arts of dream and trance are used in modern, active therapies. The stories are of lives touched by evil or trauma. Therapeutic attention to individuality of experience, and its imagistic descriptors, is highlighted.

Along with individual relationship and therapy, we can also explore collective solutions to the more generic troubles. In modern psychotherapy, there is the developing tradition of the "reflecting team" (Anderson, 1991), the narrative practices of Epston and White (1990), and Erickson's (cited in Haley, 1973) innovative use of family and community in developing solutions. To those I will add a practice developed in my hypnotherapy training classes called "Passing the Trance." Examples of this collaborative search for solutions appear in the exercise, "The Problem of Evil." This approach, and that called "a problem in common," is an attempt to replace the distinction between helper and sufferer with the truer sense that we are all in this together.

The discussions in Chapter 2, "Difficult Therapy," detail relational approaches and dilemmas and their place in a comprehension of therapy and of therapists. The sections on "Utilization and Imagination" and

"The Person of the Therapist" bring the discussion back to Freud and Erickson, their notions of the unconscious mind and their different treatments of resistance and transference in the relationship between therapist and patient. The language of therapeutic communication and the language therapists use with each other are discussed here, as in "The Unconscious-Mind Metaphor," and later in "The Story Metaphor."

In this book, I have insisted that patients speak freely in their own words and that I and other therapists do the same. It is in this open conversation that relationship develops, and it is this relationship that can heal what a previous relationship has injured. Chapter 3, "Evil Influence," contains the writing of several persons about their own encounters with evil and the therapy that helped them recover from its effects. "The Unconscious-Mind Mirror," shows ways of active imagining applied to the sense of evil impulse within self-understanding.

"The eventfulness events can have or human actions can provoke" (Draenos, 1982, p. 155) are discussed in Chapter 4, "A Narrative of Images." A modern psychotherapy employs active relating, imagistic language, and the telling of stories by both therapist and patient. The ways in which a narrative hypnotherapy can be employed, and correlative notions of therapy, knowledge, power, and relationship, are discussed in this chapter.

In the first sections of this chapter, I consider types of explanation, distinguishing between scientific explanations and those of the social sciences and between causal and metaphorical language. I claim that the effectiveness of therapeutic conversation rests on stories that lead to social action, not on correct interpretations. As the philosopher A. E. Wengraf (personal communication, May 1, 1999) puts it, "I want to regard 'action to be explained' and 'agency to be gained' as different projects."

The matter of relationship entails considerations of communication, and so of language. A predilection for the common language and its richness of image informs all these conversations. Spontaneous story, enacted story, and collective story wind through this chapter, which ends with stories that develop the strong sense of self from individual images of distress and resolution.

Because the origins of problems and their sequence in lived experience are too complicated to explain, I have chosen to concentrate on solutions. Their elucidation is much simpler. After all, human competence must be available to all of us. Life must be simple enough for children to grasp and enact without self-consciousness. Damon's (1999) review of moral development reminds us that, "as far as psychologists know, children everywhere start life with caring feelings towards those close to them and adverse reactions to inhumane or unjust behavior" (p. 74). This idea may also be useful to therapists in practicing their art.

Finally, Chapter 5, "The Structure of Healing," takes up the ideas of Chapter 1, "Dreaming and Healing," and revisits them to develop connections between ancient ideas of suffering and healing and modern linguistic, philosophical, and scientific ones.

The work of ancient shamans and alchemists and that of modern psychologists and scientists are viewed through a common lens: images formed in the mind. We stand, as people always have, staring at our reflected image, fascinated and wondering. The use and misuse of ourselves, and the ways we understand and are conscious of ourselves, form the basis of questions for science, spirit, and mind. Throughout this book I have referred to certain favorite therapists and thinkers and attempted to be pointed rather than comprehensive. I discuss Freud on psychoanalysis, but not the modern intersubjective analytic thinkers; Erickson on psychotherapy, but not Satir; Wittgenstein in philosophy and Geertz in anthropology, but not Kant or Levi-Strauss; Feynman in science and Bruner in psychology. And I take these thinkers paradigmatically, as though they were scouts to ideas along broad or dim trails of thought. I've tried to keep in mind the maxim of Hannah Arendt that, "The really important things are very simple," along with her interest in those few thinkers who have invented new ideas that lead us into novel territories of thought and feeling.

The style of this discussion, like the style of narrative therapy, is not meant to be redundant, but, rather, to be recursive, a version of "retelling the retelling" (White, 1998): visiting common themes and turning them in different ways, showing them in different contexts and listening to them as sung by different voices. Throughout I am given to what Locke (cited in Geertz, 1983) called, "That wary reasoning from analogy [that] leads us often into the discovery of truths and useful productions which would otherwise lie concealed" (p. 24).

To readers wondering how to approach these materials and to learn from them, let me suggest that what I will say about therapy is heuristic: it ought to be tried on for size. If you viewed situations in this way, what would you do? How would you act? What would you say? And are these ways an aid, or at least some comfort, in rough weather? And did the person achieve what he or she came to you to achieve? Can everyone agree, no matter their therapeutic language, on the value of the therapy?

During my three decades of professional life, I've been concerned about and delighted with the range of human expression in language, and the utilization of language to heal or to harm. I've long been interested in the muscular and beguiling uses of language to evoke change and less interested in the uses of explanation to that end. This may reflect my early education with Norman O. Brown and my later training with Milton H. Erickson, or it may indicate the germination of a childhood wish to grow up to be either a ragman or a poet.

However it came about, after sitting with a thousand patients over days spent becalmed or swept by storms in the seas of feeling, I am offering up these ships' logs of a long voyage to strange and wonderful places. I'm thankful to the people I have met on these journeys.

Chapter 1

Dreaming and Healing

At the base of the southern slope of the Acropolis in Athens, on the site of a still more ancient spring, lie the ruins of the temple of Asklepios, physician and healer. This was where those for whom physical illness or soul sickness had persevered despite all human efforts at healing would repair to be treated by the gods. After a ritual cleansing, the sick person would lie on a couch in the innermost sanctuary, where the god of sleep, Hypnos, and the god of dreams, Oneiros, had their statues (Meier, 1989).

The treatment consisted of sleeping and dreaming until a dream occurred that healed the patient. Often this dream took the form of the god-physician, Asklepios, visiting the dreamer with advice or performing a sort of psychic surgery in the dream. Sometimes dreamers remained in the sanctuary until they had a dream similar to that of the priest who watched over them in their recovery. Then the dream was recorded, a fee paid, and the patient returned home.

Over the centuries, this basic architecture of clinical treatment for troubles of the body and soul—the soma and psyche—has remained, even

as the stones of the temples have crumbled. We can see the same arches
and columns in the modern practice of psychology and hypnosis, for
psychology is "knowledge of the soul" and hypnosis is "a condition like
sleep."

When Freud (1935) began his psychiatric practice, he said: "Anyone
who wants to make a living from the treatment of nervous patients must
clearly be able to do something to help them. My therapeutic arsenal contains only two weapons, electrotherapy and hypnotism" (p. 27). So Freud
would have his patients lie on a couch in the sanctuary of his office, surrounded by Freud's large collection of statues of the gods of Greece,
Rome, and Egypt. Upon that couch, in a relaxed and quiet state of mind,
his patients would remember their dreams and share them with the doctor. Although Freud later "gave up" hypnotism, he kept the couch, the
fee, the sanctuary of the office, the statues of the gods, and the telling of
dreams as a means of healing. And he held dreams to be "the royal road
to the unconscious."

Years after Freud, and on the path well worn by almost every therapist
since, I began working with dreams and hypnosis. It has seemed to me, in
these years of practice, that the names of therapies have changed, but
that, like so many fried-chicken franchises, they still put out the same
good, hot, spicy fare. The basic recipe seems to be unchanged: take a
human being who is troubled, sick, or scared, allow that person to focus
feelings, thoughts, skills, and energies until there is a healing dream,
vision, or surprising emotional event; record the dream; accept the fee;
and send the person back to ordinary life.

In the ancient temples, focusing was accomplished by gazing at a
statue of the god. In early hypnosis, this same effect was achieved by gazing at a pendulum or listening intently to the hypnotist's voice. Some
hypnotists enjoy having their patient gaze deeply into the hypnotist's
eyes. Then there develops in a patient a sort of "soft focus" or broad
attention; unhurried, relaxed, curious, and expectant. The patient's gaze
turns inward in a sort of inner search for resolution of his or her troubles, pain, or confusion. Sometimes hypnotists accompany this search
with their own words of help or comfort. As one of my patients said:
"You're talking to me, yet you're not talking to me. You're talking to all
of me. I like it!"

Do you, by turning inward, find more of you? Well, yes. And this
"more" is what hypnotists call the "unconscious mind." After all, our

hearts beat and our lungs breathe without much conscious planning, and our bodies digest and excrete and see and hear without conscious instructions. And this sort of thing also goes on during sleep, when we literally are unconscious. And so do learning, thinking, experiencing, and planning continue while we sleep. In dreams, this experimental, exploratory, and highly original thinking in images is said to be unconscious.

The notion of hypnotherapy is to help people, by focusing and searching inwardly, utilize all their learning and skills to resolve their problems, and to do so with the aid of unconscious learning and understanding. What scientists do when they "dream up" inventions and theories, what diplomats do when they "sleep on it" before solving problems of state, what athletes do when preparing for a match by "visualizing" the flight of the ball—this is the sort of thing that hypnotized patients do to apply themselves to difficult problems of living.

Hypnosis is based on respect for people as whole organisms, in all that complexity and unique experience that has made them who they are. It may be thought of as a state of mind that can imitate many of the original and useful actions of the mind, body, and spirit. In hypnotic trance, a person may experience reduced pain, heightened sensation, strong emotion, remembering and forgetting, imagining and creativity, and an enhanced sense of self. My work as a therapist consists of pointing people toward their capacities and the lessons they contain.

Patients come for hypnosis fearing that it involves "giving up your will" to another person, or being compelled to do embarrassing things, such as the antics that stage hypnotists demonstrate for the amusement of their audiences. The idea that the patients may grow to trust themselves more through hypnotic dreaming has not yet become part of their expectations. When it does, the surprise and delight they evince are very moving. The therapeutic method is a "true imagining" of the type first practiced in dream incubation in those ancient Greek temples. As Robert Hunter, lyricist for the Grateful Dead, has described it: "In the secret space of dreams, where I, dreaming, lay amazed."

Consider psychotherapy: Two or more persons sit in chairs in a room. Often, one lies on a couch or pillows. Gesture is generally confined, as is posture. Rarely are there integrated, complex actions involving the skeletal muscles, such as occur in sports, sex, war, adventure. There is talk, and the most generous range of emotion and thought and dramatic circumstance. Terror and joy are experienced intensely, but as things in the theater or at the movies, or in dreams or reverie. All therapies use the night dream and daydream and the odd spontaneous fantasy to promote their efforts.

While stressing the likeness the entire therapeutic encounter bears to dreaming, I also wish to insist on the important ways in which dreams are to be treated as situations in life. Dreams provide a picture of our life circumstances, and the dreams of therapy are often unresolved situations, interrupted by fear or anxiety. The "unfinished business," "fixation," "impasse," or "bind" of a given life is brought to the therapist's attention. He or she must guide the patient through the ambiguity and uncertainty that have brought that life's development to a halt. It is certain that the exposition of meaning or pattern in a person's life is salutary, but a type of exposition that promotes action or change is what is called for, not simply one of the several available psychological "interpretations."

In the situations that patients bring to therapy, it is not important that we try to determine what the situation "means" so long as we are capable of acting to resolve it. To accept the reality of the person's portrayal is crucial, in whatever form it is offered, and although this is easiest to describe when dealing with dreams, it applies to all disclosures: dream, play, play therapy, psychodrama, anecdotes, writing, film or tape. We treat the dream as a real circumstance requiring action, just as we recognize the dramatic imagination at work when we speak of "real life." In deciding, along with another person, what to do, it's simplest to identify a resolved situation both would value, a goal to work toward: bargaining with an adversary, binding a wound, sinking a putt, singing on key, reading a letter. The problem of comparative values is reduced in size by this approach to the dream as a life problem to solve by action. As Zucker (1967) put it, "Fewer meanings arise from direct experience as compared with the number available through cogitation."

Evil Voices

This dream, repetitive and frightening, was resolved in a single session, using image, trance, and relationship and guided by Erickson's approach to persons. Gina, a 25-year-old woman, volunteered to work with her dream before the audience at a large hypnotherapy conference:

Eric: Would you like to tell me a dream?

Gina: Okay. This is a dream that I had several years ago, and I've had the same dream several times. It starts out that I am sleeping in a bedroom in a house, and it's a wooden house with lots of windows, built right on the edge of a lake. Behind the lake are mountains, and they are across the lake from the house. It starts out in the bedroom of the house, and I am in bed. I don't know whether I am sleeping or awake, but there's a kind of message that says, "They are coming," and it is not a good thing that's coming. Then there are children's voices that I hear—not necessarily children's voices, but high-pitched voices—moving across the lake, and the sense to me is that they are evil voices. And then the thought is to say "The Lord's Prayer," and that if I say that, then the message is, "Relax and let them move through you." So then that kind of passes, and I get up and go out into the rest of the house where my childhood family is, standing by a window. I know that those voices will be coming again, and I try to tell them, and they won't listen to me. And that's kind of the point where it ends.

The first principle in this sort of work is to complete the dramatic action of the dream, using the person's own images and the structure of the dream itself as the imagined situation. The injunction to "complete the dramatic action" applies as well to life situations, dreams, imagined activities, and hallucinated or delusional understandings. Gina's dream is incomplete and unsettling and I want to know what happened next, as I would if we both were in that house with the big windows and she had said, "Oh! I had a dream of all these malevolent voices, and I know that they can pass through me, but I told my family and they wouldn't listen, and now I'm afraid they'll come again," and I asked, "Well, what happens?" as though she had told me the story and it was incomplete. The goal is to help the person successfully complete the experience.

Eric: What do you do then?

Gina: Then is when everything fades again, and the voices are coming again.

Eric: Now the voices start to come across the lake. What do you do?

"Image is psyche," said Jung (1968b) and the "reality of the psyche," expressed in dream and emotion, is treated in this work in the present tense, active voice.

Gina: I start to say "The Lord's Prayer" just to myself and to relax and let the voices move through me. It's like a physical relaxation—not to tense up. You know, you hear people say that if you could only figure out how to rearrange matter you could walk through a wall or walk through a door or something like that. So it's that kind of thing: rearranging my matter to make it loose enough to let something walk through it.

Eric: This is something that I've always wanted to know about, but I never have spoken to anybody who was really expert in this, as you seem to be. Can you *show me* what that's like: to rearrange your matter—to make it spacious enough for the voices to come through?

The simplest induction of trance consists of inviting someone to do what the person is already doing. This is a form of utilizing the person's expertise, his or her hard-won life's learning, to approach the resolution of difficult unsolved problems.

Gina: I have no idea in my waking life how to do that.

But, in her dream life, Gina does know how. The analogy that links hypnotic trance to dreaming sleep allows us to proceed. As she enacts the skill seen in the dream, she can experience trance.

Eric: Can I see an approximation of what I will see when you can do that, when your body is relaxed enough . . . (*She uncrosses her legs, closes her eyes.*). . . . that's right. . . . so that everything kind of rearranges? And you know there are too many cells and parts of the body to tell each one exactly, "Well now you go a quarter of an inch this way, and you do that. . . . ." That's right, I see that. Show me what else I'll see on your face when you are rearranging. . . . (*Pause.*) And when you've reached the point at which everything is rearranged completely. . . . That's right. . . . And the voices come closer and closer, and they blow right through. . . . and then

I guess they go on their way. . . . I imagine it's a good idea to keep your body in this rearrangement for a good long time. And I wonder if you'd tell me what you notice as you do this, after the voices kind of blow through and go on their way, and you don't have to concern yourself too much about where they are headed.

Gina: It feels limp. (*Long pause.*) And quiet. It's like relief, or release. Then, a worry—maybe that it comes back again.

Eric: This is a very difficult thing to do. Can you practice arranging your body this way until it knows the practiced arrangement by heart, like the way you practice the piano until you know the scales and you don't have to think where to begin. (*Long pause.*) Tell me when you've done that sufficiently that you are quite well practiced. {*She nods.*} Good. Do you notice anything particular about your emotions now that you have done this so successfully?

Gina: I feel like I'm floating. I guess that's calm.

Eric: And can you enjoy other emotions while you're floating like this, like sorrow or happiness or curiosity or love or whimsy?

Gina: It's a little bit harder. It's kind of heavy, like I'm not moving really easily.

Eric: Would you like the opportunity to move more easily so that your body can arrange itself correctly in all kinds of different postures and motions? Okay. Suppose you just let your fingertips start to dance, or your toes start to dance, or your eyes start to dance. . . . That's right. . . . (*Her fingers begin to move.*) And what do you notice while you do that?

Gina: It feels light, a little more energetic.

The experience of calmly focused attention, of rapport with a sympathetic other, of the freedom to experience spontaneously, of "lightness, energy, floating, and quiet" form Gina's developing trance. Now we turn to the difficult matter of helping the family to listen to Gina. Here, as in other instances of therapy, I am happy to relate to the person *within* the structure of the dream image.

Eric: Yeah. In fact, when you hit a rhythm that you like, I'm sure you'll be quite energized. Now, is the central room in your house the best place for us to meet, or is there another place in the house you prefer?

Gina: There's the full-length window that looks out over the lake at the mountain.

Eric: Is there anyone that they (your family) are liable to listen to about the best way to handle those sort of evil, intrusive voices? Is there anybody who would have enough authority to kind of make them follow a prescription?

Gina: They don't listen very well.

Eric: Mmm. (*Rueful sound.*) It's true. Is there anybody at all that your dad or mom respects in this life, anyone that you can think of, like a relative or a public figure?

Gina: (*Long pause.*) Someone from the past. . . . I don't know that they respect this person any more, but they used to. He's a minister of their church.

Eric: Okay. Just on the off-chance that they might listen to that sort of authority, if it's okay with you, I'll leave a little note in the house, sort of in the capacity of an itinerant preacher, someone to say that there's a method of dealing with these kinds of maligning and malevolent and difficult and dangerous voices, and that it involves a certain bodily relaxation and a certain rhythmic kind of rearrangement of the body. If it's okay, I'll just leave it in a kind of letter to them. Would that be all right? I don't think you should have the job of convincing them to do what is obviously so important to do.

In an ideal world, if you had such a good sense of what to do, as Gina has, there should be a way to encourage others, especially family members, to listen. And if a guest were in the house, maybe he or she could get that to happen. But Gina was convincing in saying that they wouldn't listen to anybody, and I wanted them to listen. So I said, "Well, I'll leave instructions, I'll leave a letter. Maybe they will listen sometime." Gina, discussing the work afterwards, agreed: "Well, that actually ended up being a good thing, because I think that's the thing I always think about, that some day they will be ready to hear that. So that was kind of right, leaving something for them to find."

The more modalities of experience we can engage in meeting Gina's goals, the better. To body sensation, movement, emotion, thought, and relationship we can add the very powerful notion of "the unconscious mind," which can also be influenced to help, which can also listen.

Eric: As you breathe comfortably now. . . . and really learn this feeling thoroughly so it becomes entirely yours, so that every arrangement suits you, every movement is strong and pleasing, the rhythms are right, and even the movement of your breath has just the right spaciousness to allow trouble to breeze through it . . . You probably know that as your body rearranges, so does your mind. And that you can begin perhaps to feel or see that spaciousness when you look forward or look back in your mind. . . . That's right. . . . And one other thing: I don't know if you know this, but as your conscious mind gets more spacious and orderly and you practice your body's being more rhythmic and organized in this way, there is something else important that occurs.

Everybody knows that your unconscious mind makes ideas and thoughts and feelings pop into your conscious mind—sometimes funny ideas, sometimes charming ones. And you also know that your unconscious mind arranges things in your body while you sleep deeply and comfortably at night. But you may not have known that the kind of practice you are doing now also helps rearrange your unconscious mind and makes your unconscious mind more spacious and better organized. Were you aware of that? (*Gina nods.*) Yeah. And then what do you notice as that happens?

Gina: *That it doesn't hurt. My body doesn't hurt.*

Eric: I'm so pleased and relieved to hear that and to notice that. What else do you notice?

Gina: It's like standing on top of a mountain looking all around you, turning around and looking. I can see a long way. I can see the water below and other hills or mountains below it, and it's a clear day.

Eric: It sounds beautiful up there. What do you feel like doing while you're standing there?

Gina: Flying off the edge.

Eric: Uh-huh. Have you got wings or a parachute?

Gina: (*Laughs.*) It feels like it.

A principle of this work is to use common sense to identify what must be done in imagination. Discussion with the therapist is a catalyst that allows useful decisions about action to replace catastrophe in carrying forth the dream. There's an old alchemical idea about active imagining in which it is referred to as *"phantasia vera et non phantastica"* (Jung 1968a). This is "true" imagining, not fantasy: emotional reality exists in these images—they are pictures of what we experience. And I have this odd impulse to make it real, to do only real things in the dream. If you think you can fly off a building, I get worried. But If you are *just* dreaming or fantasizing, then it's fine to fly. Some who work with active dreaming would want to say to Gina, "Oh, we'll cast a spell over your parents, and that will open their ears," and so on. I want it to be real, to involve real feeling, decision, and action.

Eric: Hmmm. Tell you what: Heights make me real nervous, but suppose you stand there and close your eyes and just dream about flying off the mountain, so that you can be safely on top and still soar and fly. Would that be all right? And fly as high, as far, as wide as you wish or can even imagine. (*Long pause.*) As you do, would you like to say what you see and what you feel?

Gina: When the bird caught the wind, it didn't have to work to keep flying. Flying didn't tire it out, the wind just carried it. It could stay up a long time like that.

Eric: Yeah. And you can feel that, can you not? It's the kind of feeling that stays with you a long, long time. (*Pause.*) What's the sound like up there?

Gina: Like wind in the trees or water rushing—like that.

Now we are revisiting the sound, which was so frightening in its original form. A kind of conservation of imagery informs this work, an attempt to relate to each major element of the dramatic structure of the dream and to engage it in the construction of a resolution.

Eric: It's the most natural sound in the world, isn't it? Sort of like the sound of all of nature's energy: It's not good or bad, it's just roaring and raging.

Gina: Yeah. It's a sound, but it's a quiet sound because it's constant.

Eric: What do you feel like doing?

Gina: I'm just kind of exhilarated. I just want to go everywhere, look at everything. Fly out over—if there is an ocean there—an ocean. (*Pause.*) It feels kind of like energy but quiet at the same time. . . .

like at the center when there is centrifugal force: It's spinning around, but that's how it holds still. It makes sense. *Finally, all the opposites make sense.* It's not like that the rest of the time.

Eric: Yeah, although you might be surprised to find that no matter where you are, this feeling is there in the background, the same way the air is, or the same way that lovely sound is there in the background whether we pay attention to it or not. (*Pause.*) When you're ready, you might like to land, and when you feel your feet on the ground, you can open your eyes if you like. (*Pause. Gina opens her eyes and smiles.*) How do you feel?

Gina: Okay. A little bit disoriented. I guess that's something that comes again and again to people in life. It's kind of like waves that are going to come back, and I guess I already knew that I knew how to deal with that. I guess the disturbing part of that dream to me was not feeling unable to deal with the evil voices but the fact that even though I knew how to deal with them, the dream still had a frightening cast to it. This has obviously taken that away because after the fright was taken out of that one experience, it didn't seem like it would come back. I tend to have dreams over and over, and that was one that kept bugging me. It doesn't bug me any more.

To complete the work, there will be a bit more practice so that this ability, a confident, practiced skill, like playing the piano, comes to take the place of the inability, fear, and helpless repetition that characterized Gina's experience in the original dream.

Eric: Now, just to show that you can do it, if you'd take a deep breath, close your eyes for about a minute, and rearrange your body the same way you did. Just so you know you can really, really, really do that. (*Pause. She closes her eyes, relaxes.*) And when your body feels just right inside, and then you open your eyes again, it can stay in that pleasing, energetic, and easy place, yes? Good.

Gina: (*Opens her eyes and smiles*) You didn't know when you mentioned playing the piano that I have played the piano for many years, so when you said that, it triggered all this other wonderful stuff. It was wonderful. Thank you.

Eric: Oh, you're welcome. I'm so pleased.

Working with Dreams

*Feelings, discriminations and dispositions and consciousness and all
such things should be thought of in the same way as material form.*

—*(Nagarjuna 1995)*

Especially in our culture, the experience of having something private,
intimate, and inaccessible to others, like a dream, becoming public, com-
munal, and accepted is both exhilarating and puzzling. What puzzles is
that dreams, unlike other intimate communications, are unlikely to meet
with criticism, ridicule, or shocked surprise when told to relative
strangers. People no sooner would call another's dream foolish than they
would say that having brown eyes is foolish.

It is possible to give adequate suggestions based on simple action
potentials in the dream situation, and these dream actions can be pursued
according to shared values for acting, even though shared symbolic
meanings are unavailable. Although the meanings of our dreams often
are not obvious and the "translation" process is difficult to describe,
what should to be done to follow through with a fearful dream is available to all. No matter what sophistication may be brought to directing
imagination, the processes of inference that relate to suggested actions are
often quite naive, and yet yield powerful results.

Another aspect to consider is that dreams have the same structure as
symptoms, they hide and reveal elements of meaning at the same time
and employ similar "condensing and obscuring devices" (Erickson 1964).
This is scarcely a new observation, yet it contains interesting corollaries,
one of which is the insulation of the dream against criticism. This parallels quite closely, I think, the inaccessibility of the symptom to "reason"
or critique: a man attempting to criticize his wife's immobilizing
headaches that make intercourse impossible for her, a woman attempting
to criticize her husband's inability to work because of low back pain, the
immense squandering of reasons in fruitless attempts to overcome phobic
reactions, ridicule directed at self-confining compulsions, all of these situations indicate the frustration of "reason" in the face of symptoms. Also,
both symptoms and dreams may contain "hidden meanings" repellent to
the conscious minds of others and shameful to the person who exhibits

them. Yet each may be easily disowned as "just a dream" or as "out of my control."

A crucial difference between dreams and symptoms, however, is that they have different social outcomes. The symptom, when exhibited, yields frustration and personal distance; the dream, when told, provides intimacy with others and high regard. Whereas symptoms encapsulate fearful events or predispositions, the working through of dreams overcomes that fear, using similar unconscious structures and with a similar disregard for the meanings of reported events, save as they signal the need for actions. The use of similar structures leads to different and mutually satisfying outcomes in the absence of conscious appreciation of the meaning of the contents of behavioral sequences: dreams, symptoms, emotions, and social actions.

In the following, I describe some guiding principles of this work of active imagining. Throughout I refer to *dreams*, which I take to mean all imaginations. Singer (1974) calls these mental representations "oneiric" events, "from those of sleep through daydreaming and waking imaginative thought under conditions of reduced arousal or relaxation." *Active imagining* will refer to dreaming guided by oneself or another person, while one is relaxed and alert.

Dream Action and Dream Meanings

The most valuable part of the dream philosophy presented that I can use and assimilate in my own life is the idea of noninterpretation. All that is needed to resolve a situation is at hand. This makes for action instead of intellectualization. The meanings aren't hidden. The dream action is generally simple and straightforward—often deceptively so.

I had an elaborate dream with four or five people chasing me and I was very uncomfortable. When I awakened I could project all sorts of sexual and social implications into "being chased." But the next morning I had a sequel dream, or rather a summation dream, and the "meaning" this time was, "Don't get ahead of yourself." The idea of not getting ahead of myself because it makes me uncomfortable is a useful idea in my life. It carries no confusion or guilt or other baggage with it.—Student in a "dream group." (Greenleaf, 1973, p. 218)

As the student's dream of "being chased" makes plain, meaning that leads to meaningful action is called for by the dream, as it is in life. The dream and active imagining of a patient in analytical psychotherapy elucidate this.

A year or two ago, I dreamed of a gigantic, sheer granite mountain, an overpowering mass, its ruggedness towering above the valley beneath, thrusting its tremendous spires into the sky. I was on a wide ledge of this mountain, so far up that the trees of the orchard below flowed together. I desperately wanted to get off that ledge, away from that threatening, cold grayness, but could find no way although I searched and searched. Finally, I saw an old white-bearded Chinese man sitting at a table near the edge of the ledge. I went to him and told him I wanted to get down the mountain but could find no way. I asked if he would help me. He took my by the hand and led me to a path.

[The patient comments: Again the dream wasn't saying anything. Where was the hint from the unconscious? The archetype of the "old, wise man" was a familiar one in my dreams, but this time he was too inscrutable. The dream was so vivid, so real, that I felt it had an importance for me that I had better not ignore. So I decided to converse with him in active imagination.]

I asked him what he had to say to me. He went and sat at a table on the cliff. So, I went to him and told him, as in the dream, that I needed help to get down. He went to the back of the ledge and wrote on the face of the mountain and stepped back. He had written in Chinese characters and I can't read Chinese. I didn't know what to do. He knew I didn't read Chinese! Being desperate, I went to him again and told him I couldn't read his message, and he told me I could learn. Feeling both a little scared and a little angry—what kind of old wise man is this?—I said to him: "I don't have time lo learn Chinese now. I need to get down off this mountain. Will you help me?" He stood, and looking very directly at me, said, "Sometimes we have to ask more than once," took my hand, and led me to the path.

The first therapeutic task is to attend to the patient's wants and concerns, especially to statements of agency ("I desperately wanted to get off that ledge"). These set the goals of the therapy. The next task is to utilize the person's own competence to allow change to occur. Taking the simple instance of the dream, the patients was asked to use her own feet to walk down the path, first one foot, then the other. She was told, "Let me know if anything difficult or interesting happens." This statement allows both the intensity of focus and the possibility of rapport with a guide or therapist that move the work along. It also sets a rule for interchange between the dreamer and her guide somewhat like the rule followed in close friendship or adequate parenting: Relationship is mandatory for novel, compelling, and delightful events, and also for events that call forth dilemmas or problems. At other times, we explore on our own.

Following the suggestion to begin walking on the path, the patient was able to come to the valley, and then to a city, and no longer was on the threatening, cold ledge. Still, such is the seductiveness of ideas, she might have stayed there indefinitely, badgering the old man for his "wisdom" and neglecting to set her own feet in motion, had she not been requested to do this. This "resistance" or "rationalizing" was overcome with a nudge, not by explanation. Milton Erickson's (1980) lifelong work is a testament to the utilization of small actions that breed small but expanding changes in large systems of human interaction.

Even with intriguing or complex dreams, it is usually possible to translate the dream material into a coherent situation and to suggest action appropriate to that situation. These dreams are often nonobvious in meaning, and the translation process is difficult to describe. In the dream that follows, for example, I had the sense of something hidden that must be found, and this intuition informed the suggested action. Cora's dream follows:

> I had gone to visit a friend, Jean, who was to be married. I was to be her only attendant. I entered Jean's home, a very large, stately house. She was excited about her marriage and explained, too, that in the spring she would be 21 and receive her inheritance. Jean then gave me a ring identical to the one she wore. We climbed a narrow spiral staircase, one complete revolution, to the chapel. Over the altar hung three heads of animals. End of dream.

Cora was asked to complete the dream as a waking imagining, and she saw Jean, but was distressed to find no groom. "The bride and I at times seemed to be one and the same." Suggestions to read a book lying on the altar led to "many rapidly changing and very overwhelming emotions":

I then turned around, and saw Jean standing next to her boyfriend. I, being the only attendant, married them. I then went to the left side of the altar and looked in my new handbag (this having been suggested) and took out a crystal necklace—a rosary. I put it on. When putting on the necklace, it momentarily became a crown of thorns. Wearing the necklace, I experienced joy.

Cora later revealed that this dreamwork had freed her from a painful and anxious identification with a martyred saint, which had held her since childhood. The implied question used to form suggestions for continuing the dream was: Something is missing, incomplete. Where can it be found? Then, when given a present, put it on, and see how you feel wearing it. Thus, it was possible to give adequate suggestions based on simple action potentials in the dream situations that could be pursued according to shared values for action (try on a necklace received as a gift), even though shared symbolic meanings were unavailable or undeveloped.

The first principle in this type of work, then, is to complete the dramatic action of the dream, using the person's own images. This may be done in some organized fashion, as with Senoi dreamwork (Greenleaf, 1973; Stewart, 1951), or it may use the structure of the dream itself as the imagined situation. The injunction to "complete the dramatic action" applies as well to life situations, dreams, imagined activities, and hallucinated or delusional understandings. The second principle must be to use the common sense of valued actions to identify what must be done. One must not attempt to fly from the cold ledge without wings. Murder and death are subject to severe constraint in active imagining, as in life. Discussion with the interior guide or the therapist allows useful decisions about action to replace catastrophe in carrying out the dream.

Human Competence

The (therapist) is . . . a serious student of practical aspects
of human personality and living.

—H. S. Sullivan (1954b)

Although psychotherapies originated in attempts to deal with human suffering and ineptitude and the literature of therapy is a record of these sufferings, there are also many examples of the way people function at the heights of human achievement. These ought to guide us. The briefest glance at the most brilliant of athletes, musicians, or scientists shows their persistence, their ability to act while in pain or discomfort, their steadfastness when fearful, and, most important for our own work, their reliance on mental rehearsal using images.

When Mark McGwire was shown on TV, standing in the batter's box waiting to hit what would be the record home run, he seemed to be asleep, his body slumped and his eyes closed. "He's visualizing his turn at bat," said the commentator. Many professional golfers won't putt until they can see the ball enter the cup in a mental rehearsal of the next stroke. Jack Nicklaus (Nicklaus & Bowden, 1974) describes it as "going to the movies."

> *I never hit a shot, not even in practice, without having a sharp, in-focus picture of it in my head. It's like a color movie. First, I "see" the ball where I want it to finish . . . Then I "see" the ball going there: its path, trajectory and shape, even its behavior on landing. Then the next scene shows me making the kind of swing that will turn the previous images into reality.*

Musicians and writers also employ visual imagery in their art. Consider Rostropovich, speaking of Prokofiev:

> *Very often he treated musical instruments as if they were living beings. For example, slow, low notes on the tuba made him think a beetle was sitting in the note. With great pleasure he would listen to the beetle climbing from one note to another. (Staff, 1979)*

Shepard (1978) quotes the writer Joan Didion as saying that plot, character, and incident in her novels develop out of "pictures in my mind," as do the syntax and order of words: "The arrangement you want can be found in the picture in your mind." He notes that Coleridge said of writing "Kubla Khan" that "all of the images rose up before him as things" (p. 127). Miller (1984) writes that Mozart's auditory imagery permitted him to hear a new symphony all at once, and Henri Poincare's "sensual imagery" led him to sense a mathematical proof in its entirety "at a glance" (p. 221).

Mathematics, thought to be the most abstract of the sciences, also is practiced with mental images. Ken Ribet (cited in "The long way round to Fermat, 1998) describes working on Taniyama's Conjecture, a difficult way station toward the proof of Fermat's Last Theorem: "When you're doing work like this, you tend to see fuzzy bits, out-of-focus images of things like these curves. It's another way to think about these complex things." Another mathematician, working in topology, had dreams each night of changing shapes in a crystal garden. When he awakened he would write down the formulas. Arendt (1959) reminds us that Plato used the term *eidos*, "the mental image, or rather the image seen by the inner eye," to refer to the mental objects we call *ideas*.

"With the help of certain [imaginary] physical experiments . . . ," Einstein (cited in Miller, 1984) wrote in his famous 1905 paper, he could picture relativity theory as a set of everyday events, such as watching a train pass by. Words or formulas were a second stage of thinking for him, as "I very rarely think in words at all" (p. 86). Because of his predominantly visual mode of thinking, he said he could "wonder quite spontaneously about some experience that comes into conflict with a world of percepts which is sufficiently fixed within us."

The physicist Heisenberg (cited in Miller, 1984), discoverer of the Uncertainty Principle in particle physics, described his thought process this way:

> So first one has what one may call an impression of how things are connected ("a picture") and from this impression you may guess, but you have a good chance to guess the correct things. . . . The picture changes over and over again and it's so nice to see how such pictures change. (p. 248)

Nikola Tesla designed complex electric motors while consciously thinking of other things. Miller (1984) says, "The wonderfully eccentric Tesla delighted in recounting that once having designed a motor mentally, three weeks later he would return to the still running motor and mentally check the parts for wear" (p. 262).

The famous instances of discovery in dreams, like Kekule's grasp of the structure of the benzene ring, can be multiplied by countless instances from the waking thought of competent persons. Since we hope to encourage people to use their own power and competence in living, we might show them the availability of the methods of competent thought and action in the commonplace activities of their lives, the most ordinary of which may be said to be dreams and daydreams. What one can do at work, say, by way of interacting with others and persisting against difficulty to solve problems, is applicable to problems at home in nonobvious ways. Erickson (Haley, 1967) is the best guide to ways of aiding people to bring existing competencies from one segment of experience to help resolve dilemmas in another part of life. Again, the examples of grace and intense concentration afforded by athletes and performers are excellent guides to the pursuit of ordinary human competence. Julius Erving ("The sky's the limit," 1997) said, after a magical basketball performance:

> *I dream about flying a lot. I just find myself floating out in space as if I had wings. I stay up a lot longer when I'm dreaming. I go sideways, backwards, do somersaults . . . It's a fun way to sleep. Sometimes your dreams just seem so real. After you understand the fundamentals of the game, the artistry and creativity come from dreams and experimentation.*

To really "see" and "do" the necessary action in continuing the dream allows access to spontaneity and to the "unconscious mind." The nasty harpies of interpretation can be silenced here, as they are for most of us while watching a play or when playing. So, using dreams and emphasizing acting in the dreams, in continuing the dreams, the therapist propels a patient through the impasse that occurs with fear or anxiety. Then "superfluous tension" disappears and natural emotions arise, and this happens without a great deal of conscious understanding of "meanings," but with agreements to act (in imagination) in certain ways. The parallels with other techniques, such as hypnosis, are obvious if, with T. X. Barber (Barber & Spanos, 1974), we note that hypnotic subjects "respond overtly and experientially to suggestions when they become involved in imaginings. Actively imagining those things that are suggested . . . precludes the possibility of simultaneously focusing on information that is inconsistent with the suggestions." Erickson (cited in Haley, 1967) put it this way:

> *The technique (of hypnosis) in itself serves no other purpose than that of securing and fixating the patient's attention. . . . There is then the opportunity to proffer suggestions and instructions serving to aid and to direct the person in achieving the desired goal or goals.*

Singer's (1974) use of the term "oneiric" includes the relaxation characteristic of states of attention and ease that the therapist, collaborating
with the patient to meet his or her needs and goals, promotes by dealing
with images. Cognitive-behavioral techniques, transactional analysis
rescripting, Gestalt dialogue, hypnotherapy, narrative therapy, and bedtime storytelling all partake of this therapeutic control over anxiety and
the safety provided by a guide to utilize imaginings or dreams by way of
helping persons in fearful situations.

Realism in Dreamwork

*The analyst may well learn from ordinary life and be guided by it. It
is astonishing to see how difficult this can be for analysts.*

—A. Guggenbuhl-Craig (1970)

The patient's involvement in his or her work and experience is held to
be crucial to change, of both emotion and behavior. The involvement of
the therapist is equally crucial, and disjunctions in involvement between
the two are evident in the patronizing, "educative" tone assumed by some
therapists, a tone that may be particularly evident when the "real meanings" of events are discussed. By comparison, complete sympathy with
the reality of emotions, thoughts, and dreams—life brought into the consulting room—often translates into some concept and experience on the
part of the patient of respect for his or her own life.

The heuristic value of this stance is evident in our dealings with the
more obtuse twists of experience—hallucinations, inchoate emotions,
uncanny dissociations of consciousness. A work of psychotherapy on
which Greenleaf and McCartney (1975) collaborated will bring this issue
into better focus, as well as indicate the interaction of hypnotic techniques, visualization, and dreamwork with human relating in the
methodologies of psychotherapy.

The theoretical orientation for this sort of work developed from the
confluence of streams originating in the family therapies, hypnotherapy,
and Jungian psychotherapy. Here I'll again summarize the assumptions
that developed out of such work so that the reader may pick a path
among the hills on the therapeutic landscape:

The therapist assumes that the dreams, daydreams, fantasies, and mental images brought to psychotherapy provide a view in visual symbols of an unresolved relationship situation in the patient's life. These "oneiric" events can be guided by the therapist while the patient attains a state of relaxed alertness similar to that of hypnosis.

The therapist suggests imagined actions appropriate to the reality of the dream situation in an attempt to complete the dramatic action of the dream sequence, using the patient's own images and the common sense of what is to be done in difficult circumstances to guide the action. Examples of human competence in action and emotion in ordinary life, what Sullivan (1954b) calls "practical aspects of human personality and living," provide guidance to the therapist.

The therapist is encouraged to pay attention to the patient's wants, concerns, and statements of agency and to alert the patient to the uses of his or her own competencies in allowing change to occur. I assume that small changes in action (here induced in mental images) yield expanding changes in systems of human interaction. Mental rehearsal of dialogue or activity affects the system of internal representation that maps relationships. Whether these relationships are conceived of as introjections from early family life, as systems of emotions and cognitions, as archetypes of the collective unconscious, or in some other manner does not affect the systems view as I employ it for this work. We need only assume a homology between the relationships of consequence and their representation as mental images. Then the conservation of images implied in our utilization of the patient's own representation and drama ensures that the therapeutic method is applied over the range of overdetermined meanings embedded in the dream images.

Meanings are affected by this method, and so are conscious thoughts, emotions, memories, and interpersonal relationships. We may also expect to see correlative changes in action and competencies expressed outside the consulting room, as in Lorraine McCartney's (Greenleaf & McCartney, 1975) story.

A Wicked Witch

We met once each month from February to July 1972, each time spending from two to four hours together. Lorraine, a lively woman in her mid-20s, entered the sessions with me in order to clarify her feelings about a complex interpersonal relationship. The first seven hours of our work concerned this relationship. The final 11 hours of psychotherapy and Lorraine's continued work with herself are described in the journals and letters she provided.

In the text that follows, dated excerpts from a diary kept by Lorraine during our meetings are followed by my comments.

May 9, 1972

This was the day I became aware of my other me. My friend Eric Greenleaf helped us today. The session started with my being very anxious—twisting my hands together, looking back and forth, on the verge of crying. I told him my dream.

The Dream: I am with Al, my ex-husband, outdoors somewhere. I ask him, "How are you?" and he says, "I'm fine, but I'm worried about Laura. She's driving me crazy. She's been sick, and she gets on the microphone at camp and says, 'ffffff,' and she never does her work. Last night I was up until four trying to get her work and mine done." We have a huge argument over the name of what's wrong with Laura. I try to tell him it's "reflective repression," because some- one told me that and I half believe it. Then, all of a sudden, on the loudspeaker near me I hear Laura's voice, "fffffffft," and then this horrible, horrible scream that I can't understand. I look at Al and say, "Go to her, help her!" because I realize she's insane and letting every- body know it. And he doesn't understand anything. He just looks puzzled. Then there's another horrible scream that I can understand. It says, "Come quick! Cat's sick!" in a terribly frightened, panicked, sick voice.

When I wrote the dream down, the voice scared me, and I cried. About a week later I told Martha the dream. When I came to the part about the voice I surprised myself and the scream come hurtling out of my guts. Uncontrollably. Then I sobbed and sobbed.

Lorraine said that she felt that the dream was related to fear of witch-craft and cats, and of being possessed, and also to feelings of "devasta-tion" when she unknowingly hurt someone. Her journal for that day continues:

> *And I told him all these things bang-bang-bang and said that somehow they're all related. I know they are, but I don't know how. And Eric said, well, he didn't know either, but he knew a place we could start working, and it would be to work with the dream and did I want to do it? So I said, "Yes," and he asked me about Laura. I told him how mostly for me she's been a person who just reminds me of me. And then he asked me to go to Laura, since Al couldn't go to her: to go to Laura and help her.*

Several important ideas that guide this sort of therapeutic work are evi-dent here: the substitution of action for explanation, treating dream fig-ures as one would treat persons in real life, utilizing the patient's own abilities to help her resolve her difficulties in living. From the hypnotic repertoire come the therapist's mood of expectation and ease in promot-ing improbable events in seemingly ordinary ways and attentiveness to the strategic situation, in answer to the question, "What can be done here?"

> *I closed my eyes and relaxed. I went to Laura—she was bent over a kitten, crying. I asked her how I could help her, what was wrong. I had a couple of false starts like, "Well, I think she says . . ." and Eric said, "Wait a minute. Don't tell me what you think she says. Just let it come, and when it comes, it might take 20 minutes, that's O.K."*

Hypnotic experience leads the therapist to encourage a person to do what she or he is already doing, in order to promote change and utilize "resistance". When fear leads Lorraine to delay, she is told to delay for as long as 20 minutes and to reduce her fear through "relaxation."

> *So I relaxed for a really long time. Then I started to talk to Laura and I said things like, "Please tell me what's wrong. How can I help you?" And she refused to answer me. At last I realized I was the one who needed help. Then I said to her, "Laura, I need your help. I really need you to tell me what's wrong."*

*Suddenly, <u>she</u> said, "I never thought of myself as a helpful per-
son—no, not at all." And she has a New Zealand accent and talks in
a very cynical way. And Eric asked her about the cat, and she started
to scream and laugh, loudly and wildly, and lash about. Finally she
collapsed back into the chair exhausted, her arms hanging over the
sides, her head back, breathing hard.*

Those readers who saw "The Wizard of Oz" while still children will
recall the piercing laugh and horrid scream of the "Wicked Witch of the
West." The scream that welled forth from Lorraine was *that* scream, and
the immediate effect on me was the same as that on the six-year-old who
first heard it, except that this time I couldn't hide.

*Eric talked to her for about two hours and it was like I was there
and I heard everything and sometimes I knew what she was going to
say, and sometimes I didn't. Eric kept trying to find out from her
what happened to that cat, and she just couldn't or wouldn't say. She
laughed at him, teased, insulted. A couple of times she tried to bribe
him by asking him if he liked to talk to her. But he was good to her,
honest and warm. He said it would help her if she would share that
information, because obviously it was hurting her. And she told Eric
that it was her secret and it made her strong, and Eric said, "Yeah,
it's about as useful to you as a stomach ache, cause you screamed in
Lorraine's dream so you must want out. You must want out." And
she talked about how Lorraine is on the outside and she is on the
inside.*

I began to notice that this difficult woman who had suddenly appeared
in place of my earnest, shy, humorous patient, that this dreadful person
with stiff mannerisms, a different voice quality and accent, different posture, opinions, ethics, style, and personality—was herself frightened,
proud, stubborn, and very lonely. I acted toward her with wary sympathy.

*She's very different from me. It's like she's another person—she's
all the things that I never am. Like when I'm scared and need help I
don't mind asking for it. I cry easily. But she would never ask for
help. When Eric told her it would be good for her to get rid of her
stomach ache she just laughed. She doesn't back down. She's always*

in control. Eric said it was like talking to someone who's been bul-
lied. If you've been bullied, you learn that if you show your weak-
ness, people will pounce on it, so you don't show your weakness,
even to yourself. And she's like that.

And she screamed at Eric and she hates Lorraine. And the whole
time I talked to him, she talked to him. I had my eyes closed and he
gave me a few suggestions. Like, he asked Laura—he called her
Laura—he said, "Laura is your dream name, but will you tell me
your real name?" And she fooled around and fooled around for a
long time and finally said, "You could call me Irene." And Eric said
"No. I want your real name." And it wasn't until he said that that I
realized—Lorraine realized—that whoever she is was trying to fool
him. And he keeps not being fooled. And she really wouldn't tell him
her name and so he said, well, later she would. Then he said, "Tell me
what happened to the kitten." She refused, showed anxiety. He said,
"I will blow my nose, and while I do, you will mouth the words.
Then I'll stretch and you'll whisper the words. Then I'll listen and
you'll tell me the words." As he did what he said he would, she
mouthed, whispered, and screamed gibberish. And she raised her
hand slowly, not speaking. Her hand dropped gradually. Eric said,
"I'll talk to you much more again, but as you're leaving, and Lor-
raine's coming back, I'm going to take your hand. And I'm going to
hold your hand." And whatever-her-name-is made a face, like
"Ohaww, it'll just kill me if you do." But he did, and it didn't kill
me—or her.

This half-baked attempt to secure repressed information through suggested approximations failed, but the interpersonal effects of *failing* to
secure the information were significant: I did what I said I would. She
could trust my words. Laura did what I said *she* would. I could Influence
her. Laura withheld the information I seemed to consider important. I
held the signal that could make her leave, or arrive. This signal, constructed from her own gestures, led to my firm suggestion that I was
going to hold her hand. And, perhaps most important for the future of
the therapy, Laura had to accept human warmth from me.

So then Lorraine come back. I opened my eyes as he called my
name and he asked me if I knew what had gone on. And I said yes, I

did, but I felt sick and I felt exhausted. It was just a fantastic amount of hard work to do it. It took work to keep from waking up. I had to keep submerging Lorraine to let this other person out, and it was hard work and I was really tired.

And then somebody had to come into his office there and so he asked me if we could go outside for a few minutes. And all I remember about that was this real sunny day. We just had a nice little talk—him and I. He told me that he didn't know how long that other person had been around and he can't help me find out about where she came from or how long she's been there, but he can help me get the two—or more—parts of me together.

Anyway, it was a very weird afternoon, finding out there's another person inside me I didn't know about, who's all the things I never can be. You know, in that movie "Three Faces of Eve," it was supposed to be kind of weird, but I think It's not so weird. I mean, maybe other people have an inside voice they don't know about. Maybe a lot of people do. Maybe just a few people find it. Maybe I made it all up. What a performance! But then I think there are parts of it that I couldn't have made up. They just came. Like the scream with Eric and the laugh and the crying and the accent just came. Also, I trust Eric not to think I'm crazy. In fact, I even asked him that. I trust him because he doesn't treat me like I'm crazy.

In our talk at the session's end, the work was established as one of reconciliation—bargaining, getting to know someone. Further personalities were not encouraged to appear and the historical and ontological questions most apt to bog down our efforts were set aside. The relationship of the two was continued in a sort of couple's therapy, with Lorraine also talking to Laura in daydreams and writing in a diary in which each could reveal her thoughts:

We can trust her—I forgot I had said I wouldn't say anything to anyone until we were ready. I guess I felt we were ready.

I'm not upset (in a different handwriting—Laura's).

This is our book—this is our place to record our days—to get to know each other. In black and white. Come here anytime.

June 15, 1972

> *I'm anxious again, but not as outwardly this day. I've moved out of my apartment. I'm waiting to hear about the job. My school is over, summer school's not yet begun. I've seen Al without much outward emotion. I'm unsure where I'm going.*
>
> *Eric had me just talk. Then he gave me suggestions to calm myself to prepare to talk with Laura. Lorraine's feelings were strong. Laura's feelings came and went, but had trouble breaking through. Eric suggested I go to Laura's house. I imagined it was on a street in the neighborhood in which I grew up, the little house next to the Wilkens, sort of in back. A little girl answered my knock. Dark inside. Then a voice from inside, "Come on in." Eric said to turn on the light as I came in.*

Throughout this vividly imagined experience in a state of deep relaxation I employed suggestions guiding the encounter of the two persons as one might do in couple's therapy or in active imagining:

> *Linoleum floor, green, overstuffed couch. To the right, a door to the kitchen. She was in there. I said, "Come out." She finally came, but there was a cloud around her face. Eric suggested we sit on the couch, that I take her hand. She didn't seem to want to talk. We went out onto the porch where Eric was. He asked her questions. She was silent. He left us alone to decide if we both wanted to stay, or what. Finally, Lorraine told Eric, "Laura wants to know if you're making fun of us, because you know there's really only one." Laura told Lorraine that Lorraine wasn't tough enough to say what Laura felt: to get mad at Eric and scream it.*
>
> *Eric asked to speak with Laura alone, so Lorraine left and went to Ann's house. Laura stayed to talk with Eric. It was difficult. Eric: "Are you from New Zealand?" Laura: "No. I feel cold." Eric: "If you reach out your hand, I'll hold it, and then you won't feel so cold. Then we'll both feel warm."*
>
> *She does so reluctantly, still feeling cold. But her hand is warm. She thinks, "I'd like to be warm all over, be held all over." Then Eric says, "I won't feel hurt or angry if you take your hand away." Laura feels so sad, sympathetic, like, "I know how it feels to feel hurt and*

angry when someone takes their hand away." She cries. Eric wipes her tears.

Then Lorraine came back and drew her hand away. Lorraine says, "She can hold your hand. I can't." Eric says, "Why, because Laura gets all the warm, sexy feelings?" "Yes, that's it," I say. I told Eric how Laura wanted to feel warm all over but couldn't tell him she wanted to be held, and he said, "And Lorraine would have an even harder time telling me if she wanted to be held. Right?" "Right!" We both laughed a lot. I really believed, up to the moment I told him, that there was something quite mature about never needing to be held.

Today we felt friendlier than before—Lorraine not so scared, Laura able to laugh at herself. At first, when Eric held her hand, Laura said, "Rather ridiculous!" Then she and Eric laughed. He said, "I can't help but smile. I like your stubbornness."

Eric was glad to see the boundary between us getting fuzzier. Lorraine just couldn't altogether go away this session. I asked him if next time he could help Lorraine go completely away. He said, "Yes, through hypnosis." But he prefers us to talk with each other. We're working on that on our own and maybe will need hypnosis to get the hurt-bad secrets out. We'll see.

Although the approaches and attentiveness of hypnotherapy were employed frequently, no formal induction of "hypnosis" was attempted. "Hypnosis," like any feared or desired mystery, can be threatened or promised in the course of psychotherapy, while encouraging people to use their own human competencies to address difficulties in living.

Driving home, I talked to her. We talked. We are friends. Not scared of each other. She doesn't hate me and she's not really so cruel and cold. She's beautifully strong and proud. We are growing closer—it's strange. In this lonely, mixed-up time we have each other and we're afraid to lose each other. But we decided that when we're ready to go on being one it'll be all right.

Thus far, through dealing with the emotions of fear, anger, and loneliness, Lorraine has been able to gain a friend who supports her, replacing an unknown enemy of gigantic proportions within. With the change in emotion guided through appropriate relational actions, she is able to reveal information to herself, and, with this increased trust in herself, she can begin the long process of recovery of memory and feeling. In this way, utilizing by herself the techniques of the psychotherapy, she slowly transforms possession into self-possession. When this occurs, she can decide to reintegrate aspects of herself into a coherent whole.

> *I asked her name. I tried to imagine it on a mailbox. Lorraine without the "L" came to me . . . Then it came. "Rene" is our name. "Irene: I, Rene." We gave Eric a riddle. We agreed to speak with each other but not to deal with the scariest parts until Eric is around to help us.*
>
> *We remembered back to the day we cut a hole in Mom's sofa. It was a hot, stuffy day on the back porch. We had on a tee shirt and pants. There was a little hole in the arm already. The scissors just fit in and cut. Other events on the porch, by the red door: "Does God love me?" "Yes, of course." Me crying, throw myself in Mom's arms. The day we asked for a bra. Mom saying it was disgusting. The blue-and-white-striped play outfit.*

In July, Lorraine wrote again. Soon after, she moved far from the Bay Area. The following January (1973), she again sent letters and journal entries to me. We corresponded for several months.

July 1, 1972

> *Up early to fix breakfast. Went back to bed. Autosuggestion to dream about Rene. The dream came: I was about to hold hands with a little girl. I became a little girl. I felt a wind on my face. I felt my two short legs and two short arms. I felt the diapers and rubber pants I had on. All my physical feeling sensations were intensified. I was walking around a white house. Knew this was the Rene dream. I let myself go into it but maintained an analytical voice too, to see what was going on. "What happened to scare you?" the voice asked. Vision of a black kitten. Feelings of anger. Reaching out and grabbing. I see only the kitten's legs under a white thing.*

January 12, 1973

    My journal is empty. Sometimes I've thought nothing has happened with Rene/Lorraine, but the farther away I get from some events the more familiar patterns seem to appear. I have this idea that whoever it is that pushes me on—sometimes it feels like a Me that knows more than I do—anyway, it's like that inner director insists upon completion of all the details, a replay of scenes until we get them all just beautifully perfect. As if I can't go ahead until the lower steps are complete. No gaps! I feel like I'm doing a pretty good 16-year-old now. If I could just run through a quick 10 years, I might get caught up in time for my 27th birthday.

    Anyway, in October I got really sick. Sicker than I've been in years. And partly it was my fever, but mostly I think it was a replay of a really hard scene. I went into the deepest anxiety I've ever experienced. I felt so guilty my stomach ached from it. And I got sicker of course. And I just couldn't see straight—I felt all the old religious guilt about not making my life count for something. I felt as if there were powers outside myself that insisted that I should never be happy, never be like ordinary people. Now when I say it to you, Eric, I feel anger at those "powers" and their cruelty. But then I felt they were right.

    Looking back on those days was like a replay. I had gone through whole years of such anxiety in Chicago, and before, in New Zealand. Only it seems now as if it was a kind of dramatic intensified replay to get the last drop of that guilt out of me. How many times, even as a tiny girl, I remember wishing with all my might that the Sunday dinner chit-chat world was the only real one—not that other world of hell and demons and angels that the preacher yelled about in church. Why did that inner world seem so huge in me? It was the one that drove me.

The feeling of guilt became the next emotion requiring careful attention. I wrote to Lorraine, enclosing the first portions of this manuscript and suggesting that, in effect, it was now time to let the cat out of the bag.

April 13, 1973

    Yeah, the cat's got to come out. And it's been asking again but I didn't know it 'til I read your question. Then all the pieces fit. The dreams are coming back—sick feeling dreams. The kind I had before I came to see you. I think that when Rene came out, lots of energy was released for new growing, and things just kept getting better, less tight, more flowing. But the sick dreams are like a brick wall. I have to smash through to keep going.

One day in February, I was staying at a friend's house, babysitting and reading, and I was rather suddenly gripped by the most terrible guilt. I was just paralyzed with the old familiar dread of being alive and there just seemed to be no end to the ugliness of it. But this time I recognized it and managed to deal with it all alone. I calmed down and saw that what was happening was not that I had been suddenly damned, but more like an asthma attack—only it's a guilt attack! So, this guilt thing feels like an illness to me. I thought I licked it in October, but then, here it rears its head again when I'm feeling most put together.

April 18, 1973

I've got this whole complex of things that feel like they belong together, only they are different than before. I'll tell you them: There's this guilt thing—like asthma attacks. Sudden, unexpected, suffocating. Maybe it's related to the many times when I was living at home when I'd wake up screaming.

Look at this dream I had the other night: I start to have deep communication with my family. It's lovely. A friend comes in, a girl with a bottle filled with liquid. I smell it and can't detect an odor. Take a deeper breath. My lungs are suddenly clogged and I realize it's gasoline. Can't breathe for half a minute.

I think the unrecognized woman in so many of my dreams is the same as the girl here. So there's this guilt thing, and the breathing, and the dreams of women. And there's also this big, empty place I feel inside about sex. I used to be terrified of anyone asking me how I felt cause it seemed as if I had nothing inside. When feelings started to bubble out I recognized that I hadn't been empty, just bottled up—a lid on.

I'm so afraid this thing will go back inside and not come out again and I want so much to let it out. The other night I dreamed: pulling a *line of fish through a long, dark tunnel. Folks are telling me they won't survive on the other side. I let go of the line, but I'm sad I haven't let them loose from it first. Now they'll all be tied together.*

I hope it doesn't mean my insides gave up. The other day I sang to myself, "I'm in love with you, oh lovely lady. Won't you be in love with me?" And right away I knew it was a message from inside: the lady inside loves me; wants me to love her. She's reaching out, kissing me, touching me. She's strong and I love her so much. I am her. Sometimes I don't experience all of me. But I go on—inside and out.

Lorraine, working with her dreams and emotions and relatedness in a prolonged and intense experience, has come to the connectedness of the various images and feelings that structure her dilemma. Her friends have helped her too, and she has employed the dreamwork she learned in psychotherapy. Now she feels more love, strength, and integrity of person than she did initially.

May 16, 1973

I'm hoping I can tell you this story in person next week. Meantime, I wanted to write it down. Guess what—I FEEL LIKE I FOUND MY CAT. The cloud is gone. The big, deep dark mystery has a tiny light shining in it. How to say it . . . I'll try. There is this anxiety for about a week. Sometimes not thinking of anything else for hours. Sometimes completely forgetting. I think, "Well, a part of me wants something awful to happen to my friend Alice, maybe even wants her out of the way." Time after time, I'm ready to admit to myself that I have such ugly feelings toward the person I claim to love the most in the world. Time after time, the admission brings no release. Anxiety is still there. I'm willing to face this horrible thing, experience the guilt of it. But I get nowhere.

I tell my roommate, and she says, "What would happen if you just let go?" I don't know, but I try it. After about 30 seconds, I just burst into tears. The pain of it was so great, right in my guts. All the guilt and anxiety were so cerebral, eating at my brain. But when I let it go, the deep down inside feeling was the most horrible pain at the thought of losing Alice. I just can't tell you how clear it was. The gnawing thing—the guilt cloud in my head—just left! And the pain just jabbed right into my guts. I could see what was happening. The sadness-pain was so much more intense than the guilt, in its way, impossible to live with. How could I go on living without Alice? I cried and cried . . . and started to remember:

I was put in mind of my grandma. I remembered a day at Grandma's house. In a dark bedroom at the foot of the stairs. I am lying on the bed and Grandma is sitting on it beside me. She's telling me things. I feel a little frightened. I sense she says to me, "You go to sleep now and when you wake up, your daddy will be here and we will ask him about the kitten." My sense is that I didn't see Grandma again after that. She got sick, went to the hospital, and died. And Sunday I finally cried for her. But I had never remembered feeling anything for her before, even when I'd talked lovingly about her to friends.

But Sunday I felt how sad it is to live in a world without my grandma. I loved and needed her so much, and I didn't understand when she went away. It was so big. What I cried on Sunday and again on Monday was a little girl's grief. This 27-year-old feels close to Grandma, has for about a month now, like she is around. But the little girl hadn't cried before.

And I remembered and sensed intense things: telling Grandma what I loved about her; the smell of bread baking in the kitchen, the warm inside feeling I get on hot days in the summer, like those days when we two were alone together on the porch and the little kittens she always had around and her garden out in back of the old house. All these pieces fitting together, like the sweet, deep ache of being close to Grandma.

In the middle of the grief, I looked at the world and it looked like the world was Grandma and her house and garden and the big trees and her and me alone together. And then she died, and all the perfection in the world left. They tore the house down. And the garden was gone, and the animals. I cried for all that was gone, and I wondered how I could possibly live without my grandma. And she died when I was four.

As a little girl I didn't think I could live life without Grandma and couldn't face the pain of that separation. So I translated it into something I could live with—guilt. And for years I've felt guilty— it's the most consistent experience of my life. But I'm just sure it's been a cover-up. I sense the grief as ever so much deeper than the guilt. Everything in me was related to this and now I see it and I'm freer.

All that fear of the cat was fear of facing the pain. Maybe I've been looking forever for someone to come and love me like Grandma did. It's so painful to have it gone, I still hurt. It's still coming up from deep down. I really do want my grandma. So often I write in my journal, "I'm lonely." I feel less lonely with Rene here, but it's Grandma I'm lonesome for.

And it keeps blowing in my mind what this means: I don't have to be "ugly" anymore. I'm not ugly inside. I was a frightened little girl, scared of an emotion—scared "to death." My survival was at stake. So, I made a pattern. It's been running me for all these years. And just this week I got to the point where I sensed I could survive even the pain. And I am surviving.

The difference between "knowing" about Grandma's dying and "experiencing" Grandma's death is indescribable. I've been reaching for this for ages—this blind spot, no feeling—and I wanted so much to know it, get the secret out. But the odd thing is, about a month ago I gave up, decided I could just live with the secret. I even forgot I had wanted it so much. But this is the secret I wanted so badly!

June, 1974 [A year later,]

Good dreams of seeing myself in a beautiful, plain white dress. And later, finding my Grandma's treasure chest of lace and trimmings and buttons. I asked whom it belonged to and my aunt said, "To you." I was so delighted—such a beautiful treasure to own and to use.

So the therapy, which totaled 18 hours during 1972, was continued by Lorraine herself for several years afterward, using the interpersonal techniques developed in dealings with her "other side." The reader may recognize in her work, both with and without the therapist present, some of the techniques and assumptions found in typical uses of psychoanalysis, Gestalt therapy, meditation, hypnotherapy, and guided daydreaming. The use of active imagining, in which personified segments of the self are treated like real-life others, eventuates in more straightforward treatment of the emotional, historical, and interpersonal information that becomes available to people.

The question arises, of course, of how we are to think about these "segments of the self." How, even, are we to conceptualize those "real-life others" whose integrity of personality we take for granted in ordinary life? A widely held view has it that personality is not a unity, but an assemblage (of habits, dissociated segments, hemispheres of the brain, etc.). In this view, our sense of "self" is illusory, or misleading. We are surprised by autonomous action by some segment to the extent that we assume a unitary self. Another set of assumptions about ordinary human experience holds that there is a bi- or tripartite division of self along lines of consciousness and unconsciousness. Here, our sense of self is tied strongly to actions of remembering and forgetting, which provide or dis-member our sense of self-continuity. The assumption is of a unitary "self" obscured by amnesia and dissociation.

Each of these ways of thinking seems to me to be a habit of mind, which, in certain life experiences, reflects quite handsomely the ontology we wish to describe. As Jung says in his autobiography, "In some analyses I can be heard speaking the Adlerian dialect, in others, the Freudian." To provide a convention for the use of the term "multiple personality" we probably ought to assume the unitary view. Then, if amnesia; autonomous action, feeling, thought, or motive, and surprise are seen in the patient, we may speak as if of another personality.

A distributed view of the concept "self" leads us to see socially or situationally derived or "state-dependent parts" of a collage portrait of persons. Somewhere between the common experience in which anesthetized patients can be brought to remember the words of the surgeon while the patient was "unconscious," and the also common situation in which persons undergo religious conversion and think, act, and feel like "different people" lies the experience of multiple personality.

When dealing with individual figures in dreams, or with "multiple personalities," "internalized others," "the voice of conscience," "hallucinated voices," or "archetypes of the collective unconscious," the ordinary and extraordinary difficulties of relating hold sway. Here one speaks of love, hate, sadness, forgiveness, lust, rage, grief, joy, suspicion, trust, and the other emotions. Following a line of emotion or emotional exchange with a person is important for clarity of relating, regardless of one's therapeutic language. In special circumstances, such as when relating with dream figures, it gives the true sense to both therapist and patient that, as Lorraine expressed it, "I trust him not to think I'm crazy. I trust him because he doesn't treat me like I'm crazy." The therapy continues, in that sense, far beyond therapeutic "termination."

Within active imagining, asking the question, as Weaver (1973) does, "What would you do in life in this case?" proves effective in dealing with multiple personalities, imagined parents or children, dream monsters, and archetypes of the collective unconscious. And, in these dealings, therapists may be guided by the interpersonal approaches of such writers as Ginott (1965) and Sullivan (1954a) in their relationships with difficult others. Then, in dealing with the relationships, one tries to push the action on to some dramatic conclusion, such as those found in life: rescue and relief, separation and reconciliation, exploration and discovery, or even death, grief, and renewal. The person's own sense of the completion of an act is usually reliable, although the therapist must watch out for instances in which fear, rather than resolution, signals the end of the work.

Many works of active imagination seem to take about an hour and a half to complete, after which people often volunteer, "I feel I worked a lot today—not physical work. I'm finished for today." Or, "I felt sick and I felt exhausted. It was just a fantastic amount of hard work to do it." The sense of effort is an important correlate of the use of one's own power to attack difficult objectives, and the sense of personal strength or activity is a commonplace of vibrant lives.

Modalities of Experience

In some ways, the use of active imagining has one do purposely what otherwise occurs to one passively, as do dreams, daydreams, passing thought, and quickly stirred emotion. Haley (Haley, 1963; Watzlawick, Weatland, & Fisch, 1974) and his colleagues often note that the suggestion or demand that one do actively what one must do anyway is by itself highly effective in catalyzing change. Similarly, treating "fantasy" figures as "real" relationships allows people to deal with those "projections" and what not they must suffer anyway, all of us having been brought up by "significant others." In addition, dealing directly with dream figures provides a change of framework, from one in which the patient is "crazy" or irrelevant or plagued or possessed, to one in which he or she is pursuing relatedness.

That reframing, or even a simple change of venue, is a useful stratagem, confirmed by works both ancient and modern. So far we've discussed such transforms of experience as the continuation of dreaming, which reframes the alien as relationship, and the active stance, which reframes an emotional dilemma as a task or practical problem. It is equally useful to reframe the modalities of somatic experience and vague or confused experience as clear images that may be dealt with.

These difficulties in living—"psychosomatic discomfort," "vague complaints," and even, and especially, the sophisticated patient's total, helpless understanding of antecedents and meanings in his or her suffering—can be mitigated when made tangible in dreams. But the dreams may also be created in the therapy itself, as when a person complaining of pain is asked, "Where is it? What does it look like there?" or of emotion, "What color is it? Where do you feel it in your body?"

For example, a man complaining of depression may be told, "Remember when you were a kid at school? We all made drawings with colored crayons and covered them with black. Then we scraped them with our nails to reveal the colors. Suppose you scrape off all the black and tell me what you see." As in all this work, a matter-of-fact-tone in the present tense—"You scrape off all the black"—is pretty good proof against objections to carrying out simple imaginings. In fact, it's difficult not to picture what the other person is talking about. When the colors emerge, compound colors may be separated into primaries and the colors given shapes by asking, "What shape is the red now?" or, "If the color were a thing, what would it be? Look and tell me." Then, balls may be rolled or thrown, curtains parted, and a general sense of purposeful motion given to a static circumstance or emotion.

Physical distress, such as headache pain, tightness of muscles, or plain nerves, can be translated into images in much the same way. I asked a woman suffering back pain and tension, "What's going on there? What do you see?" She saw two men, one at the neck, another at the base of the spine, pulling skeins of nerves so tautly between them that some had frayed and were broken. Through dialogue, one of the figures was encouraged to repair the frayed nerves, while the other agreed to leave his tugging and open an office from which to manage the woman's rather disorganized personal habits. In four days, half of her back was free of pain; in two weeks, two-thirds.

Another important guideline is the conservation of the images or system of images through reorientation, or transformations. In the "mind-mirror" exercise in Chapter 3, "Evil Influence," figures are asked to change or evolve, not to disappear. In the example above, the man is given other work to do, not cast out. In the instance of Lorraine's two personalities, a dream showed her frightened, but "doing something to get the two of us together." The metaphorical use of all of the self and all of its materials, however it's thought of—the reintegration of projections, equilibration of the system of psychical fields, or the conservation of libidinal energy—is a key element in all therapeutic work, the achievement of which provides natural closure to personal difficulty or dilemma.

Consider another instance of both translation of the modalities of experience and their integration: A 40-year-old engineer entered therapy with me in a state he described as "down in the dumps." He was asked to take on the "depressing" task of sorting through the garbage and recycling it, to which he replied: "I've thought of this disgusting garbage as attachments to past events, like adhesions. I want to get rid of it." How to do this? We agreed to compost the (mostly organic) garbage in order to provide energy by means of a methane converter. He could then put the power generated in this way to whatever use seemed important to him. His choice was to use the gas to power a burner that could cut holes through metal plates that blocked him from the outside world. As he did this, his feeling of disgust was replaced by one of calm satisfaction and smooth breathing, "like normal, everyday breaths, but easier." He had begun down in the dumps, but, after much hard work, he could breathe easier.

Vague complaints often have the irresistible quality of pathos, but they usually are not something with which we can easily come to grips in therapy. A young man was tormented by repeated, sudden feelings of humiliation and worthlessness and by severe leg pains whose cause couldn't be determined. He was asked to notice where he had the feeling of absolute or unconditional worth not tied to performance. After a moment's thought, he said that it was "in the heart" and resembled a spiky oval that grows darker and smoother with increased worth and brighter and painfully burning with decreased feelings of worthiness. He was told to let the feeling grow and was surprised to find it sending a spur into the afflicted leg, with a small, spiky ball on the end. I asked him to draw up the ball and spit it out while remembering instances of anger and humiliation suffered in his lonely childhood years. As he did this, he discovered "hundreds" of the spiky balls stored in his knee joint. He decided to get them all out.

It's long been the fashion in psychotherapy to think of the organism as an integrated system of psychosomatic events. The transforms of experience and the symptoms that compel our attention are ascribed to some interplay between anxiety and the self or stress and the organism. If we think of anxiety as a formless situation in which information is muted, lost, or distorted, and emotion as also uncertain, like a sort of white noise, we will make ready to replace this painful meaninglessness with form and image.

A patient who suffered dream deprivation and *pavor nocturnus* under the influence of antipsychotic medication said bitterly to me, "If only I had an image to hold on to." The role of providing these images falls to the dreamer himself or herself, or to the dreamer and guide. Together, they develop the means that allow safe passage through the straits of uncertainty and fear. And this role and that collaboration have an interesting history.

The Unconscious-Mind Metaphor

At the centre of each person there is an incommunicado element and this is sacred and most worthy of preservation.

—*D. W. Winnicott (1965, p. 187)*

The modern idea of the unconscious mind was formed in hypnotic investigations of the last century. As Haley (1993) writes, "When a subject in trance followed suggestions and could not explain why he was doing what he was doing, it was necessary to postulate a motivating force inside the person which was outside his awareness."

This idea of unconsciousness replaced Mesmer's concept of animal magnetism, a force transmitted by "mesmeric passes" that induced a "healing magnetic crisis" in the patient. Miller (1995) describes Mesmer at work: "Clothed in a robe embroidered with Rosicrucian alchemical symbols he stalked the darkened rooms to the accompaniment of a glass harmonica." In 1785, Benjamin Franklin and a French Royal Commission determined that Mesmer's results were not caused by magnetism, but rather by "imagination."

James Braid, a British surgeon, adopted the term "hypnotism" to describe the closed eyelids, drooped head, and slow respiration that, together with slight movements of the hands and arms, gave an impression of sleep in subjects whose attention had been thoroughly fixated. Although this view predominated from the 1840s on, a companion view was developed by the physicians Carpenter and Laylock (cited in Miller, 1995). Noting both the involuntary shifts of memory and the problem-solving consequences of hypnotic trance, they emphasized unconscious cerebration, "a shadowy province between the unarguably automatic and the self-evidently voluntary." They spoke of an "automatic self" and held that this unconscious actor was "an altogether productive institution."

This notion of "unconscious mind" is, in turn, both appealing and frightening. In Freud's view, one might fear the unconscious, which bursts forth in spontaneous neurophysiological events that embarrass, as in *parapraxes,* or disable, as did the conversion symptoms he treated with hypnosis early in his career. Erickson always assumed that the unconscious mind is a resource into which tangled problems might be dropped and in which they could be resolved. The inner searching for potentials for action and the learned skills held there construct Erickson's unconscious mind.

Konstantin Stanislavski (1926), the famed acting teacher, expresses the power and organization of Laylock and Erickson's "thoughtful," "automatic" selves in a way that informs a developing metaphor of the active, organized, and positive unconscious mind:

> Let me remind you of our cardinal principle: "Through conscious means we reach the subconscious." . . . Wherever you have truth and belief, you have feeling and experience. You can test this by executing even the smallest act in which you really believe and you will find that instantly, intuitively and naturally, an emotion will arise. . . . If you just feel the truthfulness of this (imaginary) act, your intention and subconsciousness will come to your aid. Then superfluous tension will disappear. The necessary muscles will come into action, and all this will happen without the interference of any conscious technique

The contrast between Freud's and Erickson's metaphors parallels that between the views of hypnotism as a deep sleep full of nightmares and subject to evil influence and as a forum for thoughtful organizing of unconscious learning to accomplish worthy goals.

If we were to contrast the Freud and Erickson metaphors in a more general way, we might say that there are two models of unconsciousness at work. In one, the unconscious is the *unspeakable*—those hidden events about which we are prohibited from speaking or which we speak about in whispers, or only to certain persons. In fact, we say of evil acts, "What was done is unspeakable."

The other kind of model, and the one I prefer, is that the unconscious is the *unsayable*. There is such a close association of consciousness and thought with speech that if we lack words to describe something, it is nearly unconscious. Michael Jordan, asked about scoring five three-point shots in a row during a game, said, "I surprised *myself*. I was just unconscious out there."

Another way to approach the formation of an unconscious-mind metaphor useful in psychotherapy is to ask, "*What* is unconscious?" Although the convention among therapists is that the unconscious mind is a "place" in which memories are hidden and evil motives repressed, even Freud (cited in Miller, 1995) said that "the unconscious is not a closet full of skeletons in the private house of the individual mind." Three types of human *processes* may be good candidates as answers to our question: ways of learning, bodily functions, and interpersonal relations.

A student in my hypnotherapy class puzzled herself by remarking, "What a wonderful thing I'm learning. I don't know what I'm saying." And a patient said, "The last two sessions have been specifically interesting for me in that there is an important thing that is being affected, which isn't the same as what's being discussed. I know this is true even though I don't know what I'm talking about."

The analyst Adam Phillips (1993) wrote: "The cognitive unconscious consists in an ensemble of structures and functions unknown by the subject except in their results. There was profound truth in Binet's whimsical expression, 'Thought is an unconscious activity of the mind.' " Piaget (1973), likely less whimsically, said, "The deepest functioning of the intelligence remains entirely unknown to the subject until we reach some level where reflection on this problem of structures becomes possible" (p. 250). The important commonplace that accompanies these thoughts about thinking is that we learned our ways of learning without con-sciousness: how to learn language, how to learn memory, indeed, how to learn, are processes without benefit of reflection when first learned.

Bodily functions and procedures form another set of answers to our question, "What is unconscious?" What we call "the wisdom of the body" comprises all the elaborate, organized, un-self-conscious neuro-physiological processes that sustain life, from respiration and walking to vision and physical healing. These, too, are learned without conscious thought. Erickson (1980) learned to restore his functioning after suffering paralyzing polio by carefully watching his infant sibling as she un-self-consciously learned to walk, and then imitating her learning in his mus-cles. These observations became important allusions in his trance conversations during therapy, which often revolved around unconscious learning and the discoveries of speech, writing, number, motion and bal-ance made by little children as they grow.

Expanding this aspect of the unconscious-mind metaphor, Rossi and Cheek (1988) made a case for the natural origins of hypnotic therapy in an "ultradian healing response":

> Virtually all the classical phenomena of hypnosis were originally discovered as spontaneous manifestations of altered states in every-day life (e.g., daydreaming, sleepwalking, traumatic stress syndrome, etc.). Only after they were so discovered were efforts directed to elicit the phenomena by "suggestion".....If we believe that hypnotic phe-nomena are purely the product of artificial verbal suggestion, then we tend to discount the clinical conception of hypnosis as a natural psy-chobiological response to stress and trauma. (p. 262)

This natural psychobiological response, like all responses of the vari-ous body systems, is self-organizing and not subject to specific conscious control. It operates within us whether we are awake or asleep, alert or unconscious, attentive or distracted.

The third set of unconscious processes important to therapy is that of interpersonal relationships. The English language is very thin in terms describing relationship, although there are many words to describe feel-ing states, interior states of cognition, and so on. Think about terms that describe two-person relationships: brother and sister, husband and wife, friends, and enemies. Can you think of terms to describe three-person relationships? My grandmother, my mother, and myself. The word is not "family," because my father and my sister were also in the family group. It's an intergenerational relationship. But how do we describe the relationship among my uncle, mother, myself, and my grandmother? How about five persons who communicate? Pals, friends, a social group. If you want to talk about relationships, you will run out of language very quickly.

Romanyshyn (1977) writes of "an unconscious that surrounds conscious life, an unconsciousness in the world, *between* us" (p. 215), and Jung (1966) writes: "In the deepest sense, we all dream not out of ourselves, but out of what lies between us and the other." Cast your mind back to your therapy training and think of how often the more you knew about the trouble a person was having, the more often you found that other people were involved, sometimes from many generations and many cultures, and over time. How can you talk about a complete genogram that goes back tens of generations? Carl Whitaker (cited in Keith, 1995) said, "Don't tell Freud, but with three generations in the office, the unconscious is not quite so unconscious."

To make your mind part of a relationship—to tell about it—you have to be able to put it into words. So *unsayable* and *unconscious* are in the same family. Then the question arises: How can we relate unconscious things—things about which we cannot speak? How can we say the unspeakable and bring it into relationship with a therapist, or with our friends? How can we say the unsayable things for which there are no words in the language, but of which we are yearning to speak?

Talking about unconscious "contents" or "action potentials" is difficult both in the sense that what is unconscious is by definition unsayable and in the sense that awareness of the unconscious finds no adequate expression in common language. Three attempts have been made to satisfy the demands of the problem of "speaking about the unsayable" or unconscious. One attempt led to the development of freakish therapeutic languages, such as object-relations, that employ neologisms to refer to unconscious experience. Another approach, that of Zen Buddhism, substitutes noticing or pointing for understanding and action or gesture for explanation when expressing "no-mind." The third attempt involves utilizing natural metaphor and imagery as the appropriate language with which to express the unconscious mind's thought. So, dreams, poetry, art, and the gestural language of dance are used to describe and to discuss, or make social, individual unconscious experience.

Haley (1993) writes, "In all our waking hours, if not in our dreams, we explain" (p. 111). What do we do in our dreams? Dreams are experienced as true at the time, totally absorbing. More absorbing than explanation is to dream in the safety of your bed and be full of wonder. Relating to and about the unconscious does not mean making translations, that is, making the unconscious conscious. Rather, it means speaking in the language of dreams, the language of visual images. Betty Alice Erickson (personal communication, 1995), consulting about a case, suggested, "Talk a lot about billowy pillows and blue clouds." The royal road to the unconscious has a language, and that language is the language of dream images, not the language of explanatory discourse.

Why is hypnosis the proper conversational style for this communication? In practicing hypnosis, you are learning to focus attention and to tell a story and to listen intently. Hypnotic practices invite thought and speech that are allegorical, allusive, metaphorical. Hypnosis is a good conversational style for this relationship with the unconscious because it not only employs the style of dreams and the metaphor of sleep, but it also pays attention to the human body in a way that assumes that the body is communicating with posture, gesture, and touch. Paying attention to the body, trying to utilize physical expression, and paying attention to breathing are very important parts of the therapeutic conversation in hypnosis.

To summarize: Suppose the interface between neurophysiology and social relations exists within the communication medium we term "hypnosis." Suppose the concept "unconscious mind" refers to three sets of processes: ways of learning, the un-self-conscious organization of human neurophysiology, and the unspoken network of social relations. Suppose, too, that these processes are represented in consciousness by dream images and emotionally dramatic narratives.

Now, suppose further that these unconscious processes are accessed by hypnosis, turmoil, or trauma during a state of dreamy reverie, confusion, or shock and surprise that accompanies the natural formation of representative images and narratives. In reverie, confusion, or trauma, these representations can be selected, combined, and revised (as in the inner search of hypnotic therapy) or can be expressed in action (as in helpful response to trauma). A response to traumatic experience exemplifies the social nature of the unconscious mind. Un-self-conscious process and procedure appear as natural, little-known concomitants of ordinary life:

Pearson's Brick, Wood's Break, and Greenleaf's Blow

THE ACCIDENT

One Friday morning, some years ago, while walking across the street near my office, I was suddenly struck by a car moving at 50 miles per hour. The car arrived so suddenly that I did not see it approach, but *heard* it strike me. The force of the blow below my knee drove my body up over the hood and my forehead into the windshield. I saw a bright flash of light and was thrown, unconscious, some 40 feet.

When I regained consciousness, I was lying on a traffic island, looking up into a circle of anxious faces: firefighters, paramedics, bystanders. My head was cradled by a young woman sitting on the ground behind me. I heard her say calmly, "Just lie still. You're going to be all right." Immediately I had three thoughts, infused with the strongest possible emotion:

> *I love life and I want to live.*
> *I'm going to tell everyone around me what I think and feel.*
> *I'm going to get well as soon as I possibly can.*

These three intentions guided me during my recovery, although I never consciously thought of them again. I began to speak to the paramedics and the young woman, explaining that I was angry at being hit, and frightened and sad that I was hurt. I wept and raged and joked. I asked each person's name (promptly forgetting it). I asked for my bag and I asked to be taken to Kaiser Hospital. Meanwhile, paramedics cut my clothes off, inserted IV needles, and started oxygen through a nasal cannula. I drifted in and out of consciousness.

At the hospital, I was treated by several residents and nurses, who bathed my wounds and stitched my scalp. They asked me where I was from and I replied, "Brooklyn" (my childhood home). Each decided that he or she also was from Brooklyn and we would have a lively conversation. Then I was taken to several examination rooms for X-rays and other tests. In between, left to myself in a busy urban emergency room, I spoke with any patient in proximity and exercised my swollen, edematous, cramped legs by walking and stretching as I talked.

The accident happened at 7:30 A.M. By 3:30 P.M., I was eager to go home. The nurse, and doctor agreed I could be released. The nurse tried to phone my wife to come for me, but was unable to reach her, and so I asked the nurse to call a cab. She gave me a large paper bag containing my unscarred shoes (they had flown off on impact) and my shredded, bloodstained clothes, and advised me to have my wife wake me every two hours during the night to establish my consciousness.

Wearing a hospital gown and foam shoes I left the hospital and got into the taxi. "What happened to you?" The driver asked, I told him. "You're lucky!" he said. "I'm lucky I'm alive, but I'm unlucky that the car hit me," I said.

I arrived home to find the house empty, my keys in the missing bag I had taken with me that morning. I got a ladder, climbed through a window, found my bed, and went to sleep. Later, my wife arrived home. She had been frantically searching for me, having been told that I had had an accident. The emergency room had no record of my admission, so her calls to hospitals were fruitless. I rested and slept deeply most of the weekend. On Monday morning, I returned to work a regular week in my practice of psychotherapy and hypnotherapy, as I have for 30 years.

MY RECOVERY

At some point during that first week, I asked my wife to drive me through the scene of the accident at slow and fast speeds. I wanted to see the street as the car's driver saw it. Back at work, I walked the path I always took, crossing the 15-foot crosswalk where I had been struck. I crossed this street several times each day. For several months, while my legs recovered, I carried a cane for support and took pleasure in brandishing it at drivers who came too close to me or honked impatiently as I slowly navigated the crossings. When I walked with my wife and son, each took one arm and reminded me to remain alert and careful.

Soon I began to have flashbacks of the accident, frequent and unannounced. I would hear the clang of my body striking metal, see the hood of the car and the bright light above my left temple as my head struck the windshield. I have worked with several victims of trauma and employed various hypnotherapeutic strategies to help them with flashbacks. But I found myself inclined to watch the flashback each time it arrived. Hundreds of flashbacks and several months later, the flashbacks came less often, then rarely. Finally, they stopped.

Neighbors, friends and relatives visited. I remember their expressions of care. I remember, too, one sour, inquisitive neighbor who came by to ask how I was doing. "I'm getting better," I said. "Oh," she said, "sometimes you get better, but then there are relapses." I slowly, and with great determination, said, "Sometimes people have relapses, but I'm going to continue to get better."

And I did. The doctors could discover no brain damage (although I lost words from the "tip of my tongue" for several seconds during speech and thought for much of the following year) and no "permanent physical damage" (although my right knee remains weaker than my left). Their looks of amazement when they considered the accident and compared its force with my body's "rude good health" gave me a great deal of pleasure. The positive medical reports also pleased the driver of the car that struck me, and his insurers. They settled a small sum on me in recompense for damages suffered. I took the money and traveled to Bali, where I immensely enjoyed filming masked trance dances and trance mediums at work with their patients.

THINKING LIKE A HYPNOTIST

Like everyone else, I've stumbled as often as I've been bumped and wavered and backtracked often enough. Yet in dealing with and recovering from this accident, I automatically acted toward myself as I would have toward a patient. That is, I felt positive, curious, respectful and expectant. I had a genuine curiosity to see what would happen next. And I still held my three general goals securely in the back of my mind.

The suddenness with which I was thrown into my predicament by a speeding car also seems to have thrown me into a state of immediacy and responsiveness to my previously unconscious goals and to the literal directions embodied in interactions between people. So although I was physically quite helpless, I was, from the point of impact through my recovery, determinedly active emotionally and interpersonally. When the young woman who cradled my head said, "Just lie still. You're going to be all right," I did, and I was. And when my nosy neighbor attempted to induce doubt as to my recovery, I found myself crafting a counterinduction to sustain my progress.

On reflection, I think that the active, immediate, and determined pursuit of my goals after being injured was coupled with a stance toward myself that was positive, curious, loving and attentive to the literal nature of directives: the hypnotist's stance toward a patient. In following the advice we often give to patients, "Take what is useful to you in meeting your goals in your own way and in your own good time, and leave the rest behind," I continue to wear the shoes I wore that day, which were ripped off my feet, unscuffed. The bag of clothes was quickly thrown away. Thank you, Dr. Erickson, for the words I have employed so often in my work.

PEARSON'S BRICK AND WOOD'S BREAK

The thought came to me, "Oh, if Milton was only here!" The very next thought was "Well, buddy-boy, he *isn't* here, so you had better do it yourself."

—*R. E. Pearson (1966)*

Thinking about the background from which my spontaneous reactions to trauma and recovery had sprung led me back to the stories of the experiences of two men: Dr. Erickson's friend, Robert Pearson, M.D., and my friend, Don Wood. I feel that their stories prepared my unconscious mind for the actions I took more than 20 years later, during my own experience of trauma.

Pearson (1966) reported in "Communication and Motivation" his experience after being struck in the head by a five-pound brick tossed from a roof 34 feet above him. He, like me, was taken by surprise so suddenly that his first sensation was of "an extremely loud noise." He struggled to retain consciousness and began to instruct those around him in providing proper care, transportation to the hospital, and medical treatment on his arrival. His realization that he had to "do it himself" eventuated in a spontaneous analgesia for the extreme pain he felt. In the hospital, he took charge of the treatment of his skull fracture, remaining alert to the conversations of the surgeon and anesthesiologist while anesthetized, even scheduling his own discharge:

> I said, "I have to go to San Francisco next Sunday. Under no circumstances will I sign myself out against your advice, but I do want to be discharged tomorrow. I'll make a deal with you: When you make rounds tomorrow, if you can find anything wrong on physical examination, I have any fever, I need anything for pain, my white count is elevated, or anything else is abnormal, I will stay in the hospital for as long as you say; otherwise you will discharge me.

Pearson won. The doctor could find nothing abnormal on examination and discharged him without ceremony. Pearson provides a charming example of his spontaneous emotional expressiveness during this brief hospital stay:

> My wife and a nurse were in the room, and my wife asked me how I felt. I replied, "Like I've been hit in the head by a goddamn brick!" The nurse interpreted this remark to mean that I was in severe pain, and gave me an injection. I asked her what she had given me, and she, of course, replied, "Why don't you ask your doctor?" I could have choked her with great pleasure.

Unable to call on medical knowledge or to instruct the surgeon and nurses who treated my injuries, I likewise felt impelled to take command of what decisions I could. So I insisted on being taken to Kaiser Hospital rather than to the emergency room preferred by the paramedics. I used my skills in relating to remain as conscious as I could and to have some say in my treatment and discharge. And I was most expressive of anger, sadness, and humor to those around me: I did not stand on ceremony.

Don Wood was a vigorous, athletic young man, a lumberjack one summer, medical orderly the next, psychology student during the school year. When I met him, he was confined to a wheelchair with paraplegia. He told me that he had been on a bus on his way to a graduate school interview when an out-of-control truck forced the bus over a cliff. Don was thrown from the window, and the bus landed on him and broke his neck.

He told me that he spontaneously dissociated, so that he no longer felt his pain, and then calmly directed the rescue workers in the proper manner of handling a patient with a broken neck. During his recovery in the hospital and afterward, Don told me that he made certain to respond wholeheartedly only to those visitors and staff members who understood his interest in recovery. The words of any others would be countered or deflected so that they could not impede his progress.

It is commonly known that when we search memory for the antecedents of present distress we run across instances of past traumas helplessly and painfully endured. By contrast, when we seek the origins of a satisfactory response to trauma, we remember stories told by others that display their unique, individual character in dealing with difficulties. I am sure I did not read Pearson's story between 1966 and 1988. I did not think of it, of him, or, indeed, of any precedent while I "did it myself" in response to painful trauma. Yet I think that Pearson's brick formed part of the path I followed un-self-consciously after the blow to my head.

Pearson's story, and Don Wood's example, stayed in the back of my mind for over 20 years before being used spontaneously as learning I needed when the car struck me. Certain commonalities are evident in our experiences: We all responded spontaneously to pain and were able to set it aside; actively directed our own treatment; expressed a full range of emotions, including sorrow, anger and humor; determined to recover quickly and to enjoy life fully; and kept a watchful eye out for helpful and malignant directions from others. All these combine to speed healing and rapidly to renew our engagement in life.

THE SOCIAL NATURE OF THE UNCONSCIOUS MIND

In thinking about the unconscious mind, which is a central concept in the work of Erickson, Freud, and Jung, I want to present a series of "talking points" that have oriented me in this consideration of my injury and recovery and in a search for antecedents in my life's experiences. When I say that Don Wood's and Robert Pearson's stories stayed in my mind "un-self-consciously," I mean that I never forgot or repressed them and never, or rarely, thought about or consciously referred to them for some 20 years after first hearing them. Un-self-conscious knowledge represents a great part of unconscious knowledge. When thinking about Pearson's recovery, or mine, or Wood's, we may suppose that our healing responses, emotional and physiological, proceeded in the familiar ways of our bodies whether or not we were aware of them.

As discussed in "The Unconscious-Mind Metaphor," we can also claim that systems of several people, such as groups and families, social structures, and systems of constructed social reality, may be conceived of as unconscious in the same sense as bodily process or procedure. These can best be represented in consciousness by dreams and family drama or narrative. The personal is thus always shadowed and highlighted by the social. As Singer (1990) noted:

> *How strong external social situations are in determining the specific emotion a person feels . . . It is almost as though the person uses an emotion word to label the evoking situation rather than his specific internal state. (p. 214)*

It is as though the specific emotions that came to aid me in constructing a reality of determined effort, expressiveness, and speedy healing were an expression of the evoking situation: both the tender concern of the woman who told me, "You're going to be all right," and the pattern laid down by Pearson, Wood, and Erickson in dealing with trauma. My own years of experience in hypnotizing others also helped me to treat myself with the expectation of positive outcome and the mobilization of resources I encouraged in my patients. In the relationship of a person with his or her own somatic, emotional, and mental life, stories that lay a pathway to recovery are a great aid in relating. As Silvan Tompkins (cited in Singer, 1990) wrote:

> *The world we perceive is a dream we learn to have from a script we have not written. It is neither our capricious construction nor a gift we inherit without work. (p. 488)*

Troubled Sleep

The intersection of the social world with the world of dreams, and the treatment of family dilemmas with image, trance, and relationship, are shown in the therapy of Kay. The youngest of six children of a religious couple, she was in her 20s and lived with her family. Her sister was sexually abused from the age of 3 by their father, who admitted it. Their mother still denied that anything had happened. Kay had no memory of her childhood before age 13. She said that those early years were "like pieces of a puzzle." Since the age of 14 she had had the same dream every night.

During our first meeting, I emphasize to Kay that the whole family needs to resolve the puzzle. At the second meeting, I ask, "When you think of the dream, what bodily sensations and emotions do you feel?"

Kay: It's like a net around the heart. Loneliness.
Eric: Is it tied or wrapped?
Kay: Wrapped.
Eric: When you remove the net of loneliness, what do you notice?
Kay: A strong, calm feeling. I'm not as afraid of pain. More hopeful. Clear thoughts.
Eric: Suppose you circulate these feelings. What color are they?
Kay: Sky blue.

In a solution-focused conversation, the development of improved feeling can provide a better vehicle for therapy than can a discussion of the problem. A regression along this line of good feeling highlighted the trouble but retained Kay's sense of competence.

Eric: Suppose you apply a sky-blue wash to your family members. Now, ride the sky-blue breathing back in your life: What do you run across? Gather it up, memorize it, and follow it back.
Kay: The blue-sky feeling goes back to age 5, then back from age 4 to the beginning. There's a dark patch from 4 to 5.
Eric: Suppose you air out the room [a word substituted for "dark patch"] and wash it out, but don't look inside it yet.

In the following hour:

Kay: I was able to deal with confrontation in the family a lot better. I thought of the sky-blue color and relaxed. I handled my mother and father in a calm, adult manner. I said to Mom: "This is a family issue." That really helped! I'm edgy about opening the room.

At this point, I would enter the dream space to help out, if she agreed. There was no need for her to be lonely and afraid while exploring the dark space in which her dream occurs.

Eric: I will open windows in the room, close the door, set up a fan. OK? Are there adjoining rooms to the 4–5 room? (*Shakes her head, No*) A closet?

Kay: Yes. It's small—lots of shelves with horse figurines arranged as families, stuffed animals, old, large dolls. Carefully placed. An overhead light, little girl clothes, a box with papers and drawings, story books. As I look through the pile of drawings, I remember drawing them. *I'm seeing them through a little kid's eyes again.* Not very scary. Very neat and organized. There's a rope to an attic opening above. I can't reach it.

Eric: OK if I pull it down for you?

Kay: Yes. There are seven steps up. It's dusty. There are covered things, boy clothes in a box, a carriage, old photos in black and white: my grandfather, great-grandmother, father, great-grandfather, etc. There is an adjoining room (the 4–5 room) with a bed, chest, bare walls, a toy box. Three shelves with ten porcelain dolls on them. A drawing pad and a great big box of crayons. Through a pair of glass doors with a drapery on them, there's the game room. I can see it. A pool table and jukebox.

Eric: Suppose you spend time playing in the room during the week to come. Draw lots of pictures and you can tape them on the walls if you like.

Kay: *It's not such a scary room anymore.* I can open the curtains so the outside light comes in and washes the room with sky-blue.

During the fourth hour of therapy, Kay told me the repetitive dream: She is in bed, 4 or 5 years old. A faceless man starts to fondle her. She says, "No!" He says, "Be a good girl," and he continues.

Eric: If I turn on the light in the room, what do you see? (*10-minute pause*).

Kay: *I see my father!* No beard, less heavy than now, but it's him. I'm angry, hurt, confused.

Here I can offer adult help to offset her lack of power and her loneliness.

Eric: Can I help you push him back out?

Kay: Yes! (*She nods approval.*) He doesn't belong there.

Eric: Let's install an inside bolt at a height a 4-year-old can reach.

Kay: It's nighttime still. (*She goes to her outdoor fort.*) I'm not scared there.

Eric: While you're there, suppose you just think things through. (*10-minute pause.*)

Kay: I told my 10-year-old brother the next morning. He says he'll get me help. I hear yelling and I go to the guest house. He's in the corner crying—he has a black eye. My 20-year-old brother did it when he told him what Dad did. He says, "It didn't happen." I'm the baby.
        Now I don't feel so scared, not unreal. This is what it was. I feel like that was it—the only time. The room is mine again!

When fear leaves, so does "unreality," although the means to this combines real relationship and help, as from an adult to a child, with imagined or metaphorical space from the awful dream. At the fifth meeting:

Kay: I had the dream two times this past week. I saw my father's face in the dream. They weren't violent dreams and I wasn't scared. I did not awaken in the fetal position like I did before. Went right back to sleep. I was fine. *Remembering that has unlocked all the memories of those years. That's been kind of nice having the light on in the room (in the dream) and being able to lock the door has been wonderful!* I have a right to feel the way I feel. I'm tired of the ripple effect in the family being negative all the time. I have a tee-shirt: "You're never too old to have a happy childhood."

The sixth hour began with Kay saying she hadn't had the dream of being molested again but had had other violent dreams. She had been crying and felt depressed during the week. An orientation toward the future, often contrasted in modern psychotherapy with a fascination with problem-saturated narratives (White & Epston 1990), leads naturally to viewing emotions as "forward-looking" too. The relational context of emotions, here those connected with leaving home, was also an important guide for us:

Eric: What are you planning once our work together is done?

Kay: (*With determination in her voice.*) I'm going to finish my college degree, move out of the house, get a job, and be out of debt by August!

Eric: Were you crying for your mom and dad?

Kay: Yes.

Eric: Suppose you tell your mom and dad that you're crying for them.

Kay: I feel freedom and strength. The depressed feeling is like a volcano in my stomach.

Eric: What happens when you relieve the pressure from the sides of the volcano?

Kay: It cools off. I get exhausted.

Eric: Suppose you have a steady, warm flow all over?

Kay: It's better, more in control, more relaxed, less anxious. I can get things accomplished without feeling burdened. I can think clearer and hear my own voice. *It helps to break up the ugliness of the past.*

At our final meeting, Kay told me that she had spoken with her aunt and uncle, with her sister and her kids, and with her brother and his wife, explaining what had happened to her and discussing ways in which they could all protect the children.

Kay: I've felt happier and a lot stronger these past weeks. Every night I lock up the room.

Every day I concentrate on the sky-blue color. *I don't feel isolated.* It's not this deep, dark secret anymore. I've joined the choir again. I'm preparing for future relationships. I told my mom that I was leaving my abusive boyfriend. She said, "Oh, you'll sleep with him again," but I said, "I won't share your fear." And I told my boyfriend, "I deserve better than you." *Now I know my own heart. I've got the foundation.*

Kay demonstrated the integration of dream meanings, trance learnings, relationship, and social actions. She restored her self-esteem and self-knowledge and began to influence her extended family to help them reshape a community whose practices protect children and express respect for persons. In the next section, we'll explore means for developing such communities of practice within a professional group, using, again, the means of image, trance, and relationship.

Passing the Trance

An Ericksonian psychotherapy is meant to be individual and idiosyncratic, taking its lead from the unique life patterns and expressions of its clients. In spirit it is pragmatic, aimed at encouraging action, change, and experiment, even in the timid. The relational styles of this therapy employ all manner of communicative devices, from play and imitation through directives, storytelling, and the exchange of activities, knowledge, and secrets. Rapport is engendered through, among other ways, humor, challenges, and the use of shared figures of speech.

Milton Erickson was an innovator in the use of hypnosis in medical and dental settings, in family therapy, and in brief treatment in emergency medicine. Practitioners have learned from his hypnotic experimentation to actively focus the attention of both the patient and therapist. The result of this focusing is a sort of naturalistic hypnotic trance or mutual intense engagement in experience. From hypnotic practice also comes the use of dissociated attention in response to trauma, in pain control and in active imagining. The powerful concept of the benign unconscious mind allows therapists to entrain their treatments with what Rossi (1996) calls natural ultradian cycles of bodily and emotional healing.

Prior to his interest in hypnosis, Erickson (cited in Bandler & Grinder, 1975) had become a student of communication:

> An attack of anterior poliomyelitis in 1919 . . . rendered me almost totally paralyzed for several months, but with my vision, hearing and thinking intact. . . . My inability to move tended to restrict me to the intercommunications of those about me. . . . I was amazed to discover the frequent, and, to me, often startling commu-

nications within a single interchange. This aroused so much of my interest that I intensified my observations at every opportunity. . . .

Also, it became apparent that there were multiple levels of perception and response, not all of which were at the usual or conscious level of awareness but were at levels of understanding not recognized by the self . . .

Then, I was introduced to experimental hypnosis by Clark L. Hull, and I became aware of the possibilities both of decreasing the number of foci of attention and of selecting and manuvering specific foci of attention. This led to the combining of my awarenesses of the complexities of communication with my understandings of hypnosis, for experimental and psychotherapeutic purposes. (pp. vii–viii)

The hallmark of Ericksonian relatedness in therapy is its variety. Everything from challenging a child to a bicycle race to infuriating an arrogant man to inviting a woman to imagine a hungry tiger is employed to aid patients to meet their own goals in therapy (Haley, 1973). As a therapist, Erickson was attentive, kind, and respectful in tone, even when engaged in difficult exchanges with difficult persons.

His constant use of metaphorical communication in images and story-telling was central to his effectiveness. Erickson maintained that there was no reason that a person need know the semantics of a cure or the origin of his or her difficulties in order to be helped. There also is no necessity to examine and make public in the therapy the private and idiosyncratic meanings of phrases or of symptoms. As Ginott (1965) says of a child, "He wants to be understood without having to disclose fully what he is experiencing." The unconscious-mind metaphor allows Ericksonian therapists to offer this sort of respectful treatment to their patients.

Still, Erickson was fastidious in his use of certain terms and phrases. This care with metaphorical language functions in the following ways: (1) The central themes of therapeutic discussion are taken directly from the person's report of his or her problems, interests, and work. These themes, and the person's most idiosyncratic and vivid phrases, are incorporated into the therapist's statements. (2) Interpersonally, this provides a sense of exactness to the hypnotherapist's remarks; a sense of the appositeness of the remarks to the person's compelling needs. (3) No one—hypnotist, patient, Freud—need know the many possible or few probable and idiosyncratic meanings of the patient's linguistic and symptomatic utterances. Metaphor is at work. If asituational, fantasy, or overdetermined meanings exist, metaphors trap and utilize them for communication. (4) Hypnotic practices mobilize people's energy and direct them toward change. The particulars of this change are directed by the meanings of the phrases they themselves have used. (5) This approach, Erickson (1964) has noted, affords individuals an opportunity "to achieve successfully contradictory goals, with the feeling that these derived out of the unexpected but adequate use of their own behavior."

A tent under which all these concepts loosely fit is the idea of "utilization" (Erickson, 1980), which we may take to mean the use of all aspects of human life—emotions, communication, actions, sensations, thoughts, patterned activities, memory, imagination—to coordinate desirable change through therapeutic relating. This chapter began with examples of the utilization of dream imagery, hypnotic trance and the social network to induce therapeutic change. Later chapters will emphasize action and relationship and the epistemology arising from novel forms of imagining.

"Passing the Trance" discusses and demonstrates a social form of hypnotic experience through which solutions to difficult problems are approached and exemplifies the powers of metaphorical speech realized in states of hypnotic trance. This work is an ongoing improvisation in psychotherapy, attempting to harmonize themes from ancient and modern practice. The rhythms for the piece come from the old music of hypnosis and dreams, practiced in many cultures and revived in modern times in the work of Freud (1935), Erickson (1939), and Epston (White & Epston 1992) among others. You will recognize the themes as metaphorical communication and visualization.

The ensemble that performs here consists of members of my six-month-long hypnotherapy class, each an experienced psychotherapist with a different set of skills. We are playing various melodies with a reflecting team motif (Andersen, 1991), in which solutions are developed collaboratively. In our practice, we have passed the trance from one member to the next, using a faceted crystal as a focus, and developed solutions to human dilemmas by passing an image from person to person. This improvisation is also a method in much of modern therapy. You may hear echoes of strategic therapy, psychodrama, and therapeutic rituals in our work.

The method of composition involves a radicalization of some signature assumptions in therapy, a "going to a root or source of something" (Morris, 1969, p. 1076). This method was used in producing the spare, lovely pieces of the Milan team (Boscolo, Cecchin, Hoffman, & Penn, 1987) as they go to the root of strategic therapy. Here we radicalize the notion of unconscious mind, taking seriously the assumption that this "mind" cannot be consciously known and Erickson's insight that this "mind" can be utilized in a positive manner.

Passing the trance is a hypnotic simile for the discussion that takes place in a reflecting team or consultation. Imagine hypnosis as a sort of conversation that enables the discussants to imitate all types of felt human experience. Imagine, too, that the language of this conversation is dreamlike, that it is pictorial and emotive. To realize solutions, we follow a rule of thumb: "Treat the imagined situation as real." And we propose possible courses for action that would obtain if the situation were actually occurring. This advice may be proferred by a therapist, by the client, by the family, or by the team, just as interventions and directives are constructed in modern therapies. The task is to utilize a person's own competence to allow change to occur.

A main principle is to complete the dramatic action of the dream, the imagined event, using a person's own images. These dramatic actions may be considered a sort of thought experiment in the development of possible solutions. Another principle might be termed "conservation of imagery," the attempt to relate to all aspects of the image and to involve them in prospective solutions.

In my view, we have very highly organized systems of action, feeling, thought, relationship, perception, and sensation, and they are analogous, or one can make analogies among them. It is a common practice in folk medicine and shamanism to analogize one thing to another by way of effecting some change. Thus, you perform sexual ceremonies in order to make the fields grow. It's change by analogy. But, more immediately than ceremony, language itself has that analogic function. All words are analogous to something else that we are talking *about*.

An implicit directive in this work is: Treat what we are saying as though it were the thing with which we are trying to deal. Treat our words as though they represent and can effect the relationships you had with your parents when you were a kid. Treat our words as though they could represent, engage, and resolve the grievous loss of your uncle. Treat this image as though it were a treatment for and a healing of the pain in your foot. To quote Jung (1968a) about psychotherapy: "He must try to get his mood to speak to him. His mood must tell him all about itself and show him through what kind of fantastic analogies it is expressing itself."

In psychotherapy, our intention is to do no harm and to ameliorate the suffering of the people we are with by helping them to use their own means, their own subconsciousness and intuition, to meet their goals. And if we are to do this "in our own way, in our own time," and leave what's not important to us behind us, and do it just as we wish and find it in our own inner search—all these protections Erickson (1980) built into his therapy—we can take the image and imagine possibilities and move through emotional states without having first to risk our actions directly in the world.

The Problem of Evil

In this class session, we had been sharing stories about difficult work experiences from the week's practice, including work with adults ritually abused as children, participants in therapeutic cults, and survivors of political torture. Now we were sitting together with images, memories, and emotions from all the stories we had told.

Eric: Suppose we take a very difficult problem, the problem of evil, and let's think about contamination by evil: "What's the way of avoiding contamination from the feelings and experiences of others?" It's a very good question for therapists, all of whom are empathic. So let's think about contamination and complicity, and sanctity, and integrity, and we'll see what we can come up with. This will be a very hard assignment, the worst form of insoluble problem, because people have struggled with it for thousands of years.

This will be an induction to solve the problem of evil with images. What I'd like to do is to induce a trance with you, and let's develop the image as we go around the room until Tom delivers the solution to me. (*General laughter*: "*How long will that take?*" "*Thousands of years.*") We are going to develop the solution to an insoluble problem of feeling—not the problem of a world of evil, but the problem of feeling, engaging ourselves with other human beings who have experienced mistreatment or evil, or perpetrated it, in a way that cannot be called back.

The induction I'd like is a sort of dissociative one. In other words, we are going to consider this image as though it were separate from us. We are going to imagine an image of the solution, not of the problem. We are going to pass the image around, like we did the faceted glass. Pass it when you have seen the image and said what it is, and when your body can relax with it. An image of the solution will come right out of the box, because it is a kind of black box problem. You don't know how it works. The solution will come out of the black box.

Alicia: And the image is the solution?

Eric: It's the solution. It is whatever image answers the question, "How can I feel, or what is it like to solve the problem of evil?"—the problem being the feelings of the person coming into contact with it, contaminated by it. How can you be helpful and not contaminated when you have ordinary human feelings of fascination with evil, of repulsion and dismay, of fear or anger? Is that a fair way to put it to you? Is there anything you want to add to it?

June: I already have an image, so. . . .

Eric: Wonderful. Then if you'll allow me to hypnotize you . . . (*Takes June's hand.*) Be comfortable and just say what you see.

June: I see myself in a newborn nursery at the hospital, my hands in an isolette. There is a fragile premature baby in there who desperately needs a lot of help, and the only way I can make contact with this tiny person is with gloves through these holes in the sides of the box. The feeling is wanting so much to do something that will comfort this little person and help nurture it and help it grow. I feel it in this part of my abdomen. It's a gut-wrenching kind of feeling, a turmoil. It's wanting to do something and not being sure how to do it. It's a feeling that in my just touching it some way it can get better. So for me it's a feeling of some confidence, but some fear for its safety.

Eric: Would you be willing to watch the baby until you have more and more reason for this confidence?

June: Yes, I have a feeling I will be willing to stay and watch this baby for as long as it takes.

Eric: Now, to pass this to Eleanor, I'd like you to help her to be hypnotized comfortably and then to let her either have her hands on the baby or to watch and to add to it what she sees and feels—if that's all right with you.

June: (*to Eleanor*) Just breathe very deeply and try to see this tiny infant, which is really a tiny problem or a tiny form of a big problem. You can see that in your mind as you relax. I'm having a hard time giving you this idea, but you can see it and imagine your own response. Do you have any kind of feeling about it at all?

Eleanor: I'm confused. Of course, I have a response to an infant: It's a nurturing response. And I have the feeling of rage and fury that such a helpless thing could be hurt. And what do I do with that rage and fury, because there is nothing I can do about whatever it was, whoever it was that hurt this infant? I want to drape this infant and wrap it to protect it, I want to keep it warm. I want to communicate to this infant with this gossamer, yet protective, covering. It is even beautiful as a kind of protecting—a kind of antidote to this evil that is dark and awful and ugly. And somehow I have pulled this out of myself, out of inside me. That's where I have resources. There is something about spirit, there is something about willingness. Not just to be helpless before this.

Eric: When you talk about the image, you want to talk about the beauty of the gossamer blanket, the strength of it, the lightness, the warmth—not the meaning of it, just the blanket. Just the baby, just the blanket. You are going back and forth between the reality of the image and the reality of the feelings, not the meanings, but the real image, the real feelings.

Eleanor: It's so light, it's not even a blanket. It's almost translucent; it's brilliant. It's almost insubstantial while being warm and brilliant and light. Just to have thought of something to do for the infant makes me feel resourceful. There's something inside me I can turn to, pull out. I'm not so frightened. I'm not so angry any more. I'm not so full of rage. That part melts away because it's not important anymore. I took something out of myself here (*puts hand on chest*). The first gut-wrenching feelings, the hard ones, the angry mixed-up confusion really started here (*puts hand on abdomen*). I essentially pull out from higher up a sort of an organizing or quelling of that so you can have its energy and it's not splattering all over the place. The energy actually makes the blanket, the gossamer. It's light and warm.

June: I do have that impression—that it is a very strong, very real thing. If you would take that image now and give it to Andrea, so that she can experience it too . . .

Eleanor: (*to Alicia*) I'm going to entrust you with my image. I want you to look at this, to let your mind roam around in it, your feelings wrap around it. Pull it into you deeply as you go into trance. Take it inside to your deepest feelings, to make it your own, to transform it as a fetus transforms inside of a womb. This is a baby that grows inside of you, and it changes. When you are ready, you can tell us how it changes and how this infant is transformed.

Alicia: First is that my hands feel as though they are very full of blood, and I have a lot of sensation in my hands. I don't really understand what I am doing, but it doesn't bother me so much either. I feel my own blood. I feel the sensation of my own blood. This isn't a premature baby; this is a healthy baby. A baby that has me watching it, and me holding it, and the class watching it. There is some protection for this baby. There is the intention to keep it from evil, to keep it from harm. What I feel is a lot of sensation in my own hands, when the baby is in my hands. And the baby is wrapped in some kind of light, shimmering something that has a lot of energy.

Eleanor: So you are giving the baby feelings, good feelings in its body, through this shimmering. Can you describe how the baby feels now?

Alicia: Moving, feeling it, contentment, smiling a little. I feel good, and if I can give this, if I can be in this state and give this kind of protection to myself and to a baby and to a client and to anybody, it's the same as when you talk about a gossamer scarf.

Eleanor:	Would you like to take this infant that's wiggling with new life and give it to Vanessa? Can you help Vanessa go into a trance and contribute to the growth of this infant?
Vanessa:	I have the infant. I'm really just content with this baby. Close to me. It's just maybe a month-old or a 6-week-old baby, and I want to protect it with the gossamer, but somehow I want to hold that flesh, that nice soft warm wonderful feeling, the bottom and shoulders and a little peach fuzz on the head.
Alicia:	So you are really feeling each part of the baby, the bottom, peach-fuzz hair, shoulders, right close.
Vanessa:	It bonded to me in some way. In a minute I'll want to take a look, but right now I like this feeling of its just being next to me. Yet I feel too that I don't know what the protection is for this baby that's so innocent, because there is that evil. I can't protect the baby forever from the evil, but I want to do something for it for now, maybe so it will always have some sort of idea of good and evil—be able to choose. When I see clients, I picture them as having this invisible covering that protects them—so that we won't contaminate each other. I guess I'm thinking of the light around this baby as being a protection from that, from evil. I'd like to be able to find a certain stone or crystal or something that I'd like to put in the baby's hand, something that is there but isn't there in a certain sense. I can't explain it any more than that, but it's as though embedded in the palm of that baby's hand.
Alicia:	Suppose you go around and look. While you are holding the baby.
Vanessa:	Oh! To go and look for it. The baby is very content. I am by the lake, in the sand. As the water comes up in the sand, there are a lot of little pebbles, but there is one that is clearer and also washed like the sea-washed glass. As I get closer to it, it is quite flat. It would just fit in the palm of the hand, and that would become the baby's protection and connection with what's of real value—nature, I guess. What would be true nature would also protect the baby from outer forces of evil. I can feel it in my own hand as the baby feels it. It's as if it just transferred from my hand to the baby's hand.
Alicia:	When you're ready, find your way to pass the baby on to

Tom and help hypnotize him to see what he can find for that baby.

Vanessa: I'd really like to keep the baby, but I do want also to share that life. Just lots of feeling of life in my hands, and so I would like to share that. When I pass it to Tom I think I want him to feel the baby just like it is, with all that nice soft firm flesh.

Tom: Energy!! It feels like a gossamer blanket of energy. I see colors. I don't feel any weight from this baby, it's all energy. I feel light in my chest. It makes me very happy. I feel a blending of energy, feel a form in my hands, but I can't see a shape. I feel it in my hands and my body. I see reds, greens, blues. And I feel a shape in my hands, I feel it. It has a little weight. It's light. It could be a child. It has a soft blanket. The blanket feels very good to me. There are stars on its blanket. The baby's face is very fair. Its hair could be red. Protect it? But it doesn't seem necessary. It seems to have the energy. It seems very connected.

Vanessa: So it's protected by its own energy. When you feel ready, look at your energy in your hands, and when you feel as though you want to come back into this room, come and join the group.

Tom: (*Pause.*) Now what do you want me to do? (*General laughter.*)

Eric: Everybody did really well. It's a great baby. It's a baby that started out injured and helpless, and premature and needing faithful care. It started out with just the faith that you had to do something, but without any hope that you could accomplish it. You (*June*) added your faith that something had to be done; and you (*Eleanor*) added the strength from yourself; and you (*Alicia*) added the lively energy, the blood, the birth, as you (*Vanessa*) added and you (*Tom*) added.

And so it lived and became infused with self. Contrary to the view that knowledge of good and evil is dangerous, you had knowledge of good and evil as a protection for the infant because it allowed choice. There were good and evil; therefore, the infant would be protected by choosing. There was danger, uncertainty, so the infant was protected by faith and by whatever you could give, which was your heart, your hands, your love and energy. It is a kind of parable of hope: When one has suffered evil, there is still hope that others— the survivors, the children—can be graced, and that is a natural metaphor for resolving this question of the problem of evil.

Eleanor: Actually, we each did that. I guess what I did was to turn the anger and the terrible powerful emotions I have about evil into energy to comfort and protect. I had a sense that today's class was a poetry-writing class, only it just happens in one person when it's a poem.

Eric: I want to read the Stanislavsky (1926) quote again. "Let me remind you of our cardinal principle: 'Through conscious means we reach the subconscious.' Wherever you have truth and belief you have feeling and experience. You can test this by executing even the smallest act in which you really believe . . ." Here you really believe in something gossamer, insubstantial, of the heart, spiritual, but you really believe it. That is to say, you truly experience it: the giving of it, the energy of it, the search for the stones. "Executing even the smallest act in which you really believe and you will find that instantly, intuitively and naturally, an emotion will arise. If you just feel the truthfulness of this (imaginary) act, your intention and subconsciousness will come to your aid." Your intention ("Find a solution to the problem of evil, this insoluble problem") and subconsciousness ("I don't know how we are going to do this") will come to your aid. "Then superfluous tension will disappear," which everybody experienced. "The necessary muscles will come into action . . ." There is all that engagement of power, energy, strength. You could protect that baby. You could hold the baby. That's also very nice: Nobody dropped it; everyone knows how to do it. "And all this will happen without the interference of any conscious technique." In other words, the conscious technique for solving a moral problem isn't in operation here. Here the technique is: What do you see? What do you feel? What are you moved to do?

The uses of analogy in healing pain, fear, and uncertainty through the development of a mental image are accentuated in our use of the social group form, passing the trance. Experiences encoded as emotion, sensation, thought and action are utilized by the group to develop solutions to difficult problems. In Chapter 4, we consider the epistemology of this approach. First, though, we discuss the use of these methods and their relational forms in dealing with some troubling dilemmas of psychotherapy.

Chapter 2

Difficult Therapy

Utilization and Imagination

The relational forms encouraged by a hypnotic psychotherapy lead in different directions from those engaged in by dynamic psychotherapies. In the latter, the concepts of *resistance* and *transference* predominate, whereas the former are guided by notions of *utilization* and *imagination*.

In Freud's (1935) early experiments, he used hypnosis for purposes other than enhancing suggestion:

> I used it for questioning the patient upon the origin of his symptom, which in his waking state he could often describe imperfectly or not at all ... It turned out that ... symptoms had a meaning and were residues or reminiscences of ... emotional situations. (p. 35)

There is a wonderful quality to Freud's observations. A careful reading of his allusive qualities of speech might have saved later analysts from reifiying psychological knowledge. If symptoms are residues *or* reminiscences, and if, "as a rule the symptom [is] not the precipitate of a single traumatic scene, but the result of a summation of a number of similar situations" (p. 35), we have lattitude in understanding the interactions among painful events, memory, and recovery. This difference in residue or reminiscence between the hypnotic experience and waking consciousness was demonstrated again when the trance concluded.

> *When the subject awoke from the state of somnambulism he seemed to have lost all memory of what had happened while he was in that state. But Bernheim maintained that the memory was present all the same and if he insisted on the subject remembering, if he asseverated that the subject knew it all and only had to say it and if at the same time he laid his hand on the subject's forehead, then the forgotten memories used in fact to return, hesitatingly at first, but eventually in a flood and with complete clarity. (pp. 50–51)*

Freud's lively image of Bernheim's *insisting* that patients remember, and accompanying his words with pressure on the patient's forehead, gives us some sense of the experiences that generated the concept of resistance as an analogy to physical events, such as hydraulic pressure. And the rhetorical element in this hypnosis, the relational aspect expressed in ordinary language, reminds us that across the room from every resistant patient we may encounter a stubborn therapist.

Freud's observations on the social interactions in therapy were lost in the later development of psychoanalysis as a theory of intrapsychic conflict and accommodation. In modern narrative therapies (White & Epston, 1990), resistance is once again used to denote an interpersonal refusal to allow influences from another and is encouraged as a means of recovery, rather than disparaged as an impediment to desired change.

The entire strategy of *utilization* derives from the highly original work of Milton Erickson. This concept, like Freud's *resistance*, was developed in hypnotic work with difficult patients (Erickson, 1980).

> *Ordinarily trance induction is based upon securing from the patients some form of initial acceptance and cooperation with the operator. In techniques of utilization the usual procedure is reversed to an initial acceptance of the patients' presenting behaviors and a*

ready cooperation by the operator however seemingly adverse the
presenting behaviors may appear to be in the clinical situation. (Vol.
IV., ch. 3, p. 178)

This explanation covers some charming and spectacular therapy. Erickson (cited in Haley, 1993), confronted with a man who believed himself to be Christ, opined that the man must have had experience as a carpenter, and helped him to develop work and a life with other people. Met at an initial session by a man who cursed Erickson, psychiatry, and much else, Erickson said, "I'm sure you can say that and even more," opening the conversation between them to therapy.

We have been taught that acceptance of emotion in therapy is communicated to patients by saying, in effect, "I understand that you feel such and such to be so." Differences between the therapist's formulation and that of the patient are often ascribed to patient resistance. Utilization approaches to communication take the patient's formulation as a given and extend it to action that helps meet the goals of the patient: "You are (Christ) a skilled carpenter, therefore, take on meaningful work," or, "You have a lot to say (of a rude, negative sort, about me), so you can say even more (of a helpful sort, to me)."

The difference between the therapeutic concepts of resistance and utilization was captured by a man who, as a child, had been raped by his grandfather. After years of psychoanalytic psychotherapy, he had learned to identify his reluctance to trust, his prickly wit, his aggressive self-protection, and several other powerful aspects of his personality as "resistance." While discussing his love of music with me, he described the basic beat of native rhythms as being similar to the human heartbeat. As he sounded out the rhythm on the arm of his chair, he said, "Resistance is the skin of the drum." I replied, "Keep it tuned," and we both laughed.

In current usage in many therapies, transference has come to mean a response to the therapist that imitates the pattern of the patient's childhood relationships with parents. Freud's (1935) own use of the term is much broader:

> *Transference . . . decides the success of all medical influence, and*
> *in fact delineates the whole of each person's relations to his human*
> *environment. We can easily recognize it as the same dynamic factor*
> *that the hypnotists have named "suggestibility" which is the agent of*

hypnotic rapport and whose incalculable behavior led to such difficulties with the cathartic method. When there is no inclination to a transference of emotion . . . then there is also no possibility of influencing the patient by psychological means. (p. 80)

The difficulties to which Freud refers in this treatment of human relations are those that gave rise to the grave doubts about hypnotism with which generations of therapists are familiar. The origins of both doubt and transference are found in this narrative from Freud's (1935) *An Autobiographical Study.*

> *One day I had an experience which showed me in the crudest light what I had long suspected. One of my most acquiescent patients, with whom hypnotism had enabled me to bring about the most marvellous results, and whom I was engaged in relieving of her suffering by tracing back her attacks of pain to their origins, as she woke up on one occasion, threw her arms round my neck.*
>
> *The unexpected entrance of a servant relieved us from a painful discussion, but from that time onwards there was a tacit understanding between us that the hypnotic treatment should be discontinued . . . I felt that I had now grasped the nature of the mysterious element that was at work behind hypnotism. In order to exclude it . . . or to isolate it . . . it was necessary to abandon hypnotism. (pp. 45–50)*

It's striking that Freud allowed "tacit understanding" to replace "analysis of the transference" and that the drama of this event was used to clothe Freud's scarecrow conception of hypnosis and of the unconscious mind. Dynamic therapists came to adopt versions of this point of view, and therapists employing hypnoanalysis also wrestled with the narrow notion of transference as a patterned reminiscence. The analysts held that analysands imagined the nature of their relationship to the analyst. Rossi (Erickson & Rossi, 1981) wrote: "In every analytic treatment there arises, without the physician's agency, an intense emotional relationship between the patient and the analyst which is not to be accounted for by the actual situation" (p. 156). Ericksonian therapists, taking responsibility for their influence on relationship and guided by the principle of utilization, seek ways in which to use imagined relationship as the actual situation to aid their patients in reaching their own goals.

Restoring Freud's original, broad use of the term "transference," with its homology to hypnotic rapport and suggestibility, we can proceed to develop the modern sense of hypnotic psychotherapy as a focused and collaborative relational enterprise whose meanings are constructed through imaginative acts during a continuing conversation.

Erickson's (Erickson & Rossi, 1979) "February Man" monograph is one striking example of the uses of imagination in forming therapeutic relatedness. Here Erickson utilizes the patient's feelings toward him—her rapport with him, her liking of him, her dependence on him—to help her meet her goals in therapy. He does this by informing her that she can revisit troubling times in her life with him as company. The widely quoted induction of this companionship is familiar to most Ericksonian therapists (Erickson & Rossi, 1979):

> And I want you to choose some time in the past when you were a
> very, very little girl. And my voice will go with you. And my voice
> will change into that of your parents, your neighbors, your friends,
> your schoolmates, your playmates, your teachers. And I want you to
> find yourself sitting in the school room, a little girl feeling happy
> about something, something that happened a long time ago, that you
> forgot a long time ago.

Erickson's approach to or attitude toward patients is clear in this: The patient has freedom of choice and can seek a positive outcome according to her goals. Her imagination can include Erickson, her past, and her strong emotions in a safe and interesting relationship. Erickson chooses to utilize transferential feelings unconsciously, in pursuit of desired changes, rather than to convince his patient of their interpreted meaning.

Freud (1935) was clear on the distinction between the use of the transference and the analytic concept of working through the transference, with its implication of interpretation and conscious understanding.

> It is perfectly true that psychoanalysis, like other psychotherapeu-
> tic methods, employs the instrument of suggestion (or transference).
> But the difference is this: that in analysis it is not allowed to play the
> decisive part in determining the therapeutic results . . . The transfer-
> ence is made conscious to the patient by the analyst and it is resolved

by convincing him that in his transference-attitude he is re-experiencing emotional relations which had their origin during the repressed period of his childhood. (p. 80)

A modern understanding of the difference between Erickson's approach and that of dynamic therapists is expressed by a psychologist and hypnotherapist who herself has experienced both dynamic and Ericksonian therapies as a patient. Stott (1998) writes:

I remembered that I had been trying to explain to my analytically oriented friend how it could be acceptable for me to attend a seminar that my psychotherapist was presenting. "It's not a problem to see him in these two roles," I explained. "In fact, the two contribute to one another. I think it is not problematic because the transference in our work together is so different from what I've experienced in the past." "What do you mean?" she asked.

My response: When Eric and I work together, there is an area between us where we meet and work. We both come there out of our own lives, bringing with us what we need to do the work. I am usually there as myself, but with a willing vulnerability to be open and direct, and as disclosing as possible, sometimes with a curiosity to understand something, and sometimes with just a need to be understood, knowing that as Eric understands me I will come to understand myself.

There's the third place in the room: there's him and there's me and there's the place we work together. If there were a transference, it would be to the relationship. But I don't think you can really call it transference. It allows the work to develop, it enables it and it's quite freeing. It allows for basic processes to occur in a very supportive, nurturing, holding environment.

You don't go through all that stuff about boundaries. You effectively strengthen ego functioning as opposed to the traditional transference of attachment-individuation. It is more direct, but an entirely different experience.

He seems to come as himself; his personal life is somewhat visible (though the details are unknown) but largely irrelevant except as it lends understanding to something I'm trying to understand. It is present in a pleasant way; it imparts a kindness and a keen interest in people, but is nonintrusive in the work. Thus the "transference" is much less personal than in a more traditional framework. He never feels like my father to me, for example, even though there are times when I take from him the kindness and gentleness or the wisdom or the challenge that one would wish to receive from a father.

It is as though the interpersonal aspects of the therapy are all channeled through this working space between us, and in that way becomes personal yet impersonal and has to do with our work in that room, not who Eric is when he is presenting a seminar. Much as one can learn to dance from a talented dance instructor, experience the dance, learn to whirl and soar on the dancefloor, by experiencing the instructor without ever needing to know him or her, it's that way with therapy. Thus seeing him in a seminar setting has very little bearing on the work we do together in the office. They are just two different ways of experiencing the same person.

The Person of the Therapist

I know a great deal is said about this transference relationship, and
while I like to have my patients like me, and like me immensely,
I want them to like me in such a fashion that I, as a therapist,
can be pleased.

—*Milton H. Erickson (cited in Haley, 1985, vol. II, p. 68)*

Freud's patients came to his home office, read his books, knew his colleagues. Erickson's patients came to his home office, read his books, met his family. In distinction to the idea that the therapist can be a blank screen for a patient's projections, Ericksonian therapists hope to use their own persons—voice, posture, humor, presence, social circumstance—to influence the other person's recovery and growth. We assume strong emotional responses, positive and negative, as a correlate of any real human relationship.

Negative countertransference was used by Erickson to train his medical students in developing a therapeutic attitude toward and feelings for their patients. He describes his approach to the therapist's emotions using the analytic language his students understood. His description (Erickson, 1983) comes from a 1965 workshop on using hypnosis in pain control.

Now here is an important question: In your endeavor to analyze and control the attitudes of patients, how do you subdue your own countertransference so that anxiety is therefore not aroused?

I have often taken my medical students through cancer clinics because I think they ought to see terminal cases of cancer; I think they ought to see all the ulcerations and all the very difficult things that result from neglectful cases. This was in the County Hospital ... and my medical students were rather repulsed by the appearance of the patients' wounds and by their generally depressing condition.

After my students were thoroughly repulsed and had manifested thoroughly their adverse reactions, I pointed out: "You are reacting adversely to these patients. Why? Aren't they the patients that are affording you a medical education? How do you expect to make your living except by meeting your patients, by respecting and liking them—by thoroughly liking them. ... Don't you think you ought to be grateful to those patients?"

I also would take medical students through the back wards of the psychiatric section and do the same thing with them. You simply ought not to have any other attitude toward patients but one of sympathy and liking and respect. (Vol. I, pp. 271–272)

In his own experience as a therapist, Erickson tolerated all manner of emotions toward patients, as he had in his students, but with the same emphasis on providing the patient with sympathy, liking, and respect. His response (cited in Haley, 1985) to his own emotional adjustments is both characteristic and charming.

I had an experience of countertransference the other night. This woman irritates the life out of me. Horribly so. The previous patient had come in a bathing suit and got the chair of the seat all wet. So I got a towel and draped it over the seat of the chair. Then the patient that irritates me so much came in, sat down on the towel, and irritated me very much. I suddenly realized, with a great deal of amusement, that after she left I had taken hold of the corner of that towel and very carefully, gingerly, picked it up and put it in the laundry. (Laughter) That really amused me. My own more or less phobic response to the towel—which took up all my anger. I think I must have looked funny taking that towel out to the laundry. (Vol. I, p. 89)

The most difficult therapy relationships often lead to ineffective inter-pretative commentary, followed by the cessation of the therapeutic rela-tionship. Termination of treatment or a collapse of the conversational relationship into sexual or violent acts are common outcomes. How then may we view the system of the relating of the therapist and patient so as to maintain effective therapeutic conversation within the transference of therapy?

The Therapist as Stand-in

Even the most brilliant results were liable to be suddenly wiped away
if my personal relationship with the patient became disturbed,
proving that the personal emotional relation between doctor and
patient was after all stronger than the whole cathartic process, and
escaped every effort at control.

—Sigmund Freud (1935, p. 48)

The stand-in, as a member of the cast of a play or movie, takes the place of the major character and says the lines, and allowing the other players to block their scenes and take their cues in the absence of the star. At the actual performance the stand-in waits in the wings while the main actors take the stage. In active therapies, such as psychodrama, with its metaphorical space of theater, a stand-in's role can be central to rehearsals of the action.

Traditional therapies might benefit from this way of thinking of rela-tionship. Rather than taking umbrage at being enrolled as a stand-in for parents, friends, or lovers, therapists may enjoy and encourage this use of their abilities. They may say, "Let me talk to you like a mother (or a Dutch uncle, friend, or brother)." They may even say, "If I were a differ-ent sort of therapist, I might say . . ." In a recent session where an inter-faith couple was trying to decide whether future male children would be circumcised, I said, "Let me speak to you like a rabbi: 'Pray for girls.' " Then I was able to discuss the context of religious choice and ritual action with them. The place of solution was shifted from the couple toward the councils of rabbis, whose job it is to satisfy ritual criteria in a human fashion. At their wedding, the groom consulted the rabbi and was offered

a ritual solution. He reported to me, "Only three drops of blood are necessary, not the mutilation of my son's body."

Another example of the stand-in approach to troubles and of the idea
of imagination replacing that of transference is found in my case study,
"Conjoint Therapy with an Imagined Co-therapist" (Greenleaf, 1985),
which begins with Melody Palmer's dream.

> *I remember later, in another part of the dream, I am in an upstairs
> room of my grandmother's house. My husband and I are going to live
> there and I am complaining about the lack of mirrors. He suggests
> bringing one from our bedroom but I don't want to do that. I want a
> new one.*
>
> *Then I begin to notice many small doors along the bottom part of
> the wall, and I remember that one is a secret passageway to an attic
> area, and that I used to know the way there as a child. At the same
> time, I have the feeling that I have visited these attic rooms in my
> dream life as an adult.*
>
> *Yet I am afraid to open any of the doors. It has been many many
> years since anyone has opened them and looked in and I think there
> are probably terrible, awful things behind them now which I
> wouldn't want to see.*

I was consulted by Melody, a happily married woman, who, although
orgasmic with her husband and experiencing a wide range of sexual
activities and emotions, felt sexual restraint. Her inhibition, although
shameful and secret to her, was made manifest in a reluctance to undergo
even routine gynecological examinations. She also experienced nausea
and dizziness when attempting to insert Tampons. In addition, and more
unsettling still to Melody, herself a psychotherapist, she had had a series
of crushes on a succession of therapists she consulted, the first one some
three months following her marriage, and the others over the course of
the next 15 years.

Melody's therapy with me began in September 1981 and continued
through the resolution of her inhibition in April 1983. We met for an
hour each week and dealt in turn with themes in her life that seemed to
offer a way to relieve her distress. Each path in dreams, relationship,
strategic intervention, hypnotherapy or conversation seemed to reach

some resolution, only to turn into another unsolved puzzle. Meanwhile, Melody's crush on her therapist grew and flourished. As Melody said, "I need to keep doing this until I exhaust myself and let go of it."

Melody was encouraged repeatedly to express all her sexual feelings by words and in letters and to enjoy these feelings as the natural expression of her womanly emotions. As she said, "It happens a little bit with the writing, but the experience of relief is much stronger after I actually have put these letters and dreams in your box."

The experience of having an attractive, intelligent woman of honest conviction declare sexual passion week after week is a heady one, no matter how trivialized, demonized, or interpreted in the therapeutic literature. My box was piled high with letters. I thought I could use some help and so suggested that Melody solicit a woman's view of her intense emotions. To save the expense involved, she was to consult, in her active imaginings, with a woman therapist of her choosing. She chose the distinguished and innovative family therapist, Mara Selvini Palazzoli. Then, at home, she held the first of four long conversations with Mara.

In the first talk, Mara gave Melody a blue and red blanket. She told her that this blanket "belonged to your grandmother many years ago. She gave it up, put it away, far away, so that it was lost even in memory, when her first love died. This was the mantle of her womanhood. Under its warm protection, she would surrender fully to him—but, more important, she would yield to the mysteries of her own nature." Mara told her, too, that Melody's husband would be enriched, as she was, by her "secret treasure."

The second conversation had Melody ask Mara for understanding of "the dream about the small girl child and the male torso with the large penis." Placing Melody and the 3-year-old girl on the magic blue blanket, Mara transported them to the hill that was the dream's most frightening place. She said, "No harm will come to either of you. I will help you discover what to do." Melody and the child were naked. "Suddenly I was aware that a shadow had fallen over us. Mara called to me, 'Melody, open your eyes and look now.' "

There stood a tall, dark, handsome stranger. Mara coaxed Melody to speak with him, sit with him, touch him, make love with him. Mara took the child with her to the tree. Melody and the man were caressing each other. "Suddenly I felt afraid. At that moment, Mara's singing came to me with the breeze—she was comforting the child, and I, too, felt soothed."

Melody and the stranger made love until both were satisfied. The child returned and Mara told Melody, "Your body holds all the meaning you need."

So, Mara brought together the themes of the frightened little girl, the alluring stranger, and a grown woman's sexual knowledge. And she placed these in the context of the patient's history—her imitation of a grandparent's inhibited love. For their third conversation, I asked Melody to speak with Mara about her sexual feelings toward me.

Mara led Melody to describe her sexual imaginings and emotions. Then Mara suggested that she imagine being in the office with me. Melody asked that Mara accompany her in this fantasy and warned her, "If you get me into hot water, I'm leaving!" She was encouraged to express her natural feelings in words—they turned out to be words of warmth and affection—and was told, "It's the holding back that creates difficulty. Long ago you learned to suppress these natural and very right feelings."

The fourth conversation with Mara concerned ways in which Melody might schedule her time and care for herself in the world, at work, among her friends. Of the conversations with Mara, Melody said:

> *They seem to be supporting this important shift from my regard-*
> *ing you as the one to be revered and idolized to simply one who is my*
> *equal. I'm not speaking here of the content of the conversations, but*
> *rather of the structure itself.*
>
> *In addition, Mara's femaleness.... in some way is allowing me to*
> *re-own my own wisdom and power, rather than projecting them onto*
> *some male figure (you, most recently). I feel happy. Yes! I feel happy!*
> *I think I am finally falling in love with myself.*

As before, the resolution of issues of emotion was not accompanied by sexual disinhibition, although it did produce real changes in Melody's sense of herself, changes noted with approval by her friends and her husband. Even into the next year, Melody insisted on bringing out the remaining aspects of her family drama for experiencing, talking about, dreaming with, and understanding:

> *I dreamed that as I was looking into the deepest part of the water,*
> *which was at the beginning, a man who was alternately my husband*
> *and my father came up behind me as I was looking.*

Also, feelings about her grandmother and great-grandmother surfaced again, as well as feelings about her father's rages and sadness. In February 1983, Melody tearfully "confessed" that she had yet to overcome her sexual inhibitions. In March, she asked to discontinue therapy, then changed her mind and continued until her successful completion of the sexual experiences she had set for herself as the task of therapy. She displayed the ability to endure gynecological examinations comfortably early in 1982, the disinhibition of her sexual fear in April 1983, and the ability to insert a Tampon without nausea and dizziness was hers by September 1983.

Before she could accomplish these tasks, it was important that she relate the emotional distress in her family life, in part, because undiscovered questions—such as, "Can I let go of 26 years of feeling ugly?"—had to be brought into the therapy before the goals that were the ostensible reasons for treatment could be accomplished.

These sexual goals had to be attained, as Erickson always insisted,"In your own way; in your own good time; in the right way; at the right time." The acknowledgment of sexual passion as a natural emotion, the expression of sexual activity toward the right partner, respect for the emotions brought out in psychotherapy and between the therapist and patient, and trust in one's own wisdom, power, and love, one's right to one's own life and liveliness—all these themes of emotion coexist and must be expressed. As Melody put it: "The charm would be to feel what I feel neither more nor less than what is actually so in the moment, and to find a way to stay in contact with you at the same time."

To illustrate the work further, the following is a transcript of the October 12, 1982, session in which Melody and I met and employed the aid of Mara as an imagined co-therapist. Here, "G." is Eric Greenleaf and "P." is Melody Palmer:

G.: I thought we might have a joint session today.
P.: A what?
G.: A joint session with Mara.
P.: I thought about that the other day. (*Laughs.*) And?
G.: I had the idea that she and I could show you something about this dilemma that you're in. Suppose you just sit back and close your eyes. (*Pause.*) Now, I don't know when you started going to "blue movies," but if you started going to blue movies a long time ago, you probably remember that the male characters in those movies

often wore masks. If you didn't start going that long ago, take my word for it. (*P. laughs.*)

Now, in the letters you wrote to me you told me some interesting things. One was that it's different to have sexual feelings in a daydream than it is to have a variety of feelings right here, talking with me, and that the contrast is intriguing to you—isn't bedeviling you. So, I thought, Mara and I would sit with you, and let you see a blue movie of your daydream, and then, at some point, when you are satisfied with the erotic content of this daydream, the male character in it would peel off his mask, and then you could see, and then he would peel off his mask again, and then you could see, and then he would peel off his mask again—as many masks as he has. Mara will turn on the film. You can watch to your heart's content. Just watch the screen—you'll see it. She'll sit at one side of you and I'll sit at the other, and you can just watch, and when you finish watching the movie, open your eyes and tell me what you saw.

P.: And this male is supposed to have a mask?

G.: Well, you know, he'll probably look like your therapist, to begin with. At least, that's the mask he's always had in the past.

P.: How true. (*Laughs.*) Oh, God.

G.: Now, while you watch the movie, I'm not going to watch you. I'm going to go out to get coffee. Do you want coffee? Do you want tea? Do you want milk?

P.: You're supposed to say, "Coffee, tea, or me?" (*Laughs.*) All right. Tea, with one sugar. Thank you.

(*Ten minutes pass while P. sits by herself. G. leaves to get coffee and tea. Then he returns.*)

P.: You came in just at the good part. Now, what about this "mask" business?

G.: Just keep watching and see the guy take the mask off. (*Pause.*) It's very possible he'll take several masks off, one after another.

P.: But am I supposed to know who he is?

G.: No. No, not really. Not necessarily at all. He might look like a complete stranger. If you have any questions, ask Mara what she knows about this odd event, that this complete stranger has such strong sexual attraction for you.

P.: So strange. I have this little, vague image of this older man. I imagined there'd be more masks, but it's the same. I'm sort of surprised though that even . . . when I saw this older man who's a stranger, *I didn't feel horrified.*

G.:   I wonder if you'd ask Mara if she's felt in her life strong, powerful sexual attraction for strangers, or if she knows that in other women? Just listen as she tells you about it.

P.:   She has a very positive view on this subject. (*Laughs.*) She says that it's an experience many people have and it's not something to be afraid of or ashamed of, but something you should be glad about.

G.:   Why "be glad"?

P.:   Just a different way . . . sometimes it's easy to have your head up in the clouds, and these feelings can be reminders of something more rooted.

G.:   Something more lifelike. Is her stranger an older stranger?

P.:   She doesn't have only one. Well, she's older. (*Laughs.*) She has older and younger ones. Likes variety. (*Laughs.*)

G.:   Yes, she does. (*Pause.*) And you can just open your eyes. Well, how did you enjoy it?

P.:   What do you say I do when I do that? When I get into my thing, what am I doing? When I get into these fantasies, it's like I give over conscious function to you. You being the teacher or being in charge. And then that lets me imagine myself getting more and more intensely into sexual feelings. But actually, I'm doing the whole thing. I'm just using you in a sort of convenient way.

G.:   Ah! That's me—a sexual convenience!

P.:   (*Laughs.*) But here that's appropriate.

G.:   I think that's exactly so.

Following this exchange, Melody was treated to a long, complicated lecture on the various psychoanalytic and Jungian analytic interpretations of the "stranger" in sexuality and of the utility of denial as a way of gradually allowing information into consciousness. The concept of the archetypes of the collective unconscious was invoked to encourage a rearrangement of emotions and actions better suited to Melody's individual needs and sensibilities than the arrangement bequeathed to her by her family.

Then, in the last minutes of the hour, we spoke about relationship.

G.:   So, what makes people special is the experience of doing something unique together. You know the story about "The Little Prince"?

(Saint-Exupéry, 1943) You know what the fox says to the Little Prince when he's leaving? He says, "There are millions of little boys in the world, and millions of foxes. But what is it that makes you special to me? You're special to me because you've 'tamed' me," says the fox to the boy. "So, wherever I go I will see the color of your hair in the waving wheat and the color of your eyes in the blue sky."

P.: While you were telling that story, I said to myself, "Listen, Eric is saying something about *this* relationship." And then I felt pleased, and then I felt myself go in a sort of haze, and take it in.

G.: Do. Take it in. And see how pleasurable it is.

P.: I don't trust the pleasure.

G.: Feel some more. It is pleasant, is it not? No matter what you think about it, taking it in is very pleasant. So, you're welcome to think what you like, but you do have the experience of the pleasure of taking in that special feeling. And what you discover is something about your special quality of feeling. You're not a boy, I'm not a fox. I'm not a little boy, you're not a fox.

But you want to know what it means to be special to someone. That's what it means.

It is important, when doing psychotherapy, to respect the emotions brought forth and the reality of the relationships formed during the work. Even Freud (cited in Bettelheim, 1983) said, "Psychoanalysis is in essence a cure through love." Everyone has recognized, though, that these relationships and emotions are embedded in a complex context, now thought of in terms of narratives, structures, or families, or conceived of as complexes or introjects.

When interacting with others, we are all aware of the "voice of conscience" and some of us, too, of "voices" or "visions," the haunting presence of our dealings with others, or of the aspects of our unconscious minds carried in dreams or in waking life. Wise counsel from friends, family, and therapists also provides us with authority for our conduct. We may remember the voice of a friend, or of Milton Erickson, during periods of doubt or struggle.

It is easy to see the usefulness of the imagined co-therapist in psychotherapy. But it is a hallmark of effective therapy that people come more and more to depend on their own wisdom and emotions in living their lives and to feel equal to all other humans they may meet along the way. As Melody said to me that August:

> You will perhaps enjoy hearing what my friend said to me this morning as we were standing on the porch at work: "Melody, you have been looking so sexy lately. Are you going through a little sexual revolution or something?" I said, "Yes!!"

Together with differences in approach to resistance and transference, some of the other important differences between older "dynamic" therapies and the modern strategic and narrative forms explored in this book ought to be kept in mind. To summarize: (1) The therapist in the dynamic model is meant to be emotionally neutral and reflective in tone while oriented toward the patient's past. Modern therapists are urged to be emotionally positive, humorous, and expectant, active in tone and future oriented. (2) The patient in a dynamic therapy is held to be responsible for change, and yet is enjoined to understand rather than to act. Modern therapists hold themselves responsible for change and encourage the patient to act, although the responsibility is often held to be collective and the actions may be imaginative or speech acts or small "unimportant" changes in simple patterns of action. (3) Dynamic therapies entertain the concept of resistance and hold that the goal of therapy is to make the unconscious conscious. Modern therapies utilize the unconscious as an ally in change. (4) The method of dynamic psychotherapy is interpretation, an analytic tool with which to conceptualize the past differently. The modern method is storytelling, a didactic tool with which to imagine different futures. (5) Insight is held to yield change in dynamic models, whereas change is held to yield foresight in many modern ones.

The practices of hypnotherapy involve a focus of attention on the entirety of the person before us: his or her posture and physiology; language, spoken and unspoken; figures of speech; patterns of action; culture and personal style. Although it is true that hypnotherapists learn to give directives and to tell stories, they also practice a mutually focused relationship of ease and intensity, which contrasts with both the stereotyped authoritarian hypnotist and the stereotyped neutral analyst.

Hypnotherapeutic practices encourage surprising and imaginative possibilities in social roles, as well as in dreams, images, and actions. They inform the more difficult therapeutic relationships.

Struggle and Cooperation

I don't focus on an issue. I focus on an antidote.

—*Twyla Tharp (New Yorker Magazine, 1995)*

Those patients who are the most difficult or eccentric communicators are characterized in the worst way by their therapists: paranoid, narcissistic, schizophrenic, or borderline. Their styles of expression are termed projection, projective identification, delusional, defensive. In therapy, much effort is expended on securing and clarifying boundaries between persons, on encouraging realism in thinking, and on reorienting the sense of self and other that the patient has brought to therapy to accommodate the sense of self and other maintained by the therapist. In this work, often enough, a mood of dismay, suspicion, despair, and outrage grows that becomes an obstacle between the struggling patient and the struggling therapist.

This struggle of two or more persons can be said to be about *locus*, or the place of origin attributed to certain emotions and thoughts in a conversation. It is highlighted in conversations of intimate couples. In difficult times, they may be heard to argue, "This is your emotional stuff, not mine! You handle it," or "This comes from your (mother, childhood, selfishness, rigidity). Don't put it on me!" Or, "Don't tell me what I'm feeling." Carol Feldman (cited in Bruner, 1990, p. 24.), in another context, used the term "ontic dumping" to describe this struggle over the placement of the ownership of certain experiences.

Most people would agree that it matters a good deal in adversarial relations to establish who does what to whom. The legal system is adversarial in this sense. In cooperative relations, it often matters little who does what or who originates which communication. In good times, couples are heard to say: "We feel the same. We're both coming from the same place," "How did you know what I like? You must have read my mind," "What fun this is!"

Think of such situations as making dinner together or putting up a fence. Sequencing of actions is important, as is a division of labor, but whether you or I beat the eggs is of little importance and we must each carry an end of the beam to hoist it into place. The structure of the job or system of activities allows each of us to participate in many tasks according to our skills. Cooperative conversations are similar in kind to these tasks. Brainstorming does not require authorship or ownership of ideas.

An example of this kind of cooperative conversation, which happened in my hypnotherapy class, led me to many of these thoughts about placement of emotion, ownership of experience, and responsibility for action in therapeutic contexts. Fran (Stott, personal communication 1998) is an experienced psychologist. This is her story of the events of that afternoon.

> The setting was that it was my turn to hypnotize a subject and due to a major highway jam I was late for the session, meaning that I not only missed our presession planning time but I arrived after the subject got there. So I was really distressed, and was also feeling embarrassed and irresponsible. I came into the room, which was a blur to me, and the group was sitting quietly, discussing something. I had secret hopes that since I was late, Eric would just go ahead and hypnotize the patient. I was really upset that she had to wait too. Eric greeted me and said, "How are you doing?" I was speechless, came in and threw my stuff down, went to the bathroom. Jean brought me a cup of tea. That was comforting. I was torn between offering an apology and just getting going: we were some 20 minutes into the session.

> Eric showed me where he would like me to sit and invited me to try out the chair and the microphone. I'm trying to think about what to do next and Eric says, "Fran, I'm not feeling very well today. I've been rushing around since six this morning and I didn't get enough sleep. I feel jumpy and tired and I need to pay attention for the next three hours in class. I wonder if you'd do me a favor before you begin the session. I'd like you to induce a trance in me and help me to be more alert during the session."

> So I was amazed and wondered how in the world I could do that, but my attention became immediately focused on Eric! And I remember thinking, "Well I can't possibly do that; well, how do I do that?" Then my next thought was, "He seems to really want me to do it and I probably can do something." So that was the turning point and I just decided I would try something that I knew how to do. I asked him to close his eyes. I started thinking I was doing a lot of things that he wouldn't neccessarily endorse in inducing trance, but I just had to go ahead and do it. I asked him to relax and focus on his body. Then he was extremely cooperative and seemed immediately to be

able to respond, so I just kept going and I remembered thinking, "Oh, thank goodness, this is working." Eric seemed to be getting into a light trance and that was so reassuring. I just became totally engaged with his problem and I became calmer. Eric said he felt much better and he looked better and then I felt much better.

It was delightful in the sense that I knew what he was doing but it didn't matter. It was absolutely genuine at the same time. And I thought, at the same time, that there was a part that was true and a part that was strategic and it didn't matter. The process was so genuine that understanding it didn't detract from it.

I felt reassured and thought, "It's O.K. You can do this. You can just do what you did with Eric and you don't have to rehearse it." When I worked with the patient, I felt perfectly comfortable. It distracted me from all of the rules or models I was trying to live up to. It just gave me the confidence to go ahead and do what I knew I could do. I had much more confidence that that would be accepted. Then I remembered our preparatory work from the previous week and just let it flow.

The therapist in me was just amazed! Particularly with an anxious situation like this, it was so effective to pull the problem out of me and focus it somewhere else where I could do something about it. It felt like a partnership along these lines: he would help me help him so I could help my subject.

Locus, Structure, and Meaning

In most human interaction "realities" are the results of prolonged
and intricate processes of construction and negotiation deeply
imbedded in the culture. Put this way, constructivism hardly seems
exotic at all. It is what legal scholars refer to as "the interpretive
turn," or a turning away from "authoritative meaning."

—J. Bruner (1990, pp. 24–25)

Among the interesting corollaries of working in relationships cooperatively and without concern for ownership of emotion is the indifference of the therapist to privileged placement of his or her ideas, what Bruner calls "authoritative meaning." As Fran's narrative reveals, interpretation of another's experience has no particular pride of place in the effort to be of help: "It was delightful in the sense that I knew what he was doing but it didn't matter."

In dynamic psychotherapies, the therapist's sense of meaning typically has been privileged. In such a therapy, the conversation might have concentrated on Fran's description of her own inner states of feeling, coupled with my sympathetic comments about their meaning and a resolution proposed through understanding of their antecedents in her life. Thinking of the interior experiences of individuals in this way, we may view them as rather helpless respondents to past patterning, whose patterns must be elucidated through therapeutic interpretation of meanings. We may imply that their actions, emotions, and ideas are out of place in many different ways, that they "are" anxious, depressed, dissociated, and so on. We may even imply that they don't "know their place," as we do with people who stretch the boundaries of our comfort or expectation.

In the exchange that Fran and I actually had, forsaking the luxury of interpretative privilege and individual attribution of feeling, we acted as one might who imagines the entire social situation rather than its individual elements: Here, *some* distress needs comforting by *someone* in order to calm the class and prepare for learning. The therapeutic task is not determined by the question of the origin of particular feelings in the past patterning of relationships, but rather of how to utilize the feelings to determine effective communication toward meeting a common goal.

Systemic thinkers, viewing a couple or a therapist and patient as they communicate, will have in mind a second meaning for locus aside from "place." Locus is also defined as: "the set or configuration of all points satisfying specified geometric conditions" (Morris, 1969, p. 766). This idea of a configuration of points is like the notion of relational structure. Piaget (1968) saw structure as "the set of possible states and transformations of which the system that actually obtains is a special case" (p. 38). Now we are close to imagining a strange landscape in which individual feeling and thought are seen as special cases of social systems and in which persons may take up various positions, states, or places within these systems. The version of this view that has seeped into therapeutic communication and relationship is that we are all in this thing together, without privilege by virtue of position or the stored commodity of expert knowledge.

What follows from this sense of flexible placement and relational structure in viewing human communication? Suppose we saw the culture of psychotherapy through this lens. If free association is important to the activity of therapy, does it matter whether that task is done by the patient or the therapist? If dreams are the "royal road to the unconscious," can the therapist sometimes blaze the trail? Therapists may think of balancing or sharing emotional attribution among individuals, as they do in work with families, or even of shifting the attributed origin and ownership of troubles, as is done when narrative therapists "externalize the problem." Erickson-influenced therapists will recall his habit of shifting the seats of family members to influence change in feeling by change in place.

To investigate this set of ideas as they occur in practice in a systemic therapeutic culture and to examine the communicative relationships whose rules form that culture, we ought to be participant-observers, not analysts from some Olympian plain. We can follow the advice of the anthropologist Clifford Geertz (1995) that "what is needed, or anyway, must serve, is tableaus, anecdotes, parables, tales; mini-narratives with the narrator in them."

Misplaced Locus and Relational Solutions

> You know, ordinarily, what is what about yourself and the other
> person. When confused you suddenly become concerned about who
> you are and the other person seems to be fading.
>
> —*Milton H. Erickson (cited in Havens, 1996, p. 33)*

Consider the problematic attribution of locus mentioned earlier and consider an antidote to such troubled communication: B. J. sat in my office, alert and intense at our first meeting. His huge frame filled the large chair as he had completely filled the door frame. Prison time and mental hospital time: violent encounters. He had learned to wait. Feeling "dissociated, unreal," he came for help. I asked him a question about his life. B. J. glanced at the wall behind me: "I could take that wall apart with my bare hands. I've done that." "I like that wall," I said. "I've liked that wall for many years."

For the rest of our conversation, I spoke only about myself, my thoughts, my feelings, and my dreams. He spoke, more sparingly, of his thoughts and experiences. After the third conversation in this manner, B. J. said, "You've done something all the armies of lithium pushers and padded cells didn't do. They always told me what I was like, and I shut them out. You talked about yourself: your thoughts and feelings. I feel like *my*self."

The next time we spoke, I told B. J. a dream. I am driving an old red sports car on a cliffside road. The road diverges and I choose to drive the way that careens down to the beach and strands me in the sand, rather than to continue on the highway along the cliff. B. J. listened to the dream, then said, "I dreamed that a park is being built in the wasteland of Beirut. I feel this session really flowed." In the next three conversations, B. J. said, "Things are developing at a pace that makes a lot of sense to me. I'm happier. . . . I want to take care of myself. . . . Everybody wants to act better."

This simple notion of pitching in to do or demonstrate what is necessary to the activity of therapy, without fussing about who is responsible for doing it, obviates any need to discuss or interpret what is not being done and why it is not being accomplished. A fancy way of saying this might be, "The attribution of locus of experience is arbitrary in systems of two or more persons." A therapist comfortable with this outlook will appreciate Chloe Madanes' (1990) many therapeutic inventions, as when she encourages minor children to care for their troubled parents or shifts relational tasks to those family members best suited to carry them out.

Flexibility of attribution can help reorient the meaning of feelings without their having to change in form or intensity. It can also help develop meanings that were obscure and help them flower in the person's life. A professional musician, first chair in a symphony orchestra, came to therapy with negative feelings and thoughts about her musical performance and troubles with a "shaky bow." Asked to describe the feelings of playing the violin, she said, "Feelings of love in my heart." Asked to describe the negative, fearful feelings, she said, "Feelings in my throat and the pit of my stomach." Asked to show how she feels when she practices, she said, "I relax my feelings into the bow," and demonstrated a beautiful bowing motion. Asked, "Why have these problems come along now?" she said, "I feel that I can be considered a world-class violinist." And when asked her place in the world, she said, with her "pit-of-the-stomach feeling," "When you come to no. 15 on the list of violinists in the world, you come to me."

Instead of asking about her ideas about the origin of her shakiness or about her fear of success, I asked about her relationship with the conductor. I was told that he was arrogant and controlling and uncertain in beating time. I said, "*He* is shaky." She said, "Yes!" She described her attempts to help him keep the music under control from her place among the strings. I asked her if she would be willing to lead him to a better sense of the beat and a more collaborative sense of making music. Her reply was forceful and direct, "I want people to know I can play!"

Eleanor Maccoby (cited in Tavris, 1998) showed some years ago that the gender composition of a group rather than personality traits accounted for gender differences in children. The behavior we attribute to gender is "an emergent property of relationships and groups." For example, female intuition was found to be the intuition of subordinate social partners, to depend on place and position rather than on trait:

> *Both sexes are equally intuitive when they have to read a superior's mood, non-verbal signals or intentions—and equally thickheaded, when they are the bosses, about their subordinates' feelings.* (*p. 126)*

McIntosh (1988), in an account of her investigation of her own "white privileges," draws the cord that connects social experience with states of feeling:

> *In this pot pourri of examples, some privileges make me feel at home in the world. Others allow me to escape penalties or dangers which others suffer. Through some, I escape fear, anxiety or a sense of not being welcome or not being real. Some keep me from having to hide, to be in disguise, to feel sick or crazy . . . Most keep me from having to be angry. (pp. 10–11)*

Emotions themselves are sometimes held to be the grail that we seek when searching for our "real selves," or for the means to authenticate communication. The place and timing of emotional experience can be shifted to allow varieties of authentic experience to replace internal conflict between relational emotions.

My friend Shirley each year held a Christmas breakfast at which all of her friends would gather. She enjoyed the cooking and conversation and looked forward to the yearly event. One November, she told me that she was sure she would be depressed on Christmas. Her husband was depressed, her job was in jeopardy, and several close friends were seriously ill. But, she said, she didn't want to cancel her party, so she had decided to "put the depressed feelings aside until the New Year." Shirley's party that year was as delightful as always, and when I saw her again in January, I asked how things had gone. "Oh, I had a lovely Christmas, I so enjoyed the breakfast party. But on New Year's Day I woke up with the worst depression I've ever had and it lasted all day. Then it was gone."

A counselor I helped prepare for the licensing exams used hypnotic imagination to corral her nervousness. When taking the written exam, she sat in front and imagined me and some friends at the table before her. When the question was difficult or odd, she reminded herself of us, saying to herself, "That's a stupid question. Just go on to the next one." At the break, she did cartwheels on the lawn. She was at ease until after the exam, when she found herself very anxious about her answers and talking obsessively with others. She passed both the written and oral exams.

The therapist may also participate in change along with the patient. I offered to stop fiddling with my beard and moustache, "a really difficult thing for me, to stop fussing with myself," if my patient, Margie, would stop "threatening herself" by pulling out her hair. Between mid-October and the end of December, she pulled only a single hair from her head, after months of pulling hundreds of strands of hair, resulting in bleeding and scabs. Margie told her best friend, "I didn't feel like I wanted to do it anymore." "How did you stop?" asked her friend. "We made a deal," said Margie. Sometimes it is difficult to "make a deal" through negotiation in psychotherapy. Still, as Freud (1935) said in *An Autobiographical Study*, "Anyone who wants to make a living from the treatment of nervous patients must clearly be able to do something to help them" (p. 27).

People called borderline are like the illegal immigrants once derisively called "wetbacks." They appear in one's emotional experience like intruders and are repelled forcefully, only to show up at the next session, heralded by armies of telephone messages. What can be done to cooperate effectively with a patient who claims that the therapist has malignant motives and emotions? The attribution is made to explain or justify strong feelings in patients, but without their claiming these feelings as their own. Such a patient may say to the therapist, "You're trying to influence me!" and storm angrily from the office, slamming the door. In one case I supervised, the therapist responded to this with a letter "to express my thoughts about our last meeting." She said, "When you notice the inevitable accomplishments and improvements you will make yourself without undue influence from others, write them on a postcard to me, so I and my work with others can be influenced and affected by your example." The patient resumed their meetings saying, "I'm honored," and gave the therapist a book, *How to Argue and Win Every Time*.

Suppose a therapist were to speak aloud the putative emotions of the patient as though they were the therapist's own? The therapist might say, "I *am* trying very hard to influence you! But I feel frustrated and angry. When I can't influence you, I feel helpless and empty and really scared."

Kill the Children

Another supervised case that required breath-holding as well as hand-holding was that of Yvonne, a 50-year-old woman "with a mother like Hitler. I learned to be cruel through her modeling." Raised in Las Vegas "to be a beautiful young wife," Yvonne resented caring for her younger sisters. When a sister died in a car crash at 18, she refused to attend the funeral. Yvonne married and divorced twice. She "broke down" after the first marriage at age 20. Her unwanted daughter from that marriage was being raised by relatives. The psychiatrist who "saved my life" died of cancer when she was 35. Yvonne has been on Valium since 1965.

"Work was beneath me, always abhorrent to me." Her one year of college was followed by office jobs. Unemployed and with all her money gone, she left Las Vegas and moved to San Francisco. Her new goal: "to meet a lifetime female partner." She found work as a receptionist and her anger at men increased: "They make so much money." She mismanaged her own money and in fear turned to her parents for support. When in Las Vegas, she once had had sex for money and was drinking heavily. Feeling that she was losing control of her body with age, Yvonne dreamed of money for cosmetic surgery.

Yvonne found her therapist, Roberta, through a support group. Roberta encouraged "a walking program for health," which Yvonne later said, "saved my life." In therapy, her feelings of love for the therapist grew, along with desperate feelings of suicide and anger: "I'm in such pain. No one really likes me. I didn't deserve this." Her mother sent Yvonne $1,000 and Yvonne thought, "This is it. No more money until she dies." Her credit card expenditures zoomed.

Three years before moving, Yvonne, angry at her mother, had threatened to hurt her sister and the sister's family. Her mother gave her $20,000 to stay away from the family. Restraining orders were placed on Yvonne. Now, once again angry at her mother, she threatened, "I'm not going to go quietly. I'm gonna take people with me." She mentioned her sister's children as targets. They're in Las Vegas. "I can hurt my sister and mother that way. I'm in such pain. I want to hang myself. I want to kill myself. I feel like shooting you. I'm tired of being nice and tired of fighting."

In October, Roberta and I met. We put together a "Lethality and Legality" intervention: Roberta explained to Yvonne what her own legal obligations were—to warn upon a credible threat of harm to others, and to call the police upon a credible threat of suicide. Yvonne knew the rules and was willing to agree to a contract: No suicide or homicide would be considered until January of the coming year. Roberta told Yvonne, "We're going to set that aside." They would be engaged instead, said Roberta, in "learning-to-live therapy." Yvonne would learn how to handle money, budgets, and debts. To express her "big emotions," she would send postcards to Roberta, telling her how she felt and about the things she was learning to do in her life.

Roberta endorsed Yvonne's need for revenge by informing her that "evidence of living well is the best revenge." She asked, "How will your mother suffer when you present her with the evidence of living well?" Yvonne was coached to send her mother paycheck stubs showing raises she received at work, photos of her having dinner with friends, pictures of her newly painted room. "Dear Mom, I'm having a good day. Your daughter, Yvonne."

Yvonne sent the cards and her mother responded with friendly notes. This indicated to Yvonne that the approach was working. She went on to further outrage about her work life and her various coworkers, but there was no more talk about killing the children. She decided that she wanted to live. January passed.

Over the next year, there were some job changes, but no money or love. She felt bereft. Her therapist would be her lover, offering only to serve as a "stand-in" until the real thing came along. Yvonne raged at Roberta and about everybody in the world. In a "Leaning Forward" intervention, Roberta countered her own feeling of running away and encouraged the full verbal expression of the rage, "the landscape of her large emotion that gets in between us." Yvonne wanted people to treat her like a "lady." Roberta spoke about "the feminine essence of your emotion. Clarify this and you will draw to you people who'll treat you like a lady." Yvonne made lists of the qualities of her feminine essence. Roberta taught her trancework, "about learning new things without even knowing it."

During the next two years, Yvonne had to declare bankruptcy and threatened suicide. She ate compulsively and worried about her inheritance. She was paranoid about work and raged at life. She had asthma. But she increased her work skills and had several successful job changes. Two years later, she took a stand with her coworkers and set limits. She now lived on cash, not credit. Yvonne had a long-term rooommate. Two years after that, she explored returning to Las Vegas for financial reasons. Her father became ill and Yvonne reconciled with her mother and they had many supportive phone conversations. She planned her move to Las Vegas and sent Roberta a letter: She had found a nice apartment and possible jobs and had contact with her parents and with her sister, niece, and nephew.

The following workshop role-play of a client by her therapist shows how much work is needed to communicate effectively with some persons. Patient persistence is helpful, as is a work apron full of the nuts, bolts, and screws that can support agreements between persons under great stress. Solution-oriented comments, externalizing, future orientation, and utilization of the patient's skills, styles, and metaphors, and flexibility in *locus* of emotions and identities are some of the fasteners applied to this therapeutic conversation.

Do You Think I'm an Idiot?

Eric: What's another case we can wrestle with?
Linda: This is a woman. My experience with her is like I'm walking on eggshells, and if I say the wrong thing, I'm going to get chewed out. She sits just as I'm doing now and it's very hard to get a conversation going: "Well, tell me how you feel about that," or "What do you think about this?" If I try to get her to engage in something more visual, like talk to parts of a dream, say, "Pretend you're the baby in the dream," she says,

"Well that's absurd, I can't do that. A baby can't talk."
There's no ability to be flexible.

And if I should, by accident, repeat anything she has said,
she will experience it as my trying to take credit for her
thought. I can't even see what this woman's strengths are. I
just know they have to be there—that she's got more than she
can show me. She is petrified. I want ideas about how to
move her.

Eric: Why does she come to therapy? What's her goal?

Linda: To get her eating under control. You know what? She won't
           let me talk about me either.

Eric: She won't? Oh she's very good.

Linda: She doesn't want to hear anything about me. She's got this
           idea that I am the therapist, I'm a professional and she is a
           patient, and so we can't talk, we can't mix. I'm supposed to
           dish out some expertise that is going to make her not eat.

Eric: But if she's going to diet, you don't want to dish out too
           much. Tell her you're going to have to put her on slim rations
           if she is going to accomplish her goal. (*Laughter*). Does she
           have work that she does as well?

Linda: She's not quite a secretary. She is going to school too. She's
           taking a history course. It's rather interesting: She was telling
           me about genocide. It's interesting when she does that . . .

Eric: Could you role-play her a little bit. And I'll call her by your
           name.

Linda: I'll give you a chance. (*To Eric*) Go ahead.

Eric: So, I don't know, I just get the saddest feeling.

Linda: About what?

Eric: You know, I'm not sure. What's been happening?

Linda: I've been working. You know, I've been filing, and I've been
           doing some computer work, and it's going okay. And I've
           been having trouble with the eating. You know, somebody
           came by and asked me to do something and I didn't want to
           do it, and I said no and I immediately saw a picture of
           myself wanting to eat. And I tried talking to myself, I tried
           doing the things you told me to do, and they just didn't
           work.

Eric: Yeah, the things I told you didn't work at all, did they?

Linda: A little bit, but. . . .

Eric: I feel a little sheepish about that. I gave you these things to do, and then I guess you didn't have any good effect with them: They were sort of punk, they didn't work.

Linda: Well, it makes me nervous if you don't know what you're doing. If you don't know what you're doing and I don't know what I'm doing, then how am I going to get anywhere?

Eric: You know about Carl Jung, the famous psychoanalyst?

Linda: No.

Eric: You don't? He used to say that he would send a patient who had a problem to see a therapist who had the same trouble. He said if you put two idiots in a room together, one of them will figure out what to do.

Linda: Do you think I'm an idiot?

Eric: I think *we* are idiots about this problem.

Linda: My father used to say I was an idiot.

Eric: I'm sorry to hear it. I think you would like to accomplish this goal of being thinner. Have I got that right?

Linda: Yes. No. Well, not so much that, I just don't want to feel out of control when I eat. It's not so much how much I weigh: I just want to feel that when I say I'm going to eat I don't want to be eating more than I really want.

Eric: Yeah. And how do you know when you've reached that point inside?

Linda: That scares me. It makes me feel like you're watching me.

Eric: You know, I *was* watching you. I was watching you so closely just to see how you manage these things.

Linda: That makes me feel like I'm going to go home and eat.

Eric: I would guess it does. I sure hope you don't. I hope you go home and don't eat. What do you hope?

Linda: That I don't go home and eat.

Eric: We agree on that for sure. This is really a fervent hope of mine. Do you hope it really strongly?

Linda: Mmm hmmm.

Eric: It's real important isn't it?

Linda: Mmm hmmm!!

Eric: Because it is to me, you know. I screwed up our first two sessions so badly. Anyway, I really hope very much for that. And I can't see how you know when enough's enough with that stuff. Like when you know it's been enough and you don't have to eat any more. Can you help me with that?

Linda: I can just tell. And when you ask me that it makes me feel nervous again, like I don't know—and that makes me . . .

Eric: Yeah. But you see I really don't know that because I eat like a fat person.

Linda: Really?

Eric: I really do. If you gave me a plate full of stuff, a table full of stuff, I'd eat everything there. And if it's not there, I don't eat it, so I don't understand how someone like you has the fineness of feeling to know the difference between too much and not enough.

Linda: You are making me feel like I don't know. It's scary. It makes me feel out of control.

Eric: Yes, and can you tell me how it feels when you *do* know?

Linda: I feel comfortable. I feel like I've had enough, and then I just go off and do something else, and I feel good about it.

Eric: Then you can do that. You feel comfortable.

Linda: Yes, I feel good about that.

Eric: Can you tell me—can you tell me how I would feel that comfort, where I would feel it if I were able to do that too? Like if I could go over to the table over there with all the muffins on it, and if I could feel comfortable inside so I'd really know that I didn't want any more. And then I could go home, and I wouldn't eat. It would be out of my mind, and I would be comfortable with it. Can you tell me where I can expect to feel that comfort? Is it a stomach comfort?

Linda: Well, I don't know for you. . . . .

Eric: Just guess, because I'd like to have something to look forward to.

Linda: I guess in the stomach. I feel it in my stomach. That's how I know when I've had enough to eat.

Eric: So you think I might feel it there, kind of in my stomach.

Linda: Yeah.

Eric: I know we're different—you're a woman, I'm a man, and all these differences. . . .

Linda:	You'd feel it in your stomach. You'd feel like that's. . . . comfortable.
Eric:	Comfortable. Just comfortable.
Linda:	Not too full.
Eric:	Not too full, not too empty.
Linda:	Not too full, not too empty, had enough and aren't thinking about having the next bite.
Eric:	And what kind of things would I expect to think about when I'm comfortable like that, would you guess? Again, you don't know me really well, but if I'm not thinking about food—you know, I'm not going to look past you to the table. . . .
Linda:	Right, kind of like that: You don't think about the food, you think about, you know, going off and doing some work.
Eric:	That's for sure. And if it were you, what kind of work would you be thinking about doing?
Linda:	I'd go look at some brochures on travel. I might go study my work and read over my assignment and start writing the paper.
Eric:	And what is your next paper, Linda?
Linda:	Uhhh. Genocide. Genocide that occurred in Africa.
Eric:	I find that in myself such a helpless feeling. And it makes me angry too, because I want to feel like there's something that can be done about it, but these terrible things have already been done. How is it with you when you work on this?
Linda:	Um. It's interesting, um. . . . I don't know what more could be done. And I'm not really sure I know how to write a paper.
	So I've been writing a lot of notes and trying to get some ideas about how to write a paper because I haven't written a paper before.
Eric:	Can I say something to you that might be difficult to receive? (*Silence.*) When you speak about these matters, I hear the speech as highly articulate and intelligent. It starts me thinking and wondering and waiting to hear the next interesting thing you have to say, even though you are just speaking aloud what's in your mind. Do you think, as I do, that writing and speaking are very similar activities? Or different?
Linda:	I don't know. I haven't studied that.
Eric:	But you do know how to speak very nicely.

Linda:	Hmmm.
Eric:	And you don't know how to write.
Linda:	Right.
Eric:	I can only write if I'm kind of speaking out loud to myself when I write.
Linda:	You speak out loud when you write?
Eric:	Yes. I transcribe what I'm saying.
Linda:	Well, don't you read something first? Read it in a book? Before you write it?
Eric:	No. Do you?
Linda:	Well, of course. I read all the books, and then I write the paper.
Eric:	And you have done that before?
Linda:	Just this last paper.
Eric:	How did it turn out?
Linda:	I got an A on it.
Eric:	You know, here's another difficult thing. Can I dare to ask you a difficult question?
Linda:	Mmm hmm!
Eric:	When you received that A, did it give you a pleasant feeling?
Linda:	Well, yeah.
Eric:	I would very much like to know how that feeling is felt.
Linda:	It was good. I was pleased. It was pleasing.
Eric:	I've always found those difficult moments, you know, when you get the A that you've been trying so hard for. It's just very perplexing.
Linda:	But didn't you get a lot of As?
Eric:	Don't you?
Linda:	Well, I haven't taken that many courses.
Eric:	But you've had As?
Linda:	Two.
Eric:	Well, I took a lot of courses, and I think I got five A's but out of a lot of courses. And each time—I'm a little embarrassed to tell you this, but I was sur—
Linda:	Well don't tell me. I don't want to know.
Eric:	Too late. I was surprised. (*She makes a sound of amusement.*) Were you surprised? At the A?
Linda:	Yes

Eric:	Given that you didn't know how to write papers and you got an A.
Linda:	Yes. I was surprised.
Eric:	How would you explain your ability to do this thing you don't know how to do?
Linda:	I don't know.
Eric:	Because I've had that experience where I was convinced that I was going to fail a very big exam. I was so convinced that when they told me I got the best grade, I accused them of cheating. Can you imagine that?
Linda:	No. Why would you do that?
Eric:	I was crazed for a moment. I felt very suspicious. This is a true story. I took an exam that was five days long. I walked into the room with my tutors who were going to deliver the grade. A tutor said to me, "Well, you got honors." (*That was the top grade.*) I said, "This is a trick!" I said this to the most honorable person in the room.
Linda:	Who was this person?
Eric:	He was a philosophy professor, Louis Mink.
Linda:	It makes me nervous when you talk about yourself.
Eric:	Oh, I understand that. And Louis Mink—I turned to him and I said, "This is a trick, Louis. This is the kind of trick that someone like you would play," to the most honest man in the room. Can you imagine that?
Linda:	No.
Eric:	It is scary, isn't it? It's very scary.
Linda:	But I asked you not to talk about yourself.
Eric:	I understand that, and I have to beg your pardon for having done it so much. Because it is a kind of sad and disconcerting thing.
Linda:	What is?
Eric:	The way I responded to this.
Linda:	Mmm. Well, then, why did you do it?
Eric:	You know, that's a very good question. I don't know why I did it; I just know how I did it. And the way I did it was to get very worried and feel very helpless.
Linda:	What were you worried about?
Eric:	About failing the exam.

Linda: And so that's why you are telling me?

Eric: I'm telling you because I'm trying to sort out these different feelings.

Linda: Your feelings?

Eric: No, **these** feelings: The feelings of getting A's, feeling comfortable, holding oneself away from food that's unnecessary, having a conversation in the midst of some fearful moments, but keeping relating. That's what I'm up to here in this conversation. And I find it very interesting to talk to you, I like talking to you, and yet there's an atmosphere of fear and difficulty and doubt kind of circulating around, like the air conditioner. Have you noticed that?

Linda: Do you have a lot of doubts, or . . . ?

Eric: Yes, we do.

Linda: Hmmm. You have a lot of doubts, and I have a lot of doubts.

Eric: So we have a lot of doubts.

Linda: Well, then, how are you going to help me with my eating?

Eric: Because we have a lot of that comfort in—

Linda: How does that help though?

Eric: In looking forward to going home and working.

Linda: I know, but how does that help?

Eric: I'm not sure either, but I do remember that you showed me that nice feeling of comfort that we can have. And that we can go home and work on our papers and feel comfortable and not think about food. And so I'm looking forward to going home later on and working on a paper about my workshop. What are you looking forward to when you go home?

Linda: Umm. I'm going to go and start doing some reading for my paper.

Eric: Is it all right with you if I wish you luck in dealing with that topic?

Linda: Sure.

Eric: Can I do that?

Linda: Sure.

Eric: Because I think you are taking on a very difficult but important kind of work. The most difficult matters. So I don't know how you'll do with it, but know that I admire you for looking forward to working on it.

Linda/A.:   *I'm coming in as myself at this point, by the way. (General laughter.)*

Eric: This is one of the very most difficult people I can imagine, and you do a great job of presenting her. Can you tell me what our conversation felt like?

A.:   It gave me some ideas of what to do, which is what I was focusing on. I'm going to try what you did: I'm just going to insist on talking about myself and try doing it that way. What it felt like? I was trying more to focus on being kind of scared and doing my part. But I had to ignore you in order to do that.

Eric: Yeah. But you did it really well. I suppose you could try to picture this woman in some way: It's like a stained-glass window where the lead has been pulled apart You don't know if you could ever get a coherent picture. But within that distortion, let's say, there is the possibility of a lot of feeling and thought and even relatedness, because she's making forays all the time; she's not just like this (*folds arms, crosses legs*) all the time.

A.:   No, she doesn't do that; she's trying.

Eric: And since that's there—I will put as much into it as possible and I am not going to be dissuaded by doubt. If the person can't hear me, like someone in a coma, I'll keep talking, because that's all I can do. It's a scary sort of thing for the therapist. It may have seemed like a facetious gesture to say, "Well, I'm scared, I'm not certain," but I'm telling the truth: I don't know what to do. And I only know how I feel about these things, and that was a true story about Louis Mink.

A.:   I'm going to take more liberties with talking to her about myself. She practically issued a proclamation: I don't want you to talk about yourself. Because she will worry about me.

Eric: But I would want to say, "Well, that's very decent of you." And I could honestly appreciate that. You want to be very courteous too in this kind of interaction, because there are things of grave importance going on in the person's feeling to which you can't have any clue. It's like a foreign language: She is speaking Bulgarian and her heart is pouring out, and I'm scratching my head, and saying, "Was that the word for milk or for engine? I don't know what that was."

A.:   That's exactly how I feel.

Eric: So my only expertise has to be with myself.

A.:   Right.

Eric: I know about that college kid and Louis Mink, pretty well by heart. And if I could get her to do this thing about describing what the successful feeling was. . . .

A.:   You said, "How do you know when you've eaten the right amount?" Her husband actually said that to her, and it flipped her out. She felt totally out of tune when the guy said, "Well, how do you know if you are comfortable?"

Eric: Well, I think if she can't or won't do it, you could do it: You are a self, you're a demonstrable person, flaws and troubles and all, so if that's all you've got, okay.

A.:   That's what I'm going to start doing. Could you tell us why she's so averse to storytelling about someone else?

Eric: She keeps talking about me and telling me what to do and what not to do, so, strangely, I think it's a very intimate relationship. Diagnostically you'd say this is the furthest thing from an intimate relationship. You practically don't know who's who. So I think it's already very intimate, and I want to speak in intimate terms. That's really my feeling about it.

A.:   She won't get the relevance of it. It's weird, but she won't apply it.

Eric: Yeah. You won't get the kind of thing that you'd want in Rogerian therapy, an acknowledgment by the client that the reflection is occurring: "Oh, you understand me, you see me clearly, you listen so well to me, I'm so thankful to have this quiet place to speak," you know, as genteel people speak in therapy: "Can I raise your fee? (*General laughter.*) You've been working so hard." But this is a different sort of person.

       All you can do is relate with what you know, which is yourself in your vulnerability. You can't tell stories of great success. I told the worst story—a true story—awful! You can't imagine.

A.:   That's helpful. Thanks.

Eric: Yes. And the big problem, the unshakably insoluble problem I can empathize with—the problem of genocide that she is trying to write about. Nobody knows what to do. And I imagine her to be like that: She knows a lot, but she doesn't know what to do. She's got helpless big troubles. And maybe she takes on the troubles of the world, but she sure doesn't know the difference between her and me and food and not and . . . You could see her as very confused about boundaries and all that, but I don't prefer to see people that way. I just figure, well, if she doesn't know the difference, I don't have to know the difference either. We have feelings: I have feelings, she has feelings. There's a kind of a pool of feeling in the room. And if we talk she can mistrust me, that's okay, we can both be helpless, we can both struggle with eating.

So the important thing in this kind of therapy is to be very honest in telling the story as it was, so that your feelings will be fairly transparent. You don't want to elaborate a story for her sake. Just pick the right one that's the worst one and tell it.

A.: I've often thought that I've struggled with food too, but I think she'd flip out because then she'd feel hopeless that If I struggled with it, how is she ever going to get over it?

Eric: I did that essentially.

A.: Yeah, but you eat everything at the table.

Eric: Well, you don't know that.

A.: (*Laughs.*) No. But what if I were to tell her truthfully that you and I struggle with it too and are ultimately successful?

Eric: I just think so that you could demonstrate what a person is like. A real person is like somebody who sits there with the whole tub of ice cream and says, "My god! What have I done?" That's a real person. Why can't she be a real person?

We are taught, as therapists, to accept the emotions our patients bring to our meetings. We might as well learn to express those emotions as well as to request their expression by others, and learn to utilize them to help others meet their therapeutic goals. Speaking the other person's interior experience as though it were one's own, or shared, provides a means by which to "join" the other person and to develop a mutual relational experience. A therapist was being criticized, harrangued and emotionally battered by a patient who had experienced depression and loss of a sense of herself after sadistic relationships. I suggested that the therapist say,

"There's so much hurt in the room. But adrenaline numbs the pain. Later, we'll be heartsick, tired, and sore. But now, this anger is exciting!"

The therapist may act as a stand-in to help with the dramatic task at hand, remembering, as Sullivan (1954b) said, that, "a great many of the techniques of interpersonal performance continue to be just as applicable (in therapy) as elsewhere." In most matters of communication between persons in therapy, I recommend that when the patient speaks his or her mind or emotion, the therapist not only accept that communication, but justify and utilize it: "Of course you feel that way. I treat you with care and attentiveness, and we have fun talking together. No wonder you feel (loving or sexy or moved)." When a mature woman who had been seriously and maliciously abused as a toddler asked if we might stand together under the tulip tree outside my office, I agreed. She said, "There's something about safe intimacy that's so special. It's what I missed." Another time, when she drew back in numb confusion and hurt at the thought of my coming vacation, I said, "I will pay any price to be back in relationship with you."

What guides the therapist in these relationships? I hinted, earlier, that therapeutic relating is a communication by conversation, and that "relate" is taken primarily as meaning "to narrate or tell, to interact with others in a meaningful and coherent fashion" (Morris, 1969, p. 1097). In system-considerate relating, the telling may be seen as metaphorical and the tellers may easily switch places.

Particular actions, especially sexual or violent ones in therapeutic relations, are prohibited by law or custom. Part of the art of psychotherapy is to so enlarge conversation that it allows the participants to meet their goals without trespassing into prohibited exchanges or a cessation of relationship. A thoughtful narrative by R. N. Dart (personal communication, 1999) expresses the clear sense of how to keep one's footing in therapeutic relating:

> Two dreams in two days. I awoke feeling that I had been given therapy, and my feeling of renewal grew as the day progressed. When marveling over these dreams I realized that something had changed inside me without my noticing it. I felt empowered and free in a way that was new, and it seemed to involve my perception of the rules of relationship.
>
> Eric had always emphasized the rules of relationship in therapy,

partly because I was always pushing their limits, partly because a therapeutic relationship is unique and seems to require some definition, and partly because he believes that "Rules are relationship." My intellect has always concurred completely. Since no one draws the line between privacy and company in quite the same place, ground rules save us confusion and distress.

So I concurred completely intellectually, but never wholeheartedly. I felt hurt by these rules governing the relationship in therapy. Eric wasn't unreasonably rigid: When I was homeless and arrived really hungry, he would buy me milk if I asked, an action that I imagine could be construed as "unethical." But, we kept to The Rules. This hurt: I felt excluded, and the rules meant to me that I was not part of the real world of adults. Too often I would lose respect for feeling in the process of controlling or arguing over the means of expression. I would end up feeling as though I couldn't breathe.

So sometimes I breathed in my dreams, and we talked about them in the safety of knowing that they were only dreams, but knowing that they would not be acceptable if literally transferred to waking life. In disclosing any dream of intimacy I was always aware of and wary of The Rules.

However, I gradually learned that there was one invariable rule that included me. Genuine emotion was always permissible because it was an inescapable reality for everyone. An emotion cannot be made to disappear through exercise of will power or logic, and it cannot be hidden from anyone of perspicacity. The causes of it can be misunderstood or misrepresented, and one's response to it can be practically anything, but the emotion itself stands as fact, and so it generates a rule: "Acknowledge it in relationship." The other rules constrained the mode of expression of emotion, not its existence.

When I realized that I could actually use an emotion, even an unpleasant one, to make myself more powerful and alive, I established ownership. Whatever the rules governing their expression, the emotions were mine, they were palpable, and no one could deny me the experience of them. I owned the tools for making my life better, and the interface with other people was derivative: It began to take care of itself. Eric and I could enjoy the interface of rules between us as a subject for imaginative thought and experiment, and I even thought up some rules of my own.

I guess that this enabled a new kind of dream that was directly translatable into waking life without interpretation or expurgation. I thought of T. S. Eliot's "Burnt Norton": "Footfalls echo in the memory/Down the passage which we did not take. . . . My words echo thus in your mind." In therapy we had used words in such a way that their echo was emotion fully realized, and the experience as dreamed was complete, as though we went down the passage together.

As I become more whole, many of the rules become trivial in their power to restrict, although they retain validity in their power to protect. If one modality of experience is not feasible, there are others that follow the same road, and I am free to keep moving forward. Perhaps the rules in relationships are not bars to keep people in or out of particular life territory. They are more like bars in a gymnasium, defining a locus of activity around which one can pivot. They are handles to grab hold of in a dynamic system in which relative positions are always shifting, and I am part of the world in the same way that I can be part of the activity in a gym: I can't change the law of gravity or the position of the bars, but I can use them with flexibility and imagination. The set of rules that I thought was restrictive of living was in fact an interface for relating, each rule a pivot and a place to begin.

When making the appointment for today's session, I had told Eric that I wanted to talk about sex. Somehow we ended up talking about rules in relationships, the two recent dreams, and the thoughts expressed above. At the end of the hour, I said, "And you thought we were going to talk about sex." "We did," he replied. "Was it good for you?" My answer was an unexpurgated "Yes," and I left the office laughing.

Michael Hoyt (personal communication, 1995) has suggested that in writing about these matters of relating to patients in psychotherapy, I make some attempt to indicate the limits of these approaches, the ways in which one may know what to say or do in which circumstances and the manner of evaluating whether or not things are going well. Most of the examples in my discussion have come from therapeutic situations in which duress or difficulty required some experimentation to advance communication and where the guidelines of the various therapies haven't been a complete guide to action. These very guidelines have pressed against my desire to view matters systemically, as though my face were pressed against a window. Still, through that window I can see diners enjoying a meal of diagnosis followed by a rich dessert of treatment protocols. I will try to sketch out some rules of thumb.

On the matter of misplaced locus, I would say that feelings of extreme discomfort in the therapist while communicating with a patient are signs leading to a consideration of changing the locus of that communication, or shifting its metaphorical space. Also, when the therapist finds himself or herself feeling less and diagnosing more, or slandering the patient in confidential gossip with colleagues, that is a sign to "change places," expressing those emotions held to "belong" to the other party to the therapeutic conversation.

About communications loosely termed "transferential," the rule of thumb might be to accept the communicated emotion, amplify and praise and justify it, and use that emotion to help the patient meet his or her own goals. Don't worry about "whose" feelings these "are": the interpersonal field is large, and largely unbounded in time and space.

The language of psychotherapy should be the rich, varied common language within a culture: family talk for families, wiring talk for electricians, sports talk for athletes, and always the language of dream, metaphor, and story. This use of language enables patients to utilize their own best skills to address the resolution of their troubles, and it allows them to instruct the therapist about life. I have noted with alarm that most patients coming to therapy these days speak a dialect of Freudian psychoanalysis, or even one of the offshore patois like "Co-dependency." They have learned this from therapists. *Caveat emptor.*

No matter what language form seems correct or useful, these forms of speech and action I am suggesting will only be appropriate if one relates out of genuine emotion and with genuine emotion. The perception of emotion derives, I think, from the acts of attentive listening and empathic feeling that we have all been enjoined to practice from our first days of training. Simply, a "genuine emotion" can be any of the several feelings expressed by any party to the system of therapy. "They cannot be made to disappear through exertion of will power or logic, and cannot be hidden from anyone of perspicacity." We know therapy works when all agree, from whatever perspective, that the goals of the person in therapy have been met. This knowledge is similar to that which allows us to judge when a meal is ready, a dome is complete, or a painting is finished. The quality of surprise, satisfaction, and delight is an emotional guide to this experience.

Chapter 3

Evil Influence

Evil is unspectacular and always human
And shares our bed and eats at our own table

—*W. H. Auden (cited in Rawson & Miner, 1986, p. 80)*

Experiences of evil are highly complicated human events and their resolution can benefit from some of the gestures and conversations adumbrated in our discussion of locus and relationship. In the series of psychotherapies before us, questions of evil influence and complicity, secrecy and loyalty, temptations to evil, and compassion and reconciliation are raised. Light is cast from several directions to illuminate Medusa's head and the voices heard are those of the persons who lived through and came through such fearsome encounters.

110

A Knife in the Heart

Alice, a 50-year-old woman, sought hypnotherapy to resolve a severe hip pain she had suffered for eight years. No positive medical diagnosis had been found. The pain would occur after visits with her family. She had acupuncture treatments but the pain in her hip increased as she was encouraged to talk about her problems. Alice had, like many modern patients, questions about possible preverbal abuse by her father. Therapy took place in three hourlong sessions.

At our first meeting, Alice declared that she had great anxiety about hypnosis. I asked her, "What is the worst that might be expected?" She answered, in tears, "I might remember things about my son and my father." Her grown son had been seriously injured in an accident while riding his motorcycle and was now, with her help, living independently.

I asked a series of questions.

E.:   What color is the feeling of guilt you bear from your son's accident? Where is it felt?
A.:   A slate-gray color. In my heart. I feel a headache too.
E.:   What color is your headache?
A.:   Pink. Like a hood over the top and back of my head.
E: Where else do you notice the gray color?
A.:   In my right foot. I have residual nerve damage there from surgery.
E.:   Where else does the gray color in the heart lead?
A.:   It ends on my hip: a jagged, bright red.

This inquiry established a sort of pain map, without her having to discuss the painful details of her feelings. We proceeded, as though in a medical protocol, to establish the sources of possible remedies.

E.:   Where are the colors of comfort clearest?
A.:   My arms are a strong, glowing, vibrating white, strong and pleasurable. My legs are blue. I'm a strong hiker and runner.

The next conversational step we took involved an experiment. We applied the remedy to the painful areas.

E.:   Suppose you place the white color over your heart.

A.:   It's better. Feels like it's not so gray. My head is lighter, like there's more space inside. It's black in my head.

E.:   Suppose you bathe your head with vibrant white. Suppose you send vibrating white through your unconscious mind; send vibrating white circulating throughout your body.

A.:   I feel purple. I have shuddering breaths, like in a dream of mine: I see pews in a church. I remember my father in the pulpit, his black robes. It's foggy.

E.:   Suppose you blow the fog away.

A.:   It starts to feel better and there's more shuddering too. That's why I'm here: to do that!

E.:   How do you feel when the white feeling spreads and circulates?

A.:   Things are in perspective.

We can think of this therapy as one that shifts the sequence of expectable events from "history, diagnosis, treatment" to something approximating "treatment, history, diagnosis." Application of the "color of comfort" to the heart and head leads Alice to feel a new color, purple, and the shuddering sensations that indicate to *her* that she has come to the point of the therapy. The dream accompanies these experiences and the result is a surprising sense of perspective arising from the experience itself, rather than from education.

The second session began with Alice's remarking on the first hour and offering another surprising consequence of the work.

A: It was effective; really good. The blackness in my head is not as black as it was. Whatever happened with my father—he's dead. There's no need to revisit that black robe. It's not anything that warrants my misery anymore.

Then Alice told me a story about her son's neurologist, who criticized her harshly for verbally "forcing" her son to drink milk by using his injured hand to hold the glass in order to help him rehabilitate it. The young man, as she described him, turned out to be highly determined and self-reliant, although still impaired and impulsive. About the neurologist's criticism, she said, "Those words have been like a knife stuck in my heart." I replied, "Suppose we pull the knife out, carefully." She did so.

The final hour of therapy began with Alice's noting another emotional conclusion arrived at during the week between our meetings. I replied, speaking like a hypnotist:

A.: I did a good job with my son. I will just live with the sorrow and I can look back at his progress.

E.: Suppose you spread the sorrow more evenly (from the heart). Breathe all through, and the colors change and rearrange. And the unconscious mind breathes too, to bring fresh air to your memories. (*There follow 15 minutes of silent breathing.*)

E.: What do you notice?

A.: Images of his accident. I'm looking at them, realizing it happened. It's not happening now. And not being afraid.

E.: Take all the time you need to do it thoroughly and well.

A.: I have a memory of myself in the hospital as a 10-year-old. I feel really light. Silvery white flashes are going through my head. I feel myself spread out as a part of the universe. Like a nice, restful feeling.

E.: And that can become well established with you.

A.: My whole body is open and it feels good. I don't have to have the whole burden myself: it can be spread out through the space beyond me. It feels wonderful. I have thoughts of my father. I feel relief. I can look at this stuff. It feels really white.

E.: Breathe through the muscles and bones.

A · I feel light and powerful too. Peaceful. Happy, like running on the beach.

E.: Yes, and enjoy that, too.

A.: There's a sense of excitement. (*She gets up, laughs.*)

A reorientation of perception, emotion, memory, self, and relationship occurred as Alice applied and spread the comfort of her own strength throughout her experience. The untangling of hurts known and unknown was both conscious and unconscious, like cold, dirty laundry, tangled together in a knot. Soaking in the warm solution of the unconscious (with shuddering agitation) allowed a cleansing and sorting out to occur.

A Case of Incest

BACKGROUND

Isabel has suffered seizures since she was 3 years old. At the age of 10, in the Philippines, Isabel cared for her grandfather, who was the sole support of the family. When she was alone with him, the grandfather exhibited himself to her. She had a seizure and, in her helplessness, he raped her. This was discovered by the family doctor, who was called to treat her. The family warned Isabel never to tell what had happened because everyone in the family depended on the grandfather's financial support.

Now Isabel was 18, living in California with her father and brother and attending college. A pretty young woman, she was intimidated by the football players who flirted with her at school. I asked her neurologist if he had ever known patients with a long history of seizures to recover spontaneously. He said that it was possible.

TREATMENT

We did an hour's hypnotherapy with 12 members of the clinic staff present. (The full transcript can be found in the Appendix.) Isabel sat in a dramatic, fearful posture. I sat far from her and spoke in a friendly, matter-of-fact way. She told me that her goal was to use hypnosis to relax, to be less scared. She had had a seizure that morning. I said, "Show me how your face will look when you relax; show me so I'll know when I see it." She did, and then showed her "warm, relaxed hands."

I asked, "When you're relaxed, what will I notice about the way you show your feelings?" I asked to see sad, silly, happy, angry, and disgusted feelings. I had her choose a "Yes" and a "No" hand and say the words, coaching her to project the "No!" and grading her performance.

Isabel asked, "Are you supposed to touch me?" I said, "No," and talked about doctors touching their patients without permission and how my son hated "having his hair mussed." I spoke of his childhood diseases and recovery, his fears, hurts, and triumphs, and about how he "will reach his majority at 18 to 21, when you get to say 'Yes' and 'No' and people have to listen."

I told Isabel the opinions of her neurologist, psychiatrist, and psychologist about how long it takes to outgrow certain difficulties, as they nodded agreement. Then, in a deep hypnotic trance, she saw a screen of the past–present–future, of success at school, a friendly boy, laughter, the people in "this room, this city, this country."

When she opened her eyes and looked around the room, Isabel laughed and asked, "How do you do that?" She giggled happily, "I saw some weird things, funny things," and then, with determination and resolve, she said, "Now I can face my father!" Isabel left with thanks and a warm handshake.

Follow-up: A month later, her psychologist told me that Isabel was no longer so frightened out in the world: "She rides the bus and looks around. She has new clothes, a new hairdo. Now her brother praises her: 'You used to be a tomboy.' She notices some of the nice young men in her computer class. No seizures during the month."

Isabel was growing up, becoming the woman she was meant to be in a way that could please her while keeping her safe. Her dramatic sense of life and good humor carried through her fear and hurt and injury to reach me and the others in that room. In these next two sections, written by two individuals, we will meet this same sense of life carrying through against odds, injury, and betrayal toward a renewal of the meeting with others.

Before Hearts Are Broken*

> Try to remember when life was so tender,
> That Love was an ember about to billow. . . .
>
> —T. Jones and H. Schmidt, (1960, p. 4)

I can remember, if I really try, I what it felt like to be a 12-year-old girl whose capacity for romantic love was stirring but was still only a potential, evidenced only by new responses to warm summer evening breezes filling her up until she thought she might burst and wondered why.

And if I really try, I can remember what it felt like some years later to

*By Ruth Dart.

be in love with an actual person for the very first time. What was unique about that was the complete certainty of reciprocity, of resonance between oneself and the loved one. Love occurring in concert: as palpable as a ball tossed back and forth.

Too often the happy certainty of first love is attributed to inexperience. On the contrary, perception of love as innately mutual is not naive: It is accurate. At this first beginning, no one has yet confused the issue: No one has tried to impose stasis upon flow, to be someone he or she is not. In my very first interval of romantic love, I was utterly content to be exactly the person I was, and delighted that the other person was exactly himself. Love bypassed disguise then, and I would add to love's innate reciprocity its attribute of recognition. Not everything is known, but nothing is denied.

Out of this recognition and resonant feedback between persons grows the empathy that accompanies many caring relationships, family love and friendship, as well as romantic love. One continually imagines *being* the other person and feels a measure of that person's joy or pain. One can hurt so terribly for a friend or loved one as to wish it were possible to do the suffering in his or her place, or be buoyed up for days by imagining the person's joy over some happy event. More commonly, empathy takes the form of willingness to "try on" another person's point of view, even if one does not concur with it.

Loyalty in friendship is much like first love in its essential resonance because close friends are, in their imaginations, continually trading places. I can remember being 10 years old, looking across the classroom into my friend Nancy's eyes, knowing that she was thinking about climbing trees behind the school even though the class had been told that it was not allowed. Now, decades later, we can still look into each other's minds and laugh, no explanation necessary.

Reciprocity, recognition, imaginative empathy—all are internal capabilities and yet innately interactive. What happens when an individual suddenly, paradoxically, impossibly, finds herself *alone* with these processes, receiving insult after *returning* a smile, reflecting light into a black hole? Where is her identity when her loyalty is continually evoked to point the way for attack? In a person who is empathic and loyal, evocation of resonant emotion as a prelude to assault can lead to terrible distortions of the self because the self is necessarily complicit in its own battery. What follows is the story of one person's involuntary conspiracy against herself through her own characteristic responses of loyalty and empathy.

> I know who I was when I got up this morning, but I think I must
> have been changed several times since then . . . and being so many
> different (people) in a day is very confusing.

—*(Carroll, 1946, p. 46)*

It began with confusion. Life has rarely presented me with a perfectly controlled experiment, and its traumas have never arrived neatly wrapped, analyzed, and classified. As the object of whispered gossip, I began the slow journey toward awareness of my selection as social scapegoat in simple perplexity.

I was talking with my lover, Walter, at his studio when Ed dropped in. Ed had always managed friendly banter with me, but on this occasion he glanced at me coldly with no greeting, delivered his message to Walter, and headed back out. "*Cunt!*" was Ed's parting word. Startled, I looked around. "What was that all about?" I asked Walter. "What did I ever do to him?" Walter looked sheepish and told me that the night before he had excused his extreme drunkenness by telling Ed that I was a "cock tease," and that any man would get drunk under such circumstances. "It wasn't true," Walter said, "but I needed an excuse for being so drunk." In my disorientation I mistook his attitude for regret.

This was a first for me: I had never been *rewritten* before. I had a happy childhood in a family of people who loved and valued one another. We did things together as a family: singing folk songs, gospel hymns, and six-part madrigals; traveling and camping out in the summers; cooperating with chores. And we did things apart according to our interests. My brother became a skilled luthier and singer; my older sister an ethnomusicologist, dancer, and math teacher; my younger sister a linguistics professor and horticulturalist; and I graduated summa cum laude from Harvard in mathematics and English literature. Learning was a lifestyle, and the possibilities were so endless that no one felt the need to write a restricting part for anyone else.

Many times, in looking back, I have wondered why I failed to see Walter's casual willingness to sacrifice others for his own convenience. This insight would have ended our relationship immediately and saved me years of suffering. Did I lack exposure to malice in others? No! Walter had just given me a live demonstration. What blinded me was that I did not know how to act or where to move when addressed as someone I was not.

Assuming that Walter would straighten things out with Ed *later* was my way of reclaiming my identity. I didn't take warning from the hollow sense of unreality they had created moments before by dramatizing a lie. Their exchange had been the opposite of recognition and of emotional reciprocity. They had tossed a ball back and forth high over my head with no intention of letting me touch it. They had called me someone I was not.

My Quaker upbringing offers a valid response to the question, "Where is God in this situation?" The response is: "All He has is thee." During those moments of abuse, God did not have me. Nobody did. My self was gone, and without it I had no handhold.

Walter had been introduced to me by Ben, a Quaker friend of 10 years' standing. When I was a 19-year-old getting to know Ben, he asked me why I wrote down my thoughts. I said, "I want to express thoughts so clearly that if anyone were to read the words 10 years from now they would know exactly what I had meant." He smiled.

One evening, looking down from the foothills at the lights of Claremont, Ben asked, "Why do people live in cities?" I thought for a bit. "To be near other people." Again, he seemed to enjoy my being simply who I was. Ben and I told each other pieces of what made each of us who we were. As a family friend, he dropped his finals to help search for my cousin when she was lost in the mountains of Baja. I had faith in him. I liked feeling that there was someone who would always be a friend. Ben and I went our separate ways but remained friends, catching up with each other from time to time.

Emotional resonance enriched my contacts with Ben until sometime during the first year of my relationship with Walter. One evening, Ben and his lover, Amy, dropped in at Walter's studio. Amy and Walter went off together to a far part of the shop, and Ben approached me: "You know, it isn't kind to withhold sex from someone as a form of manipulation." "Of course, it isn't," I replied. "Then don't do it." "I'm not doing it; I have never even thought of doing it." Ben didn't continue. His eyes were flat, his face expressionless. He walked off to join Walter and Amy. I stayed where I was, trying to find myself again. This had not been a dialogue, it had been a mugging.

As I looked over at the others, they seemed a football field away. Ordinarily it would have been natural for me to join them, but now my legs wouldn't move. Once more, disorientation from being treated as someone I was not prevented me from drawing the obvious conclusion: Walter had been lying. *Why* didn't I see it? Why did I just sit there alone, confused?

In the Quaker approach to interpersonal or political conflict the first two steps toward resolution are: (1) Identify with your adversary. (2) Speak truth to power. So many times in looking back I have asked myself why I did not just walk over to Walter, Ben, and Amy and speak truth to social power—walk over and say, "Let's get this out in the open. I have been called a sexual tease, and I am not one. Look at me, look at each other, and let's clarify the misunderstanding." They might have brought out the truth and put an end to the whispering. Or if their need for a villain were stronger than their interest in truth, it would at least have led me to break up with Walter and forced them to choose somebody else to play villain. Why couldn't I make the connection between Ben and Walter's behavior and just speak up?

Perhaps I could not see the truth without taking the first step: Identify with your adversary. I was too confused to perceive them as adversaries, let alone to identify with them. I was unable to imagine myself wanting to vilify and exclude another person. I had just experienced the flat-lining of resonance between me and a hitherto trusted friend and, most important, I suffered an insurmountable handicap: I could not identify with *anybody* when my own identity had been taken away. They had called me someone I was not, and I was no longer present. My legs wouldn't move, my mind wouldn't think. I couldn't *be* the character they were calling. There was no handhold. God did not have me.

> Alice: I am trying to find my way.
> The Red Queen: *All* ways here are *my* ways.
>
> *(Carroll, 1946, p. 75)*

I remained uneasily in the dark as the gossip crescendoed to a roar. I could feel the ill will all around me but was never given enough information to address it. Repeatedly, Ben approached me alone, *ordered* me to stop manipulating Walter by withholding sex, and ignored my response. I answered the phone one day, and it was Ben's mother, Jeanette, calling to tell me that Walter's art would one day rise above attempts to emasculate him and would be known throughout the world. I obliged as well as I could, "Yes, he does make some beautiful things," thinking to myself, "*Huh?* A dramatic sentiment, but why call *me* out of the blue to express it? Maybe she's lonely." I never dreamed that Walter was lying to her too.

One morning, Walter suggested a drive his favorite burger joint. We parked and walked in the fog, talking and joking and looking at the town. At the café, I declined his offer of a gin and tonic to go with my burger. It was a standing joke between us that I couldn't bear the taste of alcohol long enough to choke down more than a few sips. He insisted: "There's a two-drink limit in here, so just order one and I'll drink yours." When both drinks were gone, he asked me to order a second, and again he drank both. We continued walking and talking, he made a purchase at a liquor store, and we returned to his van. A few minutes into the drive home, Walter suddenly slammed his hands down on the wheel and shouted, "Talk about something different!! Why do you always talk about the same thing?!" Shocked by the outburst I was silent for a few minutes. He slammed the wheel again and swore. I said, "Okay, here's something different. Why do you suppose it is that we don't live together?" My question was rhetorical. He had just demonstrated the reason for my fear of him. *Slam!* "That does it!" He pushed the accelerator to the floor. I had no idea where we were going and knew it was useless to ask, but one thing became clear: He had taken this route in this same mood of high drama many times before. Every nuance of posture and movement said that he was on automatic pilot. He took side streets with the speed and sureness of long practice. This was the ritual finale of every trip he made for burgers and gin, and the only new factor was my presence.

I was surprised when our destination turned out to be Amy's home, but given the way Walter had been driving, I'd have gotten out anywhere. Walter charged right in, and I trailed after him thinking, "*Why are we here? Why is any of this her business?*" Ben was there with Amy, and Walter stormed, "She said that we should live together! See what I mean? See what I *mean? See?*" They replied in effect, "Yes we see what you mean. How could you do this, Ruth?" *Do what? See what? What did everyone but me see?*

I tried to speak, but no one tried to hear. They were off in a discussion that they seemed to have held many times before in my absence. Apparently 90 percent of my history with Walter was unknown to me, and Amy was fluent in it, spewing 20 minutes of censorious allusion without disclosing one bit of concrete information. Quite a trick.

I left having learned nothing except that the three of them were adept at hiding the facts. Ben and Amy let Walter throw his tantrum and I had missed the point by taking for granted that our common purpose was communication. There they were, each in great need of a scapegoat and determined to create one. No one cared what I actually said or meant or felt. They had cast me in a part and were shielding their illusion from the inconvenient reality of the person I actually was.

It was after this incident that Ben told everyone, "Just assume that everything Ruth says is a lie but believe whatever you hear about her. She is capable of *anything* and will deny everything." Whenever our paths crossed, he would begin an apparently friendly conversation, and as soon as I responded in kind, would demand that I admit to atrocity. He decreed one time that I had a history of bulemia; at another, it was a history of Valium addiction. He pushed and pushed for corroboration of these lies, and then reiterated, "You lie about everything." He would phone me from El Cerrito and ask what the weather was like in Berkeley. If I replied that it was foggy, he would say, "Well, now we know that the sun is out." Over and over, for weeks and months, he would fake friendliness until my innate responsiveness came sufficiently alive that he could kill it. I would be left feeling as empty as clothes left hanging in the closet of someone who has died.

As the abuse escalated, it also degenerated. While giving me a ride home, Amy and Ben began to ridicule my voice. Amy mimicked something I had said at dinner, caricaturing the high pitch and the enunciation. Ben snorted a raucous laugh, then, "*Shshsh,*" jerking his head toward the object of their ridicule in the back seat. With only the three of us in the car, they were demonstrating complicity in abusing me and permission to escalate, with the assurance of company in wrongdoing.

The banality of the subject matter was neither paradoxical nor accidental. There is safety in doing harm in sufficiently large company, where widespread participation is assured. Whereas in most societies, an individual who commits murder is subject to social retribution, an entire society may go to war and commit murder with social approval. During the 17th century, participants in witch hunts in Lancashire, England, made no effort to deny their presence at the killing. They all knew one another.

By being present, they validated each other's behavior. The *village* committed the murder and there was no retribution.

This could not have happened without minimizing social risk. The consensus to victimize must grow safely over small issues, until participants believe that they are normal and not alone. The closer the gossip comes to being ordinary "common knowledge," the more effective it is as an exchange of permissions. Banality gives an aura of safety and the ordinary to wrongdoing and conditions participants for worse to come. Ben and Amy's trivial taunt was insidious because the behavior could not possibly stand on its own. It was meaningless without an underlying agenda of evil.

One evening, Walter lent me his car so that I could study on campus at night, and I left the keys in the magnetic box and the car in the campus parking lot as we had arranged. The following morning, I was awakened by Jeanette, who pushed her way into my apartment, grabbed my purse, and began rooting through it, babbling furiously about tires and keys and pottery. I stared at her, too stunned to give her invasion of my home and property the rebuff it deserved. For several days, verbal attacks from Ben, Amy, and Ed were repeated at Jeanette's level of hostility, always with the mention of tires and keys. They refused to explain, telling me to stop pretending that I didn't know. Finally, Ben told me that the night I had left Walter's car for him to pick up, he had arrived at a party and announced there that I had let the air out of his tires and had stolen his car keys. Naturally no one had bothered to ask the obvious questions: Did you actually *see* Ruth do anything at all? If so, why didn't you stop her; if not, why are you accusing her?

For weeks, I denied this latest accusation, and Ben took pleasure in repeating it. I retain a vivid memory of the four of us sitting around the stove in Walter's shop with Ben demanding, "Why don't you just *admit* everything and give the keys back?" I remember Amy's supporting him and my turning to Walter and saying, "Look, I really didn't do it." Walter watched us and said nothing at all.

I tried to use common sense where common sense was unwelcome. I went to the campus Lost and Found. There were the keys, with detailed documentation of their discovery on the night of their disappearance: A passing student saw them dropped by a large man answering Walter's description as he was leaving the parking lot. When the student tried to return them, the man cursed at him, and he decided to turn them in with a written explanation.

I saw Ben, and eagerly showed him what I had found. He crumpled up the papers and shoved them into his pocket. When I insisted, he finally glanced at them and said, "Well, you arranged for all of this to happen so that you could wait three weeks and then pick them up." Holding up the keys, he said, "*I* will return these to Walter and I'll tell him that *you* finally decided to give them back." It was one of the few times in my adult life that I have burst into tears spontaneously. The person I thought Ben to be had met up with a sadist, and the two of them could not occupy the same space at the same time. I could not take it in. It was impossible to imagine that Ben so desired people to continue hurting me that he would put words in my mouth and forcibly take the keys. It was easier to lose myself to numbness.

Then came the first hate letter from Jeanette, and once again I had to conclude that she was confused. "Jezebel," she wrote, "never deprived the world of great art." She went on about sluts and promiscuity and informed me irrelevantly that "shards are valuable historical documents." I thought that perhaps she was drunk when she wrote it.

Clarity of vision for me could only have come as a timely perception of opposing outlooks. I had to see the others as a group at a moment when I was both out of their reach and feeling my own power. I was running around the track on a beautiful afternoon. I could feel a cool breeze on my skin, and the meditative, dreamy part of my mind was wide open, as it often is during a good run. I noticed a group of people picnicking and kicking a soccer ball around at one end of the field. I thought "How nice!" and then realized that these people were Walter, Ben, Amy, Ed, and some others. I had not been invited. I felt shock. Adrenaline filled me with such force that I felt vibrations in all extremities, and I could hear nothing but my heart pounding.

It took my breath away, and I had to stop running. I managed to get to the opposite end of the playing field, where I sat down in the grass. Images from a recurring early childhood nightmare appeared, flashing on and off in the grass, which had become much too green, and then on and off in the sky, which had become much too blue. In the old sleeping dream, the distressing alternating extremes of size, shape, and texture may have reflected the experience of a toddler, for whom one visual reality can suddenly be replaced by another as she is whisked around by an adult. There was no transition. One moment I still thought I had friends, and the next moment, I clearly did not have friends and never had.

It was at that moment that I gave up. One can argue endlessly about who let the air out of the tires, but one cannot argue people into recognizing and including one in their circle. Shared predation unifies people even when they agree on nothing else, and facts cannot compete with its seductiveness. Ben telephoned that evening to say that it was unfortunate that I had seen them but that I had not been invited because I was the cause of Walter's alcoholism and he had been sober for two days. In those few intervening hours, some part of me must already have fallen dormant, because I, normally relentlessly logical, could not even summon indignation at the absurdity. Walter, when I first met him, had a history of 15 years of problem drinking and drunk driving accidents, with the scars to prove them. I didn't try to explain that Walter was never sober for two consecutive days, and that gin was hidden in the windshield wiper ducts of his car. I was suddenly too tired for interaction. These people who had been feeding off of their illusions about me were light years away. They had won before I even knew that we were adversaries.

> Thus in the winter stands the lonely tree,
> Nor knows what birds have vanished one by one;
> Yet knows its boughs more silent than before:
> I cannot say what loves have come and gone.
> I only know that summer sang in me,
> A little while, that in me sings no more.
> (St. Vincent Millay, 1992, p. 56)

The image of my exclusion 20 years ago will stay with me forever. On a recent Christmas, I accompanied my parents to a Quaker meeting, although I am now reluctant to take part in social activity. Ironically, the spontaneous theme was that of *community*, the first speaker saying that when he thought of *community*, he saw the image of quail huddled together in a blizzard, sheltering wings spread about each other against the storm. Subsequent speakers offered other images and anecdotes that gave life to the concept of community, and I was shocked, yet unsurprised, at the anger gathering inside of me—unsurprised, because I had lived with the feeling for so long and shocked because I had not clearly recognized it. When I think of *community*, I do not see quail in a blizzard. I see a group of friends at one end of a field having a picnic, and me at the other end, having a nightmare.

After that moment of realization at the field, I knew that I had to get away from them—especially from Ben, the most direct and persistent accuser. I thought that if I could manage to avoid contact with Ben for perhaps a month, then I wouldn't feel so crazy. I changed my schedule, avoided places that Ben frequented and events at which he was expected, and at the end of every day of successful avoidance, I put an "X" on that square of my wall calendar. I could never achieve more than eight consecutive X's. Ben could not go longer than eight days without telephoning his abuse. He would follow my "Hello?" with "Hi," not identifying himself, but expecting me to know him. This would be followed by "How are you?" If I said "Fine," he would reply, "No, you're not. Why don't you admit that you took Walter's keys?" If I said "Not fine," he would reply, "Yes, you are. Why don't you admit that you took Walter's keys?"

I began refusing to answer the question "How are you?" He would respond to my silence by beginning to chat, as though we were friends. Eventually I would take the bait. The empathy that was still a buried part of me would make me responsive to what seemed to be peace overtures, and then he would blindside me with one of the many old accusations or invent a new one. I could not defend myself without acting unlike myself. Sometimes I would hang up and scream to an empty apartment, "*Stop it! Stop it! Stop it!*" Then I would begin crossing off days all over again. I recently found the old calendars in a carton. Eighteen months were tattooed with strings of X's.

I don't remember making a conscious decision to abuse alcohol. I know that I visualized and mimetically felt the new behavior as a reactive maneuver in space, not unlike motions I used to take instinctively as a child swinging on the bars of a jungle gym. I would use whatever momentum and pivot points were at hand in order to land intact. The difference was that now I would find myself airborne without knowing how I got there.

Drinking was like executing a perfect dive, only to discover that I was plunging into polluted water. I didn't like swallowing alcohol no matter how it was mixed or disguised, and I had trouble getting it down without gagging. Then, once I had choked down enough to feel its influence, I didn't much like the effect. But I had to keep them from killing me over and over again. Ben was going to attack anyway, but if I could influence the attack's direction, I might have some measure of control. If I used Ben's own momentum and simply *did* one of the things of which he repeatedly accused me, he might be diverted to a single theme and so leave some part of my self undamaged. So instead of resisting the central accusation—that I had caused Walter to drink—I simply began to drink myself.

In retrospect, I think that when I was drinking, Ben was unable to evoke resonant emotion in me. Changing myself by drinking was the only way I could get away from him. If I had tried rebuffing the initial "friendly" overture by hanging up the phone or slamming the door, I would have immediately identified with him and felt sad for hurting his feelings. As long as I was capable of empathy, he could hurt me from inside of me, and I was not safe from invasion. When I was under the influence of alcohol, he was still abusive, but I did not end up feeling like a participant and so was spared the sickening discontinuity of having my identity suddenly disappear. I felt hidden but still somewhat present.

I drank periodically, having either far too much alcohol or none at all for weeks, and the cycle was emotionally driven. It felt too dangerous to revert to my true empathetic and loyal self, the self that could be used by others to hurt me, so perhaps the length of the cycle reflected some balance of fear with emotional recovery time. After less than a year of "problem drinking," my contacts with the others had ceased altogether: I no longer made a satisfactory victim, and their resulting frustration caused them to focus increasingly on my drinking and then go away. As a diversion, it was successful.

The price was a hideous one. There are no adequate words for describing severe alcohol withdrawal. If fear and horror could be sent to every nerve center of the body continuously, 24 hours a day, the result might approximate withdrawal. Surviving it takes every bit of strength one can summon. After beginning to drink as a panicky escape from persecution, or from a state of mind that felt vulnerable to persecution, I always tried to stop, and each time rode out the horror once again. This meant five withdrawals each year for 15 years, during a large part of which I was homeless, enduring withdrawal under bridges, without food or water. Ironically, it was my refusal to accept drinking as a continuous way of life—my determination to go through the pain and try again— that made my drinking cyclical and led others to dismiss me as hopeless.

I had seen none of the witch-hunt participants for over a year when Walter came by my apartment one day. He explained that he was doing one of the Alcoholics Anonymous (AA) steps, which entailed telling the truth to someone he had harmed and making amends. He began, "You'll be glad to know that you didn't let the air out of my tires." (What did he expect me to do—thank him for repainting white the roses which he had painted red?) I said, "You seem to forget that you are talking to one of a very few people in the world who already knew that. What are you really trying to say?"

He told me that he had let the air out of his car tires himself and had somehow lost the keys on his way to the party. He had become enraged when he realized that he was too drunk to get the key into the ignition, and he needed to blame someone for his having to walk to the party, so he vandalized the car and told everyone that I had done it. He also said that he had regularly retold the lie about sexual manipulation to everyone we knew in common, and that once a week, on Jeanette's half-day off, he would drink with her and tell her that I was saying disparaging things about his sculpture, that I had deliberately broken some of his best pieces, and that I was having affairs with all of the male potters in Berkeley. He did all this, he said, so that people would believe his drinking to be my fault and he would not lose his friends. Knowing where and when I went for my run, he had organized the soccer game with the stipulation that I be excluded so that he might take his story to its next level. The network of lies had become so extensive that it was threatened by my presence: I was not acting the part.

I was stunned. I had had no idea that Walter was the source of the rumors, and I had never dreamed that he had vandalized his own car or that he had initiated weekly hate sessions with Jeanette. I asked whether he planned to straighten out the lies with the people to whom he had told them. "I'm not ready to do that yet," he replied after a long hesitation, during which he could not meet my eyes. He never became ready, and what he told me undoubtedly was only the tip of the iceberg.

Later that same day, I decided to find Walter at the AA meeting where he was a regular, to try to persuade him to be honest with the others. I entered the foyer just as he was presenting a self-worshipping account of his "confession" to me. They all sat there, reminiscent tears in their eyes, applauding Walter's bravery, not knowing that he had confessed to the only person who would not be believed, and had left her to continue paying for his lies. He was repeating what he had done before, with me as a prop, he was seducing the people around him by offering them an opportunity to emote. It was such a perversion of everything that I value in relationship that I left without trying to talk to him. Once again, I saw *community* as a sham, and I was far removed, looking on with increasing horror.

> *Privacy is the moral fact that a person belongs to himself. (Blackman, 1995)*

Walter's confession cemented my feelings of violation. I was a victim of social rape. Everyone had known that the person I was sexual with was reviling me behind my back, and no one had told me. They had tacitly endorsed it. Instead of giving me the protective information to which I had more right than anyone else, they sat back, watched a rape in progress, and applauded. As a survivor of violent physical rape by a stranger, I can say without hesitation that violation by my "friends" did far more lasting damage to me than the stranger rape that society recognizes as a crime. My personal character and my personal history—the things that I *really* am and have *really* experienced—belong to *me*. Those people rewrote my character and my history in order to jockey for position in what they thought of as *community*, and in doing so, committed the ultimate violation of my privacy. They called me someone I was not, asserting in effect that I belonged not to myself, but to them.

My fear of my own power continued to grow, because it was my capacity for empathy and loyalty that had been used as a tool of violation. I feared that of God in me—that of love in me—and used alcohol as a protective sheath whenever I could not be alone. In drinking, I would only comprehend and store other people's insults intellectually, while my sense of self was hidden somewhere, nearly intact. I became unable even to telephone family members without drinking first. Enduring battery with a secret sense of self is less empty than participating in battery of oneself.

Alcohol turned out to be an ironic choice of cover for my identity, because society's response to a person with a "drinking problem" is to rewrite that person. A person who is already socially censured is a scapegoat for everyone else's problems. Being blamed for my niece's emerging adolescence or for my cousin's death in a motorcycle accident was not all that different from being blamed for Walter's alcoholism. Furthermore, AA, the conventional treatment, does not value an individual's uniqueness. In AA, the word *recovery* does not have its dictionary meaning of finding again what has been lost. As Walter demonstrated, it is perfectly possible to mouth the words without living them, and, in the process, to cease drinking. Do this and no one will ask, "Now, who are you?" Members are certain that you are identical to them.

It is written in the "Big Book," "We can never afford to get angry." This is wrong: There is no inevitable "we" and *I* cannot afford *not* to get angry when anger arises inside me. I was not able to forget the violation that had induced the drinking problem, and I was looking for an old and cherished identity, not for a brand-new one. AA was just another way of rewriting my character—another way of telling me that I did not belong to myself.

At the end of my first session as a patient of Eric Greenleaf, he said, "When we're through here you'll be . . . you'll be yourself!" Although I had become too deeply buried in the specifics of abuse to grasp the general problem, he went straight to it. One could describe the course of our work together as remembering or discovering parts of me that were characteristic, and following their lead. What neither of us knew at first was that my recent history had created a built-in undertow of fear— my own fear of myself— that would periodically sabotage our efforts.

At the root was the fact that the weapons used to harm me had been my own deepest innate responses. Whenever we would have a session that left me spontaneously expressive in relationship, whenever we would experience emotional resonance together, I would feel soon afterward that a dangerous weapon had been unsheathed, and I would have an irresistible urge to drink. The remedy and the danger were too much alike.

Yet they were not exactly the same, and Eric had a gift for uncovering through a person's visual imagination an identity that was as individual as a fingerprint. Remembering this part of our work always brings to my mind the watch cock in horology of the 18th century, a bracket-like plate holding bearings and supported at one end that was both a part of the watch's mechanism and a work of art. Although it was hidden from sight, it was a point of honor among watchmakers to make it as beautiful as possible, and no two watch cocks were ever exactly alike. Doing active imagining with Eric was magical, like getting a quick peek at a hidden watch cock. I shared a recurring dream of a sparkling ocean full of whales and pirate ships, the whales joyfully shooting up from the deep and colliding with a ship, knocking it into the air and scattering everything into the water, and Eric didn't think it peculiar that pirate ships made me happy. When he asked me what my present physical pain looked like, I had the fleeting skeptical thought that pain does not *look* like anything, and then into my mind popped the image of red and black thread, hopelessly tangled. I breathed and relaxed until the image changed and the pain went away.

In imagination I looked into a mirror and saw my reflection as someone we named "The Woman in Peach." She feels to me like a process or a capability, not a static image. She is always on the beach, wearing colors of creamy white, peach, and turquoise, and is an active part of the landscape. She is both serene and in motion, feeling the breeze all around her and the sun on her skin, without separating herself from them.

From one of my drawings came the Unicorn, made of light, galloping with no restraints. And out of my dreams came "The Dark Woman," self-deprecating and easily abused; "The Black Woman," physically exuberant and powerful; Andrea, an inquisitive 5-year-old; and the "King," who had all the information. Somewhat later came Wanda, who was always at the seashore like the Woman in Peach, but was drowning, struggling against undertow and clinging seaweed to get out of the water. Then there was "The Heart Surgeon," dressed in white and working to clear the sticky black coating off a heart that was still pink and healthy underneath.

They were all parts of me, and I thought of them as arranged in three-dimensional space in well-defined relative positions, like the electron cloud model of an atom in which each component is in motion but has maximum density at a specific location. Together, Eric and I were able to call me the person I really was and to make her present. It felt wonderful and sometimes I would snatch a tissue from the box on the table, ball it up and toss it, and he would throw it back. I'm not sure how often Eric's patients throw things at him, but he knew without being told that my tissue tosses were expressions of good feeling. I guess that they were confirmation of reciprocity—assurance that I was recognized simultaneously as an individual and as a participant.

But how could I maintain that presence? There was some sequence of internal events that would repeatedly lead me from joy in my identity to the need to hide and protect it by drinking. The problem was not chemical addiction but profound mistrust of other human beings in general—some hopeless tangle of red and black thread.

With experience I came to realize that by the time I felt the first impulse to drink, it was already too late to resist it, and that I needed to take warning from the state of awareness preceding that impulse. Such a fugue state would often arise from a flashback to an incident of abuse, and from within the fugue, life seemed to be missing a dimension. Past events seemed palpably present, while present realities seemed far away. I was unable to judge the relative importance of memories and actions and immediate options, just as in plane geometry one is unable to know the relative magnitudes of objects if the third dimension is not shown. It was much like my childhood nightmare in which size, shape, and texture were indeterminate and could jump between opposite extremes.

Normally I experience an emotion as a sort of flow. I have a sense of process during the minutes when I can still say, "I feel——." During the fugue state, there was pain without process: nothing moved, even though tremendous energy was being expended. The dimension of time seemed to be missing. By the time I regained the time dimension and the ability to assess relative values, I would be drinking again.

Although Eric had, from the beginning, stressed the importance of acknowledging feelings, for most of my life I had thought of emotional expression as inherently somewhat messy. Emotion was to be controlled or mitigated and so felt out of control when it emerged. I had a valid point. People are often messily emotional, mistaking the origins and objects of their feelings so that the timing and direction of expression are inappropriate. In sharp contrast to these doubts about emotion was my pleasure in the visual precision of geometry. In therapy I compared interpersonal events to particular orientations of functions in space. I visualized a person's "mood" at any given time as a vector in Euclidian n-space—a sum of the individual vectors whose lengths represented the respective intensities of each of n different emotions. I wished that the actual experiencing of emotion had that same clarity of form.

One day Eric and I had a breakthrough session on the telephone. The relationship between a therapist and client is intensely personal but necessarily involves cash transactions, and I had asked to change the timing of a payment, which was virtually asking him to lend me money. I thought that I had a good reason, and I had very little money, but, as we talked, I felt sad, guilty, hurt, and insulted, and Eric felt trapped, taken advantage of, frustrated, and angry.

Neither of us wanted to end the conversation that way, so Eric, utilizing my fondness for geometry, suggested that each of us "orthogonalize" our emotions in order to move from this stuck place. I knew the meaning of orthogonality in geometry, but I did not know what it would be like to experience orthogonal emotions. Eric said that I could have the payment timing I had requested but that now, for purposes of orthogonalizing my emotions, I should imagine that I could choose between two different powers of decision: I could either decide when payment would be made, or decide when I would make my desired trip to Los Angeles, but I could not decide both. Now, in pragmatic terms, one decision might be seen as likely to depend on the other, but it was perfectly possible to imagine giving up power over one if I chose to have power over the other. The distribution of power and powerlessness over the events of daily life often makes no sense, so the separation of the two decisions was not completely foreign to my experience.

The apparently artificial separation served as an algorithm for achieving emotional orthogonality when one does not know what emotional orthogonality feels like. Eric used feelings with which I did have experience (power and powerlessness) to lead me into a feeling state that I had not previously conceptualized.

As I imagined the choice between making one decision or the other—deciding when to pay or deciding when to go to Los Angeles—I felt the knot of pressure inside me relax a little bit. It relaxed still more as I moved from this imagining to the making of the choice. Somewhat to my surprise, I chose to decide when to pay, and to my further surprise, I chose to pay at the regular time rather than later. I did not feel so upset, and I did not feel that I had capitulated. Without my trying to please anyone, suddenly there was clarity. I had orthogonalized the two decisions.

One might draw the relationship of the two decisions as a function in 2-space with two orthogonal time axes. If I choose when to take the trip, then I must accept any decision from a hypothetical other agent about when to pay, and vice versa. Assuming that this other agent is unaffected by my choice of date, the two decisions are independent if they are represented by a vertical line and a horizontal line. Any other function indicates that one decision affects the other one, that is, is a nontrivial function of the other one. When one can have power over only one of them, the two decisions are orthogonal to the axes and to each other.

The emotions associated with the choices became independent—orthogonal—also. If x is independent of y, there is no way to link an emotional response to x with an emotional response to y. I did not interpret Eric's reluctance to manipulate our business agreement as reluctance to have me visit Joe in Los Angeles. And I no longer confused my frustration at my still unstable finances with frustration at Eric's rules, or anxiety over my relationship with Eric with anxiety over my relationship with Joe. I felt each emotion independently of—orthogonally to—the others, saw the facts the way they were, and with this clarity my distress resolved itself. I could make things easier for myself in time, just not overnight.

This first experience of emotional orthogonalization enabled me to practice the process whenever I experienced emotional discomfort. Visualization of functions moving into orthogonality eventually led me to a supplementary imagining, one of pouring a detangling liquid over a ball of tangled thread. The ball of hopelessly tangled red and black thread that had represented pain for me has much in common with emotional confusion. Individual strands cannot be followed or distinguished from each other, so it loses some of the properties of thread. It will not fall apart if you throw it, you cannot sew with it or comb out things that get stuck in it or change the pattern of black and red. *Un*tangled threads also have form. They can hang together in waves or blow together in the wind, just as emotions can coexist without confusion. There are any number of detangling substances that lubricate fibers so that they can slip and slide past each other, and it occurred to me that I could take such a super-lubricator and pour it over a distressing tangle of emotions. Untangled threads are orthogonal in that one of them can change without changing the others: you can pull on a black thread without having a red one come along with it. Once I became familiar with the feel of emotional orthogonality, I found that in an emergency I could imagine pouring detangler over thread as a shortcut for getting there.

Whatever route I took, the result was that the painful pressure inside me was replaced by hospitality, by readiness for new experiences. In a very short time drinking became a thing of the past, and life once again held limitless possibility. Eric had helped me to regain a freedom of which

I had despaired even though I had never stopped trying. Not everyone would choose geometry as a personal path to emotional clarity. I will always be grateful for his ability to look and feel outside of himself and to see me.

Formerly in my life, recovery from emotional pain had been incremental and seemingly interminable. Pain was asymptotic to some time axis and never decisively ended. With orthogonalization, however, change following pain is for me sudden, qualitative, and complete. Pain's time function has finite form. One of the surprises of the new way is the strength and intensity of pleasurable feeling that will eventually replace a painful one. Far from having to coax some happiness out of myself, I find the sudden happiness irresistible. By allowing myself to feel the full impact of each current emotion, I achieve a momentum of feeling that allows me forcefully to enter the next emotion.

Since emotions are, in part, muscle mobilizations, I compare their expression to athletic performance. The differences between my old way of handling emotion and the new way are differences in the use of momentum, in the achievement of accuracy, and in the form resulting over time from particular combinations of skills.

An athlete's transfer of momentum from one direction of movement to another is most clearly and dramatically seen when the two directions are orthogonal. Consider a gymnast executing a vault: As she runs along the mat toward the horse, her movement is horizontal, and the vertical momentum vector is zero. She reaches the horse and pushes off of it with enough force against the established motion to change her direction to vertical. If she had simply come to a complete stop and then jumped vertically, the vertical burst of velocity would have been much smaller and much shorter. Her positive horizontal velocity increased the range of achievable heights.

The article "Barry Bonds Talk Delights Little Leaguers" concludes with a nice homology of athletic and emotional sequences:

> A little while later, during batting practice, Baker, the manager, amused himself by tossing balls into the stands. Nothing too strange there, but the way Baker did it was notable. Each time, he tossed the ball so the fan had to lean way over, almost falling forward. And each made the catch, laughing at the moment of fear. (Kettman, 1992, May 24)

Baker deliberately extended the necessary reach for the catch to a point just short of dangerous imbalance. The phrase "laughing at the moment of fear" describes a change from one emotion to another in which some of the momentum of the first is transferred to the second. One can imagine the laughter to be a burst or acceleration of joy, the joy being orthogonal to the fear of falling or of missing the catch. As the catch is made, the fear suddenly abates, and some of its energy is transformed into joy.

Since first noticing the transfer of momentum in emotional sequences I have become increasingly deliberate at using emotional momentum to enhance enjoyment. I still occasionally suffer flashbacks—visceral memories of abuse—so I have frequent opportunities to wrestle with unpleasant emotion. As soon as I recognize that I am in the throes of painful feeling, I begin "orthogonalizing" all my emotions, reminding myself to notice the anger in particular. With the consequent perspective, I realize that some of anger's energy is going to be transferred to a different emotion, and I begin to take aim and plan how to use it. While still in distress, I find myself thinking, "Yes! I'll bet I can really get a *bounce* out of this one!" and I remember the vault or "laughing at the moment of fear." Then the next pleasurable activity, whether it is work that I enjoy or just singing in the shower, will have extra intensity and life. God and I have each other again.

Emotional clarity would have generated an answer to the people who called me someone I was not. Orthogonalizing emotions means, among other things, separating out and acknowledging anger. Whereas 20 years ago, I unconsciously assumed that trying to understand another person precluded being angry with that person, I might today allow both responses. The appropriate response to the injunction "Stop manipulating Walter by withholding sex" is *not* to argue its specific content. Argument implicitly validates the speaker's view of one's identity, as does any simple answer to the classic question, "Have you stopped beating your wife?" Empathy, in the sense of willingness to imagine *being* the questioner, is inappropriate, because the question itself implies a lie. It is, in fact, not a question but an assault. The right response is, "How *dare* you say those words to me?" If I had been able to say, "How *dare* you?" instead of "I never did that," I would have remained present instead of losing myself.

Empathy and anger make tricky bedfellows. Identifying with another person while protecting oneself from one person's blunderings is an ambitious undertaking for which I admire therapists, and rabbis and priests. It has become a necessary undertaking for me also, because I am still the same person, more experienced and wary, but at heart still the same. I still resonate with the person behind the dangerous behavior. I catch glimpses of what Quakers call that person's "inner light" and hear a few notes of his or her inner music as it sounds before being played by a faulty instrument. I would not have it any other way, but I must remain aware of danger in the instrument. It is all right to notice another person's hurt and confusion and badly expressed good intentions, but if the person carries a gun, one had better notice that too. I would not put someone I loved in the path of the bullet, and I must cherish myself as one of the people I love if I am to have anything left to offer. I am still new at combining vigilance with responsiveness to the spirit that lives before hearts are broken. Anger at the people whose destructiveness changed my life occasionally overwhelms me. Yet as I write this, I can imagine how sad Ben would feel were he to read it and truly understand it. As I write this, I am sharing his sorrow.

Fey*

I cannot lay claim to the usual accomplishments recognized by mainstream society. I have no children and have never been married. There are no initials after my name to give credibility and stature. I attended only a smattering of elementary and junior high school and rarely completed a grade. Nor have I built any semblance of a career: I had two or three minimum-wage, part-time jobs for a couple of years, and concluded that the humiliation I experienced was too damaging, I would have to work for myself. What have I been doing for the past 40-plus years? I have one extraordinary accomplishment that I have been working on throughout my life: *me*. It may seem odd to be saying this with such satisfaction, but perhaps only to me, since I am inevitably my own harshest critic. It is actually a heroic triumph just to be here to write this, even if I am the only one who will ever fully appreciate it. To have survived . . . to have a life. I never thought I would reach this point. I'm sure that of those who knew me no one else did either.

*By Susan Kennedy Stafford. Fey: *adj.* doomed, fated to die, unreal, under a spell, marked by an apprehension of evil, calamity and death.

I want to reveal part of this life that has, until recently, been so bewildering and encrypted. Through the process of committing those past experiences to paper, I expect to transform unreal to real, vivify wraiths and phantoms and other shadowy creatures, and then turn ether into solid matter. As I proceed with my efforts at alchemy, I am strengthened by the conviction that, for me at least, remembering is essential in the pursuit of wholeness.

I feel as if I am at the edge of a precipice with a bottomless black abyss below. Instinct tells me to carefully back away. In the following pages, I refer to "the child," not "me." This helps to keep me from coming too close to the edge. In fact, I feel as if I came into being at the age of 18 and the one who existed before was a different person. I know with certainty that writing this is an important part of my evolving freedom. I have promised myself that I won't try to escape from the telling.

THE CHILD

I am told that I was a child once and that children come into this life in a state of innocence. This is so painful to contemplate! I am told that at one time I was relatively normal, that I laughed and delighted in dancing un-self-consciously and spontaneously. I often walked up to strangers, and took their hands while smiling into their faces. I was a real child— flesh and blood, living, breathing, and presumably in that inconceivable state of innocence. Then something happened. The child vanished, or at least tried to. She was about 3 years old.

Meemo and the child lived alone in an apartment in Washington, D.C. Meemo was unmarried in an era when the word "illegitimate" was a highly pejorative term. There was only one other person of significance in the child's life, a doctor named Errett. It was between the ages of 3 and 4— after which time nothing would ever be the same—that the child disappeared. She became a wraith. Bloodless. Numb. No more child protests, child tears. The inner truth, the inner knowing, is that she died. Not in metaphor or symbol but real death. It can't be explained or substantiated, it just is true. Mysteriously, the body carried on. One might inquire, "If she died, was it from her own pain or was she murdered?" I only know that she died: murder is something I do not want to know, must not know.

At about age 4 or 5, the intrusive, sadistic fantasies began and she could not stop them. They consisted of amplified images from cartoons of women on a conveyer belt, tied and struggling helplessly, screaming in terror; finally to be sawed in half by a radial saw. Sometimes instead of a woman it was a pig (because their frightened squeals are so palpably terrified). This fantasy supplied sexual gratification in proportion to the degree of terror she could conjure up and the shrillness of the helpless victims' screams. The child knew that something was very wrong with her as these fantasies became more compelling. Sex was becoming twisted into a dark and convoluted obsession. She was definitely no longer innocent. Shame and self-loathing were spreading deep into her psyche.

THE ADULT

Throughout my adult life, I have been tormented by terrible images and unusual nightmares. Typically, I am the victim of an incredible array of bodily damage and depravity that come vividly to life in my dreams. They are often complete stories with surprising continuity, conveying the impression of an urgent message to impart. They exhibit a rich complexity and emotional intensity that is riveting. It has been common for me to be so dazed and stricken by a dream that I am in the grip of its horror for days or even weeks. The reality of my dreams is far more compelling and vivid than the reality of the waking world.

Death claimed me in every shape and form. There was excruciating pain and agony as monsters devoured me, demonic men stabbed me, cataclysmic explosions blew me to pieces or incinerated me. When I wasn't being killed, I witnessed gruesome horrors and experienced terrible grief. In the dream world, just as in the waking one, I was completely unable to scream. I would go through the motions mutely. Even if my life depended on it, I was unable to make a sound. In spite of the torment and disruption caused by the dreams, I was convinced that they were one of the few expressions of a living self within my impassive exterior and as such were the only truth I could count on. Art and creativity were also expressions of what was otherwise hidden and mute. I sensed that dreams in particular, though, were the key: they were my oracle.

In retrospect, it is apparent that the dreams' symbology was eloquently reenacting the first few years of life. It is strange that this interpretation was missed until years later. Understanding the dreams was never easy for me, or for my therapist, until I was much older, when their symbolic nature became clearer. Unfortunately for me, the interpretation of the day was that everything in the dream was the dreamer, or worse, that dreams were wish fulfillment. Both tended to support my feeling that I was monstrous, just as that little child had begun to believe so long ago. The dreams were the putrid black ooze, seeping from my rotten, evil core. I was horrified by the dreams just as I was horrified by my self. Living with such disgusting loathsomeness frequently made me feel that I was going to crawl out of my skin.

PAIN

In spite of the violence that pervaded my days and tormented my nights, I am far from insensitive to the suffering of others. I feel deep empathy for other people's pain; I seem to feel theirs even more than my own. Since I had numbed myself to traumas that were too much to bear, other people's suffering provided a glimpse into my own abyss of pain. This depth of despair and anguish was so immense, I could neither endure it nor contain it.

I have lived in utter terror of bodily damage, death, and decay, while paradoxically feeling that death was the only possible relief from these same torments. Although haunted by many things, the most pervasive was the sense that death was my destiny. Not in the manner that it is for everyone, but rather, that living was not my destiny.

Every day that passed was borrowed. I had no right to life, no rights at all. Even my soul seemed no longer to be mine. Sometimes there was the thought that if I couldn't get the evil out of me, I could kill the host. I rarely spoke with precision of what I believed had determined my fate and doomed me to this dark torment, but it was always in the back of my mind. When I spoke of it directly, my therapist tended to trivialize it. I did not want to be mocked about such a grave matter. It was also embarrassing to admit my superstitions and impressionability, even to myself. Eventually, however, this fact was undeniable: I was under the influence of a powerful hypnotic curse. I needed someone who would realize its truth, not attempt to persuade me of its falseness and archaic adaptive nature. Together we would tackle it as best we could, and perhaps we might even find a way to release the bindings of the spell.

THE EVIL WITHIN

The first time the Curse was spoken was not its point of origin. The child probably was born into it. Yet it was a landmark of destructive power because the nature of the Curse was graphically inescapable from that portentous moment. Throughout childhood and beyond, the Curse was reinforced repeatedly in deeply traumatic incidents with people. The essence of the message was, "You will unwittingly be the author of your own destruction and death, while trying to do the good and right thing. That is your destiny because of the terrible evil within you. Therefore, you are not worth saving from this destruction. No one will deem you worthy of help." It was plain to me that even if I did my very *best* to be healthy and constructive, and to overcome evil, there was simply no escape. I also knew all along, without being able to articulate it, that if, on the other hand, I *surrendered* to evil, surrendered to death, then there was immortality, immortality through power.

MEEMO AND ERRETT

As a young child, intense loneliness and disconnection from the world around her and the human race pervaded all contact with others. She discovered that other children typically had a family, a mommy, a daddy, and a home. This was incomprehensible and a source of unbearable grief and longing. The words Mommy and Daddy would never pass her lips; she could not even hear them spoken without fighting off tears. By contrast, for her there were Meemo and Errett, to whom she was bound in a profoundly tight but invisible embrace. She was the center of their lives. Their psyches all but eclipsed her own. These two eccentric people not only were the most influential people in her life, as would be expected, but they were her world and she was theirs, resulting in that influence being undiluted by contact with others. This appeared to be her particular destiny, this inescapable binding and enmeshment, in spite of her desperate need to be free of them. They all three were outside of and separate from the Big Reality. This was not noticeable to the casual observer, because Meemo and Errett had learned how to appear normal. Meemo struggled mightily to be a part of that reality. Errett deftly played the game for gratification, to attain his goals. The child didn't have the understanding or skill to be able to be in the world. There never had been a bridge to the Big Reality for her. No one had ever interpreted ordinary life and the way people relate and behave. She was bewildered by all of it and could find neither meaning nor understanding of the things that represented society and normal life. The three of them were encapsulated. They were trapped in a suffocating reality from which there was no possibility of escape. Whenever Meemo or the child had contact with the people of the other reality, the normal people, anything beyond casual contact was sabotaged by an unseen hand. The child could see, but not touch, the reality of the world; the world could not touch her, even if it had tried.

Until the time of lost innocence, she had been relatively normal and did not have the terrible thoughts. When the mind became tormented, at about age 4, the body mirrored these developments. . . . or was it the reverse? She was plagued by numerous painful, humiliating afflictions, which surely were the physical reflection of the conflicts and anguish within. In addition to the common maladies, shameful warts that erupted all over her hands, legs, and feet, burned off repeatedly only to grow back again and again; multiple allergies required a barrage of weekly shots; progressive deafness resulted in frequent painful treatments and several surgeries; painful, embarrassing constipation and rectal problems persisted and remained a mystery; progressive paralysis brought her to the brink of death; and a protracted life-threatening kidney and bladder disorder necessitated numerous treatments and surgeries that resulted in intense, chronic pain. Most of these conditions were concomitant and extended over a period of six or seven years.

Under the circumstances, it seemed serendipitous that Errett was a doctor. He could be a liaison and watchdog for the child's protection. He was a powerful man on many levels: His accomplishments in the field of medicine were considerable. He was a teacher, an author, and the editor of standard reference books on blood, statistics, and physiology, and reviewed and decided the fate of petitions from scientists for federal research grants. He had also taught physiology in Bangkok, where he helped to reform and advance academic standards. In addition to his career successes, his personal power was hypnotic and manipulative. He was accustomed to getting whatever he wanted in life, and he used people as a means to to that end.

Of the many illnesses that the child suffered, the only one he took an interest in was the kidney disease. Errett had chosen early in his career path to pursue research rather than private practice, a decision he never ceased to regret. He liked hands-on power and this sick child was an opportunity to exercise the desire for that power. Probably it was as close as he ever came to practicing medicine. He insinuated himself into every aspect of her case. He was at the doctor's office planning, advising, directing, making his presence known at the hospital, discussing her next surgery. He was doing exactly what had been hoped for, but it quickly became disturbing, then downright frightening. As she grew ever sicker with each surgery, the face of the man began to change and reveal more of the face of the predator. He was obsessed, although never out of control; obsessed with her and her illness. It was the focal point of his life.

But the animal instinct was strong within her. It told her that under no circumstances should she allow the smallest crack in her armor of stoic self-control. There must be no hint of the grief, terror, anguish, and hopelessness that churned beneath the impassive exterior. She must not be seen writhing in pain or cowering in fear, she must not even cry. Yet her control was so very tenuous given the tremendous intensity of the emotions she was holding back. Eventually, frequent and repetitive traumas left her with a strange calm. She didn't have to fight to keep control any longer. Perhaps disconnection from the body and emotions had reached the point where she no longer felt the suffering directly but experienced it from a distance.

She became too sick to attend school regularly and was falling behind. School was such a source of dread that every school morning was approached with a stomach ache. Neither the other children nor learning held any interest for her. Due to the bladder infections and the resulting pain, she often held her crotch. This was totally unacceptable among the proper and well-to-do families who sent their children to the elite school she attended. Increasing shame was the inevitable price of her effort to reduce her pain.

As young as she was, sex preoccupied her thoughts most of the time. The thoughts were ugly and dehumanizing, males were lust-driven and cruel; females were helpless vessels for male pleasure and were victimized by the brutal sex act. The penis was a dangerous weapon. It was an instrument of men's horrifying and inexplicable murderousness and cruelty toward women. The nadir of these tormenting thoughts was that as painful and disgusting as they were, they were sexually stimulating. She hated herself for this perverse pleasure. On the inside, both her world and self were shrinking as the months and years passed. Days and long lonely nights were spent focused on the unrelenting pain. Pain reduced her world dramatically as all attention and energy were focused on easing the hurt. It also had an isolating effect, which made it even more difficult for her to interact with the environment and the people around her.

THE SURGERIES

Errett was morbidly enthusiastic about the child's surgeries and the illness itself. He spoke freely in her presence, even to complete strangers, of her illness and sometimes of her impending death. As soon as one operation was over and healing in progress, he was talking about the next one. It was as though he did not want to consider a time when she would not need any more surgery or treatment. He did not speak of a cure. She never knew what to expect in either the immediate or distant future. Would she recover or die? Or perhaps she faced a future of never-ending surgeries and pain. The doctors assured her that each surgery was the last. They told her it wouldn't hurt, before performing the sometimes agonizing invasive procedures.

Among all these things and many others that created daily fear and dread, there was one overpowering fear. She was terrified of surgeries, and above all, of the anesthetic. The only time she pleaded, resisted, or cried was when they held her down and clamped the mask over her face. She felt that she was dying as she struggled to hold her breath. And yet, as terrified as she was, the hospital was her haven. For her alone (not for others), there was no safe place, nor had there ever been, nor would there ever be. She knew that the hospital was safer . . . but safer than what? She did not know. What could possibly be so terrible that facing the dreaded ether was to be preferred?

It seemed that Errett was her ally when she was most alone. He made her feel wanted and special. She might never belong anywhere else but she would always belong with him. He said he was her Rock of Gibraltar and would always be there for her. She would never be alone. Knowing her love of nature, he taught her the names of trees, and gave her little animals from his laboratory. He enchanted her. They walked in grave-yards together and spoke of magical things. The most important of these was her fantasy of escape from the human race. This dream had sustained her when she felt she could not face another day. Her dearest hope was that she would soon be able to live in the deepest forest, become an animal and never see a human again. Errett promised this dream would become reality—he would make it possible so that she wouldn't even have to see *him* any more. She wanted only to be left completely alone. Maybe then she could survive.

THE MALE MEDUSA

When she was about 7 years old, she made a desperate decision not to hope any more. If only she could go to sleep, or into hibernation forever. That was her instinct without understanding. Giving up hope ironically helped her to survive in a world as bleak as a lunar landscape.

On a particularly memorable day, not an ordinary day, since there were no ordinary days, she accidentally took one extra (harmless) dose of antibiotics. Errett had been working on a little wooden box for her to sleep in on top of the mattress. The fact that it looked like a coffin didn't register with her. It reminded her of the cupboard in his laboratory where she liked to hide. There was a pillow there. It was cozy like a rabbit hole. The box held great appeal, and it was special because he was making it just for her.

Somehow Errett discovered that she had taken the extra pill. She felt that he knew what was in her mind and could get inside every corner. He seemed to be able to do that with other people too. Errett's face was dear to her. It was usually soft, harmless, like a child's. His eyes sparkled with silliness and mischief, disarming and gentle. When he approached her this time, the friendly, familiar countenance had become a visage of hatred, rage, and vengeance. His eyes burned with an incomprehensible intensity. It is impossible to describe the unforgettable impact of that expression. His was never a rage of sound and fury or volcanic eruptions. Instead it was a single-minded laser beam of hatred, hungry for a sacrifice, an immense power concentrated with perfect control on one very small spot—her.

He grabbed her and steered her into the bathroom. He forced her head down almost into the toilet bowl and hissed through clenched teeth for her to vomit or the pill would kill her. He ordered her to stick her fingers down her throat. She tried but had no gag reflex. She had gone from a state of terror into shock. Everything felt strangely unreal; she was numb and calm. She had looked into the face of the person she thought of as her only friend but instead saw the face of a Medusa. It virtually seethed with evil. In his hands, she was now a helpless puppet as he took several fingers and jammed them down her throat repeatedly. Rough, cruel thrusts, like rape. Finally, unable to get the results he wanted, he stopped his assault and released her sagging body. His eyes, filled with hate, locked onto hers. There was an inescapable note of pleasure and grim finality as his words referred to her Curse: (Because you took that extra pill . . .) "Now you will *die!*" He then just walked away and left her. No ambulance called. No rush to the hospital to pump her stomach.

Obviously, she didn't deserve to be saved. Slowly she stumbled to the wooden box on the bed and crawled in. She folded her hands on her chest the way she had seen Errett's dead brother laid out in his coffin. She felt as if the blood had drained from her body, and remembered nothing for several hours. The vital force was ebbing from her as she awaited the inevitable consequence of her unforgivable mistake.

This incident was so like the genesis of the urinary tract disease. The doctors were puzzled in the early stages as to its cause. Then they discovered the scarring and inflammation that they said she must have done to herself by masturbating with sharp objects. She didn't understand, but they insisted she had done it. Maybe she didn't remember. The doctors told her that her masturbation caused the damage inside that led to the infections, that caused more damage, that might even cause her death. All the pain she had suffered for years was the shameful consequence of her mistakes and loathsomness.

Unaware of what had happened between Errett and the child, Meemo discovered her lying in the coffin-bed in an ashen deathlike trance. She barely breathed. It was not easy to bring her out of this altered state with assurances that she was not on the verge of death and that the extra pill was harmless (which Errett had known from the outset). With each successive surgery, crisis, and trauma, her will to live had been slipping gradually away. The ties and connections to the world were disappearing. This had been a major blow. Now she felt totally alone.

NEVER DENY HIM

Errett and Meemo had a love-hate relationship of great complexity. Errett provided a depth and intensity of involvement, attention, and interest that gave Meemo a sense of being loved more completely than she had ever experienced before. In return he demanded allegiance. Meemo had defied him. He had been stalking and terrorizing her from the time that she refused his demand for her to abort the child, the child he had once wanted. The stalking (which was not identified as a dangerous pattern in those days) had escalated to the point of attempts to kill her. She had nowhere to turn for help or escape. Most people did not believe either of them if they spoke of the stalking behavior and the other disturbing encounters with Errett. It was all too bizarre and unthinkable that a doctor would do such things. In that era, doctors were demigods. When others did believe and wanted to help, they soon would become targets too. Meemo's constant terror, frustration, and helplessness were bewildering and intimidating to the child as it contaminated their relationship. Meemo had been a playmate, they had had a close connection, but she was now transformed into a harpy. She was distant, preoccupied, impossible to please, and volatile. The loss of their connection was devastating to the child.

Errett was alluring as a strong ally and a source of diversion and escape. He appeared to be the friend who would deliver her from the painful presence of Meemo. She knew that it was her own unforgivable doing that she seemed to have lost Meemo. Every time she revealed her desire to be with Errett, it intensified the bad feeling between them. It was a vicious circle that had turned her to Errett for solace and escape. But now she had no one.

The incident with Errett had so traumatized her that Meemo was impelled to take drastic steps to enable them to escape without being followed. They would have to leave the country. They were given a safe haven temporarily in New York City with Meemo's friend as these plans were in progress. Before they could travel, one more surgery appeared to be necessary. It was performed in New York. Meemo's friend supplied the money to make the escape to Europe possible.

Recovery from the surgery did not progress well. The doctor's explanation was that the child apparently had no desire to live and needed special rehabilitation and recuperative care. Their ultimate destination was

Summerhill, a controversial school in England, but Meemo first took her to Scotland. The promise of a reprieve was almost too much to hope for. The child had focused considerable effort on not breathing for many months. She was so disgusted by the sound of breathing, even her own, that it was almost intolerable. In the same vein, she was determined to take as little nourishment from her environment as possible, willing herself to need nothing, to ask for nothing, and to yearn for nothing. But the doctor in Scotland instructed her to breathe, and she was trained to follow doctors' orders. There she was allowed to just be, so began to improve. They soon left for England and the progressive school that allowed children to be free, where she would, she hoped, be left alone. She was to have that wish for almost two years.

ERRETT'S UNDERWORLD

The Curse that haunted her did not just affect her alone. It was Errett's destiny too, but he had choices. At some point early in his life, he must have chosen to succumb to evil, and then developed an appetite for it. He appeared to be protector and benefactor for the vulnerable mother and child, while secretly sabotaging their every move toward independence.

The manner in which Errett lived illustrated his romance with death and decay: he created his own underworld, his Hades. The child he called Queen was his Persephone. Among the Greek myths that he often read to her there were certain ones that had lasting symbolic impact. This was one of them. But unlike Persephone in the myth, he expected the child to remain forever in his underworld, never to be among the living.

This hell was not born in a religious context. If it had been, there would be hope, there would be heaven, and above all, there would be God, who could save her soul from its destiny of evil torment. There was only one supreme being, of omniscience and omnipotence—Errett, and he was the master of darkness. He was outside all moral laws, he asserted, and insisted that those closest to him (or perhaps just the most helpless) be immersed in his "sewage" of amorality. His life of debasement was not inspired by a distorted sense of idealism, exaggerated asceticism, or even a result of psychosis. It was a kind of idolatry of all that offends, that causes one to recoil in shock, revulsion, and horror.

He lived in a place with no fresh air to breathe, that no sunlight ever reached; this was his underworld. In fact, it was a basement crawl space, his living grave. About one fourth of the basement at the foot of the stairs had a cement floor and drain. He urinated there, mostly at night, adding his odor to the dank, stale air. The remainder of the basement floor was dirt, and at the highest point, the standing room was no more than about three feet. He had managed to assemble a wooden bed there. In order to reach the bed, he had to crouch to make his way to the farthest corner of the dark, cold earth where he slept. This incomprehensible situation caused the child to suffer wracking anguish, bewilderment, and terror. Periodically she beseeched him to sleep in one of the empty bedrooms, to no avail.

Before buying his own home, he had rented dismal cellars in other people's houses. When Errett bought the house where he lived throughout most of the child's life, he moved into the crawl space immediately and must have planned this from the time he decided to buy it. The rest of the two-story house was not inhabited, except briefly when he rented out a room. He said it was saved for Meemo and the child. Oddly, he was an extremely sentimental man, even maudlin at times.

Paradoxically, living a debased life did not touch his professional persona. He always emerged well-groomed, whether living in a car or a crawl space. No one ever suspected his other life. He could crawl out of his dark world and shine brightly in the eyes of others.

At the age of 9, she discovered she had a father. In England, the longed-for state of being left alone was over all too soon. Even though it had been a cherished reprieve from doctors and hospitals, she remained very sick and in much pain. Still another surgery was needed and had been postponed as long as possible. She anticipated it with absolute despair. The temporary relief and freedom made it infinitely more agonizing to face surgery again. There had almost been the hope that the medical violations of her body were over. Hope was dangerous. It led to disappointment and despair.

Errett joined them in London. He had bribed the letter carrier and tracked their address at the school. He then sent gifts and letters to the child so that she became more eager to see him again. Before he arrived in London, he had decided that he wanted her to know his true identity in relation to her. He was not her uncle, grandfather, or friend, as had been insinuated, but her real father. She had secretly held the cherished notion that she had neither mother nor father, and that somehow she had just appeared as an older child, never having been an infant. This revelation deprived her of part of her fantasy and gave rise to conflict and intense emotion. Errett had a family: a wife and adult children. That meant she had relatives, like other people do. She had a half brother and half sister who were old enough to be her parents themselves. She could relate much better to adults, so this was auspicious.

Here was a terrible empty void that she lived with each day. Sometimes it hurt so much she thought the pain would kill her. This deep incessant hunger could only be assuaged by kindness, acceptance, and a sense of connection and belonging with other human beings. Perhaps here was an opportunity for that aching need to be reduced, through these newly discovered relatives. Dare she hope?

ERRETT'S CURSE

After surgery, a London smog contributed to the decision to return to the United States to recuperate. Even though the surgery was successful, she had developed postoperative shock and required periodic trips to a specialist in Boston. Her half brother was a professor at Harvard. Once when she had to make the trip by herself, she thought it was a perfect time for them to meet. He was willing for her to stay at his apartment overnight. She was sure there would be a connection simply because they were related. That was the way it seemed to be for other families. Indeed, the connection was there, but not as she had envisioned.

He knew that she had little money with her. He had a clear sense of her vulnerability, and took full advantage of his captive child audience as she listened in stunned silence as the story of his pathetic life unfolded, revealing self-loathing, sexual perversion, alcoholism, and abject despair. Errett, he said with total conviction, was so powerful, his destructiveness so consuming, that efforts to escape were futile. With what seemed like clairvoyance, he addressed her life and future with dismaying insight. He described her most intimate fears, her overwhelming shame and anguish, things of which she had never dared speak. Yet somehow he knew.

Then he revealed her future: a grim and unbearably tormented life of sexual deviancy, isolation, and self-hate, probably ending in suicide. His augury was punctuated alternately by sardonic laughter and whimpering and crying. He took her to a bar, where he picked up a man for sex. He was drunk. He wanted her to suffer as he had all his life. All she had wanted so desperately was a friend. But he was cursed, he told her. And there could be no doubt now, so was she.

When she was younger, about age 6 or 7, she almost died from a mysterious nerve disorder. Within just a few hours, her extremities felt as though on fire, her vision because kaleidoscopic, and she couldn't walk or even stand. When she was examined at the hospital, the doctors couldn't find a cause, so they declared that she must be just seeking attention. Once again, there was the Curse, she was at fault. The doctor angrily accused her of faking, and pulled her up out of the wheelchair, demanding that she stand. Instead, she collapsed in a crumpled heap, crying in agony as her feet touched the floor. They administered a battery of psychological tests to determine why she would be this manipulative. The tests didn't give them the answers they sought, but did reveal a deeply disturbed child in need of immediate treatment.

After a slow recovery from what was eventually discovered to be drug-induced nerve damage and total paralysis (she had to learn to walk again), Meemo took her to a psychologist. After the session, the woman threw up her hands in exasperation and exclaimed over the hopelessness of the situation and mental condition of the child. She said she could not help and had no advice. They left, both feeling extremely dejected, Meemo wondering, "What had the child said to the doctor? What could possibly be wrong?"

At about age 10, after returning from England, the child wanted to try seeing a therapist again. What else could she do? Her emotional suffering was increasing. Several visits to a psychologist ensued. The woman was very sympathetic, but it was beyond her to be able to help. She recommended that only hospitalization in a top psychiatric facility would offer the potential to help, and that should be soon. If she waited until age 20, the problems would become too deeply ingrained and severe to respond to treatment. This advice, although depressing, hardly came as a surprise. The understanding that she was mentally ill had been weighing heavily on her for some time. She pored over psychology books looking for answers.

The words of this therapist came back to her as the only possible solution other than self-destruction. She was in crisis. Thoughts of sexually torturing and murdering men randomly filled her mind when she wasn't planning ways to kill herself. It was apparent to her that if she had the means, she would do something terrible. She had to stop herself. Every moment was intolerable within her mind. Meemo located a top-quality hospital and they set out for it immediately. It was highly unusual for a child to be hospitalized under her own volition, especially one without behavior problems.

When the child was asked by the interviewing psychologist why she believed she was sick, she attempted to sum up the worst of her suffering. She explained that she was tortured by intolerable thoughts, didn't believe she had ever experienced love, and knew she was incapable of this emotion herself. She was convinced that love and compassion were cruel myths and, in fact, did not exist in human nature. Life as she saw it, both her own and other people's, had no meaning at all. While admitting her, the psychologist observed that she was almost 14 chronologically, an infant emotionally, and over 30 intellectually. She already knew that.

YOUNG ADULT: MYSELF

After three years of intensive therapy, grueling emotional states, and tremendous effort, I received my medical discharge. It was the first goal I had ever achieved, the first time I ever completed anything. It was a triumph of determination, hard work, and overcoming seemingly insurmountable odds.

The hospital's standard method of treatment was to gain total control, create a state of complete dependence on and trust in the relationship with the therapist, strip the person of his or her defenses, and regress the patient to early childhood. Then the therapist, playing the roles of good mother and father, reparents the person toward health, filling in what was missing in the bad parenting. Although not "cured," I was born again. A properly brain-washed convert, I emerged as fresh and defenseless as a baby.

However, I was to learn later that the process had not been completed, probably because I was deeply in love with my therapist. I had not separated, had not individuated, and had no boundaries. There was nothing to prepare me for the rough path ahead, nothing to protect me from the inevitable predators I would encounter.

I occasionally muse about how I would be different if a particular event or situation had never occurred. Especially I wonder about the events that followed my release from the hospital. How would the design and fabric of my life and character appear if my youth had not been interwoven with lies, contradictions, and unthinkable betrayals? There was nothing solid, no secure position. Who exactly was the enemy? It seemed to be everyone. The hospital had won some of my trust, demanding it as part of the therapy. I had established a degree of faith in them, in spite of the fact that my relationship with my beloved therapist eventually crossed the line of sexual restraint. I didn't perceive that as inappropriate—why would I?

There I was, 18 years old and still emotionally raw and undeveloped, leaving the haven of health with my precious medical discharge in hand. I thought of the many things that paper symbolized for me. Most important was hope. It also represented years of struggle toward survival and health that had led the person I once was to that hospital three years earlier. And it was a sort of rite of passage, my bridge to the world at last. I wanted to be a part of humanity. No longer did I yearn to retreat from others. Meemo and Errett had received counseling prior to my release. The hospital assured me they both had agreed for me to have my own place and a stipend and to handle me with care and support.

But Errett had other plans. His idea was that what I needed was a family and a home. Meemo and I moved into his house. It didn't matter that it was absurd for these three people to attempt to be a family or to create a home. He was indifferent to my pleas for my own place, saying it was out of the question financially.

There was good reason that we had never all lived together, not just because he had had a previous family somewhere else. Immediately upon our arrival, the fights and accusations between Meemo and Errett began just like before. I had crossed a threshold both literally and figuratively back into the toxic mire from which the hospital had helped me escape. Soon I would be drowning in it. Errett furtively crept up and down the basement stairs when he was "home," as he went to work in what he called his office—the kitchen.

It was standard for rotting food to be on the counter and in the refrigerator. This was not food that he had been just too lazy to throw out. It was food to be eaten, and not only by him; he urged us to eat it too. If it was too far gone, it became part of the decor of decay in which he felt most comfortable. It might remain there for years. If someone attempted to throw it out, he would react with outrage and hostility. His desk was a piece of masonite atop a garbage can, his chair an orange crate. He rigged up a bare, stark light bulb to hang from the ceiling a couple of feet above the desk. He sat there often, doing his important work, creating a scene of utter bleakness and decay.

Below ground, in his earthen crawl space, he spent most of the time pursuing his grim compulsion to dig. The digging had been going on for years to no visible productive aim. Upon entering the house, the first thing a visitor would see were Errett's underpants, by the dozens, decorating the living room rafters on evenly spaced nails. All of this produced an insidious, sinister quality that went far beyond eccentricity; that could not be explained. He was not comfortable above ground for long and withdrew to his basement lair when he was not at his desk.

This was the "family" and "home" to which I had returned. Barely a fledgling, I was fragile, but had a tremendous will. I had the emotional development of perhaps a 5-year-old, and the small degree of mental health I had worked so hard to attain was slipping away. My former symptoms were tormenting me again. I was desperate for help, but had no resources. There was no halfway house, no support group, not even a crisis line available. The hospital was too far away to be of help.

The situation deteriorated. Errett accused us of stealing his papers and hiding his underpants; then he attacked Meemo verbally and physically. I felt doomed. My hopes were being destroyed. I thought I could be out in the world with a place of my own, I believed I was healthier and had made much progress, and above all, I hoped that maybe I wasn't Cursed after all. It appeared that I had been wrong. Leaving was not an option. I was emotionally handicapped and completely dependent. I could not have dealt with ordinary problems, let alone a job. I hated myself for the helplessness and dependence that prevented my escape.

Seeing a therapist seemed to be the only answer. But my first session was to become part of the fabric of the Curse. The psychologist decreed that I was beyond help, would never amount to anything, never be successful at anything. I sat there dumbfounded, thinking about the three years of wet packs, green pajamas, total confinement, and intense emotional struggle . . . Was that all for nothing? I felt numb as I naively protested that I had a medical discharge. He practically laughed at that. But why was I beyond help? No one ever explained! This was not the last time I was to hear those dreadful words from a therapist. The Curse kept striking me down the moment there was a glimmer of life in me. I was devastated. Death had often seemed to be the only escape from my intolerable existence. It seemed like the inevitable next step for me.

THE ESCAPE

Meemo knew of my despair and had tried to assure me the psychologist was wrong. But people in his profession were the only ones who could possibly know what my problem was. At least they acted as if they knew. Neither Meemo nor anyone else ever seemed to know. All the progress I had made was lost, but this time I was not at risk for killing anyone but myself. Meemo had her own tribulations. Errett had sexually assaulted her. The combination of our distress had reached the intolerable point. She bought a van that day. We packed up my art and animals and left.

We lived in the van as we traveled to art shows around the country. Being constantly on the move was like a perpetual escape, so it was perfectly suited for me. We sold barely enough to cover expenses. There were many prizes as the judges raved about my talent and described a financially secure future for one with such ability. It was the first feeling of success I had ever had in the real world. But the belief that I had found a skill to help me support myself was bound for disappointment. The art world was not a likely place in which to earn a living, regardless of talent.

THE ADULT: THEORIES AND INSIGHT

Years passed. I was living in California and Errett was on the other side of the country. The almost daily assault of hideous nightmares, terrible thoughts, and emotional paralysis persisted. I continued my efforts to find effective treatment for my problems, and to gain a degree of understanding of this mental torture. As I read every new self-help book and kept track of the latest discoveries in psychology, people began speaking of a subject that had been unspeakable: incest. It brought confusing thoughts and images to the surface, but it went no further than that until I heard of the newly formed incest support group, Parents United. A hotline counselor suggested I look into it. And yet I kept thinking, "What incest? What abuse?" Surely the therapists at the hospital would not have steered me away from this line of inquiry if there had been truth to it? Unknown to me, the hospital counselor told Meemo that they assumed I had been molested, but I did not find that out for 20 years. True, I felt "abused" inside, but there was no evidence to substantiate it. Nothing had been identified that could explain my condition. I had never been beaten, locked in a closet, burned with cigarettes. I had never been punished for anything.

All my problems were invisible to others because I kept them contained. Unlike most troubled individuals, I didn't indulge in risky behavior, act out, use drugs, or have casual sex. I kept myself on a very tight leash because of the knowledge that I would have many of those problems, or worse, if I did not. There was no one to take care of me, so I could not afford the luxury of a mistake. I had to protect myself from any behavior that might be an expression of the evil within. I did have a painful childhood, but as people were quick to point out, so do many others and *they* get over it. So why couldn't I? If I create my own reality, as was suggested, then why would I choose to create such pain? It was suggested that perhaps I was a masochist, that I didn't feel alive without suffering. It was even suggested by one of the therapists that it was my fate from a past life. These theories did not resonate with my inner sense of truth, but, I reasoned, it could simply be that I was in denial.

I still was barely functional, couldn't drive, have a regular job or maintain any sort of routine. I couldn't afford a therapist, but Parents United had a sliding scale, so I was able to start seeing one of their counselors. With the first session, it seemed clear that this was the right track, but there was still nothing solid on which to base that feeling. As the sessions continued, I guessed that this was but a small part of the puzzle. I was beginning to realize that the mysterious attacks that I occasionally had provided a glimpse of such pain and terror that incest alone was not an adequate explanation. These attacks had initially accompanied orgasm, then, over a period of years, eventually occurred independently of sex.

I determined that an "attack" was not a tantrum, hysterical outburst, cathartic release, or, as had been suggested, a seizure disorder. Much later, it was identified as a flashback, but more accurately, I would call it a *glimpse*—a glimpse of something so terrifying and traumatic that it appeared that the body and mind had split. It was as though it were happening to someone else. I was just observing it and felt nothing. There were no feelings, thoughts, images, or impressions until afterwards, when I became deeply depressed and hopeless for days without knowing why. There was that familiar sense of not being here—that I was somewhere, but not here . . .

LIFE AS A WRAITH

Beneath my day-to-day existence I fluctuated between feeling as if I were a phantom, surrounded by real people in a real world, and as if I were real but none of this world and its inhabitants were. I felt misplaced, an anachronism. I lived in sort of a twilight zone, a surreal, Kafka-esque experience of life. However, there was one dimension, one reality, that was never illusory. I knew I could believe in the subconscious mind.

All creativity, communication, and expression born of the subconscious were to be trusted completely, however undecipherable they might be. I wished I could reside within that reality and still retain an awareness of the rest of life. Although my dreams were usually terrible, I knew that was where I was alive. My art, poetry, dreams, and the disturbing attacks were the language and landscape of the subconscious. I wanted to immerse myself in that vibrant, expressive world.

It seemed that I was arrested, held captive somewhere in the distant past of my childhood. The exhortations to cease to dwell on my archaic pain and to start living in the present were absurdly inappropriate in my case, and yet I could not explain why. I realized that this was not in the realm of choice. I had no adult life and was trapped completely in the past. That which carried on was a shell, an intellect and observer without a person inside. I was in a state of perpetual disconnection from my body and from the emotions of the past that held me prisoner.

A GLIMPSE OF TRUTH

In my mid-20s my desperate search for insight took a revealing turn. All my efforts had resulted in only slight progress. I had tried the physical approach, since the mental efforts were not greatly successful. Rolfing, bioenergetics, and other methods (in exchange for art) had some benefits but no more than did therapy. Therapy had been helpful because I had no friends to whom to turn to for support and compassion. I looked upon seeking therapy as hiring a "friend" in order to have a connection with someone with whom to share material that others found intolerable. It did little to illuminate the mysteries that held me captive.

I was still going to Parents United, but thinking I was there under false assumptions, when a call came from a man who was renting a room from Errett. He was calling out of concern for the young children in the neighborhood. Errett apparently was plying them with sexual paraphernalia. He had always given candy to the youngsters, but nothing more. Now he was talking with them about sex and encouraging them to have sex with each other. The renter added that Errett had told him that he had had sex with his own daughter when she was between the ages of 3 and 6. He did not have intercourse with her, but used various objects. Intercourse, he told the man, was for when she was a bit older. Then he said, in a rage, that her mother had taken her away before he had that opportunity. Of course, that daughter was me.

These revelations should not have surprised me, but they did. It was no secret that Errett proudly recounted to his physiology classes how in Thailand (his beloved second country) the girl babies were celebrated by their fathers' kissing their naked vulvas in a parade. Whether or not this was true, it revealed a lot about him. His sexual predilections were toward that which was generally taboo. His penis was tiny and ineffectual and he was impotent when it came to "normal" sex.

But my insulation from the pain had resulted in denial of the truth. I was stunned. With even greater shock, I realized this was undoubtedly the cause of the damage for which I had been blamed so long ago—the damage that resulted in my kidney disease and ensuing surgeries. I had the sense of something solid and real beneath my feet. Here was a missing piece of the complex puzzle.

Yet mysteriously, I began to feel that it was driving me even crazier as I attempted to process this new information. I began to resist it. Perhaps it was my fragile identity that made this too threatening to my hold on reality. Most of all, I think, if I had really faced what he did and its terrible ramifications, the pain would be truly unbearable. Denial set in. I decided that this was just a convenient excuse for my problems, a way to avoid responsibility, to blame someone else. I reasoned that Errett made up the story to impress or shock the renter. It had always been important to me to remember everything as accurately as possible. It was my hold on reality, my sense of control. It also gave me a feeling of safety. I couldn't remember Errett's doing these things. If he did them and I couldn't remember it, what else might I not remember? Everything might start to unravel if I could not trust my memory. No, I thought, Errett couldn't possibly have done the things he claimed.

As I entered my mid-40s I had a feeling of being so young that I had not reached my teens yet. I had missed out on most of life and growing up. It was so odd to realize the age of my body, like waking up from suspended animation after 40 years. For the first time, I began exhibiting some of the youth. I was earning a little money. I could carry on casual conversations and respond appropriately when someone said, "Hi, how are you?" I was relating with more ease and spontaneity. It was actually safe to move, to breathe at last.

... TO DO ME NO HARM

The most significant development was in my primary relationship. I was with a partner who was emotionally supportive, stable, affectionate, and, most important, safe. It took me several years to trust that this person was committed to being good for me and wanted to do me no harm. This experience of trust and of being deeply valued for myself was transformative. I had accepting friends who understood my difficult life and did not judge and criticize as others always had. And, I had a therapist who had the intelligence, depth of character, and perspicacity that others lacked.

These qualities were essential for a therapist to be able to understand my complexities and for genuine rapport between us to be possible. This person was not frightened or threatened by my history or by the material I presented. Everything was shifting within. It was the year of the greatest progress. I finally had an anchor to this reality, a reason to be in and of this world, to participate in it. I was invested in living at last. This was absolutely essential before I could face the most difficult challenge: the Curse.

The attacks had been more severe and frequent over the last several years. They had progressed in what seemed to be a positive direction. For years I was mute and paralyzed during an attack. This had changed to a brief frantic scramble to flee, curling up in a tight ball behind a chair or table, and finally screaming. But still there were no insights. It was as if there was something hidden by a veil. It was just out of sight, but very much there.

FACING THE CURSE

Any contact with doctors, dentists, or anyone with power over me caused me to regress or to go into an altered, dissociative state. Following a dentist or doctor's visit, if I had any invasion of the body, I was usually deeply depressed for days. Sometimes I felt so hopeless afterward it was as if I was physically melting into a pool of defeat. But I had never reacted as extremely as I did with the dental visit that took place in my year of change. Days before the appointment found me on the floor with handfuls of pills, feeling that I was facing something so terrible that I had to escape, and that the only escape was death. I could not have explained it to anyone. I didn't understand it myself. I thought of what people would say if I killed myself because of an impending dental visit. If that wasn't crazy enough, I could imagine the words, "Why didn't she just cancel the appointment instead of herself?" The desire to die was no less compelling, given its absurdity. Ordinarily, feeling suicidal was just one of my regular challenges. I was generally able to see beyond it, but this was worse than usual. I was so disconnected from self and all things that it was very difficult to overcome the impulse to die. I was tormented by a force of emotion or memory originating in another realm, something no one could see or know. Therefore, what chance was there for help? Once again, I felt doomed. Cursed.

I kept the dreaded dental appointment. I had to have an extraction. I was asked the innocuous question, "Would you like gas?" At that point, I could easily have run from the office, but I did not. It was as if I were facing execution. In this familiar state of terror, my response was (and still is) unlike a typical phobic attack. A sleepy calm overcomes me when I feel escape is impossible. Once in the chair, my terror disappears. I become peaceful and serene. Dentists have complimented me on being an exemplary patient. No one could guess what futile fight-or-flight conflict wracked my body. I myself did not know. This dental visit was worse than ever, and so was the fallout that followed.

In my regular therapy session that week, I felt an attack coming on, probably triggered by the dentist. Instead of proceeding in the usual pattern, midway into it I had a revelation. I felt a sudden knowing in my body, not in my head. With it came deep shock and grief. This was not exactly a memory, image, or thought, but I *knew*. I knew that Errett had used ether on me when I was little. He pressed an ether-soaked cloth over my face while I screamed and struggled, until I was unconscious. I sensed that this was repeated many times, combined with sexual activity. It was first motivated by vindictiveness, and then developed into something more. I thought about how he always carried his precious can of ether with him, but never would say what he did with it. He was furtive and proprietary about it, as was characteristic of him when he had sinister or sexual motives. I thought back to all the times prior to surgery, when the ether mask was placed over my face, how I felt that I was facing death, that they were killing me. Throughout the myriad of surgical bodily violations, carried out allegedly for my benefit, I always knew Errett's hand was behind most of it, steering the course. I could not escape, protests were futile. I never fought, rarely cried. But when facing ether, my greatest terror, I pleaded, I cried. That was totally unbearable.

In my 20s, I made a bitter discovery. A urologist explained to me that the outdated methods doctors used to treat my initial problem (caused by Errett) had led to the chronic infections that followed. In other words, I suffered from iatrogenic kidney disease for almost seven years, and was subjected to several needless surgeries. It was a childhood iatrogenically destroyed.

Suddenly it seemed apparent that I was not born with evil in me, as I had always believed, and that I was not "doomed to die" in some mysterious way. The only doom was to be born into a life with Errett in it—which was quite different from the doom I had always felt. He was the cause of the horrors that followed, not me. I was so emotionally starved that I would have done almost anything for love. I desperately wanted to believe in him. He sacrificed my life for his dark hungers. He sacrificed my innocence with his distorted lust. As a child, I saw, and naively loved, the face of hate, of lust, of evil. I continue to see it now, even though he is dead. As I sat there in my session with all this extraordinary material unfolding within me, I realized I was different, something had changed. Something all but impossible had occurred, and in a mere matter of minutes—the Curse was gone!

Since that session, I have wondered about the nature of this revelation. Is it the truth, or is it metaphor? Perhaps it was a conglomeration of various truths. In therapy over the years, there was circumstantial evidence that led the therapist to consider that Errett might have used ether on me. But it was purely intellectual. I had thought about it, then put it aside.

Thinking never helped me to change much of anything directly, only indirectly. Months have passed since that moment of knowing, The Curse has not returned. This is the first time I have been free of it in my life. Whatever was revealed that day, whether totally true or partially true, was clearly truth in both essence and effect.

This dramatic liberation could never have surfaced without finally having the basic anchor to the world and its reality that had been missing until recent years. That anchor was primarily derived from a feeling of acceptance and belonging from the few caring and compassionate people who cheered me on through my marathon challenges, nourishing my spirit with their kindness.

Although dispelling the Curse did not remove all hurdles or veils by any means, it is with immeasurable relief that I can say I no longer see evil as the pandemic, omnipotent force that I had always felt it to be. I realize that for all things, evil included, there are checks and balances, corrections and antidotes. For someone properly to address the effects of evil on me requires unshrinking presence and compassion (both qualities I could not feel toward myself). In the face of unbearable pain, someone must be fully human and emotionally whole, and it can't be me. Errett, this person whose genes I possess, this person whom I believed to be the only one who loved me, this same Errett chose to inflict tremendous, nearly fatal, physical and psychological pain and damage on me . . . and he reveled in it.

That is a horror that can never be felt or fully expressed. The malignant damage to self and spirit was so devastating that nothing less than its opposite is called for: genuine honor, respect, and reverence for that spirit and the inarticulatable suffering it has endured. Tenderness and sensitivity are necessary when approaching the terrified and bewildered child-animal cowering in a tiny fetal ball in the corner of my being. With each such precious, tender contact I have with another, the power of evil recedes slightly. With each kindness that I witness or experience, my belief that there is no good in the world is gradually disappearing.

Here I have offered you part of my essence, in the hope that somewhere within you, it will find a place of resonance, of connection. In the process of writing this, I have felt as if I were actually creating myself, bringing my self to life. With each paragraph, I was simultaneously filled with sorrow and a sense of triumph and exultation too: "That's me!" I cry within myself. "*This* is really *Me*!"

Compassion

Love is all we have, the only way that each can help the other.

—*Euripides (cited in Rawson & Miner, 1986, p. 153)*

We have, in the stories of our culture, many examples of the premise that the expression of love defies evil. A benign instance is Dickens' *Christmas Carol,* in which Scrooge's expression of love for Tiny Tim and his family begins to undo the cold meanness of his own lifetime. Therapeutic stories range from the provision of a gentle touch to trauma victims and of animals to be cared for by prisoners to the provision to patients of the directive to "speak only love."

In the far less benign circumstances shown in this book, questions of love are not straightforward, and the self that loves is found to be complex and at war. Here, as always, we can take instruction from our patients, whose lives revolve around these very questions. Their language of the experience of evil and of recovery from it, and of the battle against it, becomes the language of this text.

Compassion is the emotion that arises when we focus our attention on the value and goals of the other person. This is evidenced by Zen monks, expert in sitting for long periods with their minds focused on the middle distance, on "nothing," "no-mind," or the unconscious. Although anger, greed, desire, and other strong emotions are noted in passing, compassion seems to arise from the act of noticing itself. From the emotion of compassion develops the Bodhisattva's vow: "I vow to save all sentient beings."

Part of this vow must be carried out in protective acts, often those acts of greatest difficulty for those who have been victimized and have come to construct themselves like chimera and part human and part the lust, violence, blind selfishness, power, and wrath of their intimate tormenters. I remember in particular a long struggle with a woman who had been beaten and humiliated as a child to get her to wear a helmet while riding her horse, to drink water when thirsty, and to consult a doctor when injured. She had a stunning dream in which she went through an attic "full of belongings, the house of memories and children," safeguarding the children while searching for the vampire she kept trying to find and fight.

But I knew in the dream that I didn't want to kill it. I wanted to reason with it, even though I knew that you can't do that with vampires. I knew if I hesitated when I found the vampire that I'd be bitten and become a vampire too, and then the children wouldn't be safe, so I had to seek to kill. But I wanted a way to love this thing, even though I didn't think there would be such a way.

There's a puzzle in the emotions of those who have suffered abuse by intimates, shown dramatically in the reply given frequently by battered women to the question, "Why don't you leave him?" The answer, "Because I love him," can be understood in the form, "Because I *want* to love him." The first gestures of an infant are to smile and to reach out. When mature, a lover does the same. The woman who dreamed the vampire dream said about her recovery:

The point of what I am remembering isn't for the sake of remembering the trauma, but rather for remembering who I was before the trauma. The point is to feel, in present memory, the feelings of being myself, as I felt toward others then, first, when I was as one light on the water.

As Ruth Dart's narrative shows, the preservation of this desire to love and to be oneself is cruelly complicated by mistreatment by the loved one. Another woman, Sarah (personal communication, 1998), writes of the struggle to receive and practice love:

An Evil Monster

I awoke Saturday morning as usual. But today I felt inside myself something uncomfortable and unpleasant. I started my day, went through the morning routine. As I did, this unpleasantness grew. It grew fast. What started as a hint of pain grew to engulf my head, nerves, and body with misery. I wanted to leap out of my skin. I wanted to run away. What was happening to me? What was this monster inside of me? In desperation, I called my psychiatrist's answering service and left an urgent message. I waited, trying to hold myself in.

Then, the images began to come. I wrote madly as they went through my head, sobbing as I wrote: "... semen all over my face ..." I had to get somewhere. I couldn't stand another moment in my own skin. I needed help. I drove to the Emergency Room and was eventually admitted to the psychiatric unit. I don't remember much more after that, not even how long I stayed in the hospital that time.

I believe that awful image is a memory from childhood. I usually dismissed the whole thing in my daily life. I was certainly not one of these women who had been sexually molested as a child. I was "strong." Yet there were all those symptoms that I knew, from my reading, appear in those who have been sexually molested. I was a "cutter," using a sharp instrument to make cuts in my own body. I had done this dozens of times and many times had had to have stitches. Cutting myself, as strange as it may sound, brought me great relief, a feeling of contact with something solid and constant, something of which I could be sure.

One year at Christmas I visited my parents, and my mother, in a gentle voice, said to me, "Al has something he needs to tell you." I wasn't afraid, just curious. My brother told a story about something that had happened when he was 11 and I was 6. Al, a friend of his, my older sister, myself, and my younger sister were playing strip poker. It was all in fun. But there was a sinister element, shadowy figures in the background, Axel and some other guy telling him to turn out the lights. Then, Al remembers playing sex games with my sisters and his friend, stroking his penis on my little sister's tummy. But where was Sarah? The next thing he remembers is me, standing alone, crying, at the bottom of the stairs.

The dark, powerful, male shadows in the background. That's what struck a cord with me. That's what made my eyes pop wide open, when Al told the story. I'd been perplexed about the cutting behavior. Other things that spooked me were thoughts that sometimes went through my head, like, "Fuck those little girls," or getting pleasure out of some TV news that a child had been raped. I liked the idea of a grown man raping a little girl. It gave me pleasure. I was horrified at these thoughts and tried to bury them. But they kept coming up. I remember one day, as an adult, driving past my old junior high school and watching the girls walking to school, and having sexual fantasies about them. I knew I was weird, and this made me even weirder.

But as the possibility of the reality of childhood sexual abuse took shape, these evil thoughts began to make sense. Perhaps I wasn't so evil. Perhaps it was just the case, as I had read in psychology books, that I had "taken on" the identity of my perpetrator and was playing that role. When I was a teenager, babysitting one night, full of sexual energy, I molested a little boy in my care. He never knew it. He was sitting on my lap and I rubbed him against me for sexual pleasure. I was so ashamed of this behavior that I had never told anyone until I told Dr. Bloom. Perhaps I need an exorcism. It does feel as though I have an evil monster inside of me that I must not let out. An evil monster that will hurt little children.

Thoughts, Feelings, Actions, Relationships

One day, I was in Dr. Bloom's office with my older sister, Marcy. We were talking about the sexual abuse, which had come as a shock to everyone in the family. Marcy remarked, in a motherly way, that she shuddered at the thought of a little girl of 6 being sexually molested—an innocent little girl. That surprised me. I didn't usually think of children as innocent beings. They deserved to be abused and molested [the evil monster speaking]. I had never thought of myself as having been an innocent little girl. I had always been an evil, bad little girl with mischevious intentions. I mulled it over as the weeks went by. I began to consider that perhaps I had been an innocent little girl, and tears streamed down my face at the thought of her being hurt by mean boys. Instead of deserving the rape because of my badness, I was an innocent victim. The world was turning upside down.

Another source for my thinking and feeling was my brother's memory of being enraged at Axel and beating him up at school. I was surprised at my brother's loyalty, but the fact that he had defended me made me think that perhaps I was worth defending, and again, that softened me and brought tears to my eyes.

It's as if there were an oscillation between two points: At one point, I was the wild, bad woman who loved crimes and rooted for the criminals, evil men beating and raping little girls all over the world. This was the hard-edged point. The other point involved soft-

ness and tenderness. At this point, I was an innocent child of God, and tears and joy were possible.

My experience and relationships in Alcoholics Anonymous did much to influence my concept of myself and to facilitate a soft humility in the loving care of a Higher Power. My sister's and brother's concepts of me were rallying points for me, words I could turn over again and again in my mind as a defense against the evil impulse. As long as I held myself as my brother and sister held me, I couldn't be the one to have thoughts of raping little girls.

J. E. (personal communication, 1998) describes a similar wrestling within herself in an autobiographical sketch:

Whenever is done to you, you are often left unable to speak of it, believe it is taking place, or comprehend why. This paralysis of the spirit then sets the stage perfectly for doing evil to someone else. You already know in your heart that evil appears unreal, that it can never be fully understood, and that its favorite cloak is dense silence and secrecy. Having been asked to speak of this, I find myself treading water in a thick sea of emotional foreboding and forbidding. To speak of what doesn't belong in words is a strange and terrifying task. It is nearly 20 years since I first fought with myself to put into words what I had done.

When I was a child, sexually molested by my father, I didn't know the name for it. I didn't know the irreparable harm he was causing to my growing self. The loss of my sexual privacy and rightfulness, while terrible, paled next to the loss of a father and the loss of trust in my parents and in the world.

So began my long and bright career as a victim. I specialized in that particular ache, shame, and martyrdom. My eagerness to blame it for all my shortcomings and my unwillingness to ever let it go allowed the next horrible chapter to unfold.

To stop being a victim, you have to name, illuminate, and resolve the part of you that longs to punish, manipulate, and overpower someone else in a manner similar to what was done to you. I could never finish this process. I felt I was entirely good because of what evil had been done to me and I kept this passionate suffering alive at the same time that it kept me a partially developed person. I was unable to name the fury that I still felt toward my father as it came actively alive in me. I didn't recognize the urge for revenge, combined with the wish to quit being a victim by becoming a perpetrator. Without telling myself what I was actually doing, I allowed someone else's infant to suckle at my breast while I gratified myself sexually with my hand.

Thinking back now, I can see that I was able to lie to myself about what I was doing by using a distorted pattern of logic: I told myself that if breast-feeding was a good and natural thing and if masturbating was a good and natural thing, surely it wouldn't be wrong to do them simultaneously, if the baby was too little to know what was happening. In this way, I disengaged from the impact of my own actions, as if I were neatly proving a mathematical theorem. The sadness that I feel, so many years later, about having come so close to harming that baby is still very powerful and deep. In fact, I make a conscious effort to keep in mind what I did, to ensure that I never do it again.

I didn't go on to become a child molester. I never again allowed myself to take sexual advantage of a child. But I did become whole because I had to recognize, admit, and fight off this embodiment of evil in myself. I had to come to terms with my wish to become the one using somebody instead of the child being used. I had to give up seeing and presenting myself as a victim. I know firsthand how even well-intentioned people can use pain as the fuel to do terrible things, and I've used my experience to keep myself fully in charge of my own actions.

Another woman, who suffered a recurring, frightening childhood dream of her father, said, "I'm building a person in the den of the house in which I grew up." In her work, she felt herself to be "painting in an overwhelming darkness." Gazing at her painting, she said, "This stuff has energy: it's innate, not inert." "When a door is about to open about my father," she dreams, "the crazy man can't communicate, and he's falling over."

Asked, "Will he let you touch him?" she says, "No." "Will he let you sing to him?" "Yes." Asked to sing to him until "he falls in with your rhythm," she says, "I feel sick." Told to "take the lead," she says, "I can feel my separateness. I'm not him and scared of his power over me. *I want to help him out of his pain.*" This earnest request was met with the offer to "hypnotize him to listen to your words and feelings, so he can be touched, again and again. He has to learn."

The desire to help one's oppressor is expressed by a priest in his own dream in which three young birds are abandoned in a corridor and a righteous priest kills a disabled child. The dreamer builds a nest for the birds, for their safety. Then he is asked to hear the priest's confession: "What would his prayer be? How to accept God's love, given what he'd done. And the soul of the child will be asked to pray for that of the priest."

The desire to love "the vampire" can be seen in the determination of a woman whose husband tried to kill her. She escaped, but returned to care for her abuser when he was ill. We can consider this remarkable action an affirmation of her desire to love, and to grow to be a loving self.

One of the outcomes of recovery from evil influence is certainly the adoption of a compassionate protection of oneself. Along with this arrives a sense of authority, authenticity, and power, as in this letter from J. E (personal communication, 1998):

> One of the many things I have thought of telling you is that not too long ago I woke up one day and had such a clear feeling present itself in my mind that I announced (almost aloud): "I'm done being abused. I'm completely over what happened to me as a child."
>
> I'd had dreams for a couple of nights where my lifelong nightmare resolved itself. In the chronic dream, I was always trying to escape a dangerous man who was after me. In spite of my best efforts to get away, my own attempts to outsmart him had always delivered me right into his hands.
>
> Over time, the dream had developed and I could sometimes confront him angrily and even punch him, but I couldn't feel the impact of my hand and I would wake up mourning the incompleteness of it, hoping to feel it next time. Eventually, sometimes I could feel the hit.
>
> Anyway, these dreams changed. Now I could tell as soon as I saw this man how dangerous he was and I knew for certain he meant me harm, even when his manner wasn't threatening. And in these wonderful dreams I took action immediately to protect myself and successfully avoided the whole interaction. It was simply splendid.
>
> Having these dreams marked the end. I could just see and physically feel my life clear ahead of me. I took steps to prevent harm to my daughter from a sexually aggressive boy at school. She had told

him, "Don't you ever touch me that way again. You have no right to do that." I know I can't guarantee that my kids won't ever be harmed by someone. But I feel so glad that I worked so hard to redesign my own emotional house. I see clearly. I hear clearly. I feel fully.

The struggle to arrive at this self is difficult. A lawyer who had been held and tortured in a foreign prison for five years also suffered from Crohn's disease. She was asked to notice the color of hope and saw it as bright red, "powerful and authoritative. It relaxes me." Asked the color of her colon when it relaxed, she said, "Grey, not inflamed; a purple sphere with a white edge, expanding." She tells her intestine, "There's no need to be angry," and experiences a "peaceful, moving, warm, open feeling. I saw my intestines open for the first time."

When I was in prison, I thought, 'I'm a rat.' My mind has been in a cell. For the first time, it's my own power. It's the first time I have something inside myself that I have the power to do it. I don't have to be good or bad to please anyone else. I can change myself!

When these changes occur in a therapy of care, attentiveness, and rich imagery, they have the combined feeling of effort and spontaneity. As one woman said of her hypnotic work, "It self-organizes itself somatically. That's what I feel. That's what I'm experiencing." In the next section, we'll visit a use of principles of imagery to resolve the tangled sense of self and evil with which all people are confronted.

The Unconscious-Mind Mirror

We stand face to face with the terrible question of *evil* and do not
even know what is before us, let alone what to pit against it. . . .
With glorious naiveté a statesman (declares) that he has no
"imagination for evil." Quite right: *we* have no imagination for evil,
but *evil has us in its grip.*

—Carl Jung (cited in Zweig & Abrams, 1991, p. 172)

I'm going to discuss a simple exercise in active imagination that seems to have regular and consistent consequences for the experience of persons working in psychotherapy. This is to say that persons doing the exercise use the same words or phrases and exhibit similar emotions when describing their experiences. The active imagining was brought to its present form by Don Wood and myself, although the examples of its use come from my practice in psychotherapy and hypnotherapy.

The exercise is this: A person is asked to imagine and describe to the therapist a full-length mirror and to say when he or she has a clear image of himself or herself. The person is then described as wearing favorite clothes, standing with dignity and beauty, and other positive images, until he or she says that this image is clearly seen. The details of the positive description are taken from the therapist's appreciation of the character of the person with whom he or she works, or, on brief acquaintance, from characteristics widely valued in the culture, like courage.

Next, the person is asked to "step back from the mirror to a distance at which you can see clearly everything that appears in the mirror and at which nothing you may see in the mirror can alarm, anger, frighten, or disgust you. That is, stand close enough to the mirror so that you can see clearly whatever may appear there, yet far enough away from the mirror so that nothing that appears there can frighten, alarm, anger, or disgust you. And tell me when you've done so." After the person replies, he or she is told, "Now close your eyes so that you can no longer see the mirror. (This is said whether the person's eyes are actually open or closed while imagining.) Until now, you've been looking at your conscious mind's image of yourself, and when you next open your eyes to look in the mirror, you will see your unconscious mind's image of yourself. Now when you're composed and easeful, open your eyes and tell me everything you see in the mirror."

And, of course, people see some absolutely wretched "images of the unconscious self": bugs, blobs, monsters, the endless metaphors of human fear, loathing, and distress. When they've described the image fully, they're told, *"Now ask the image what you can do to help it."* Sometimes this suggestion is met with alarm, amazement, or anger, and then the person is told, "I don't want you to agree to *do* anything, or disagree to *do* anything for this creature, but just see what sort of help it wants." So far, in many instances, and with varieties of balking or vows of never aiding "that disgusting thing," almost no one has refused to ask and no one, upon asking, "What may I do to help you?" has been told other than a version of *"Love me"* in response.

I should take note, before continuing, of the importance of asking the image how *it* can be helped, rather than (as will become evident) what help *it* can render the person. Of course, a great deal of human resource has gone into the battle against *it*, a resource the suggested question redirects without a great deal of fuss or "resistance." Yet, if the question is phrased in terms of the help the person may receive rather than that the person *may*, if he or she decides to, give, "resistance" becomes a serious impediment to change. In active imagination, the resistance appears something like this:

Therapist: What do you see?
Client: The image of a grotesque face; jowly, fat lips, stubbly beard, mouth always moving, angry, hostile . . .
Therapist: Wrestle him to the ground and see how he can help you.
Client: He says, "Death," but then I realized I hadn't wrestled him yet. Then I do. He says, "Live, or I'll spit in your eye!"
Therapist: How can you help him?
Client: He says, "Cuddle me and love me." He's not so grotesque any more.

So, although other cultures fight or trick the images to gain their aid, in our culture, cooperation is recommended as a first procedure. When the image says, "Love me," the therapist encourages the questioner to ask, "What sort of help can I give you that will make you feel loved?" Again, it is important that the person not commit his or her actions before being certain that he or she wishes to and can be competent to help. Asking about the sort of help gives the person the right to refuse to help, or to secure aid in helping *it* feel loved:

A young woman, for example, saw "a bratty, dirty child" in the "unconscious-mind mirror." The child was asked, "How may I help you?" and responded with sulking, insults, and "Go away!" I asked the young woman to imagine herself as the child. Then I asked, "How may I help you?" and was told, "Love me." I asked, "What sort of help might I give you so that you feel loved?" and was told, "Teach me to share." The woman was encouraged to return to her womanly self, and to imagine drawing a hot bath. Then, with frequent coaching, she was helped to develop the "brat's" trust by ignoring the child and concentrating on making piles of bubbles with bubble bath. Then, when "the brat" grew curious, the woman was asked whether she might "blow some bubbles at the kid." This led to their sharing the bath and to "learning how to share," too.

I wish to emphasize that, in all cases of working with imagery, it is important to treat the imagined figures as one would treat living persons in similar straits. Not only will this provide the therapist with ready suggestions and spontaneous emotions, but it will lead the person working with the therapist to realize that, as the woman in this example said, "I really feel I learned something. It was real, it meant a lot, because all those parts were me,"

The next step, following some helping action directed from the person toward *it*, is for the therapist to inquire whether *it* is "ready to change yet." The woman who taught the brat to share said, "That child's got a lot of growing up to do—middle childhood and all of adolescence!" Often, though, where *it* isn't human, this request to change is enacted with evolutionary metaphors, as in the following work.

S. was seen for a four-hour session, three hours of which were spent in active imagination. When asked what image she saw in the "unconscious-mind mirror," S. said, "A repulsive blob." This shapeless *it* had a surface like mucus, and it saddened and disgusted her to imagine touching it. When *it* spoke, it asked to be loved by a powerful, tender woman, and to have that love expressed by gentle holding and touching. With much work, S. was emboldened to touch it, and she found, when she did so, that it grew hard, as though it were a repulsive insect with a carapace around its body. S. was asked to "be the blob," and with switching between her grown, loving self and the insectlike it, she was able to touch it and love it, as with grateful tears she mimed hugging it to her breast and heard it cry to her as its mother. Then, again "being" it, she unlimbered her arms and became "ready for evolution" into a human child.

Again, the person, or the "unconscious image," may accept or refuse change, and some people have chosen to retain the mirror image in unchanged form. M., for example, had a snake as her mirror image. Instead of evolving to human form, she chose to retain it "as a pet," and reported spontaneously imagining placing the silver-and-blue snake around herself and her husband while they had a severe argument, just as she had, by suggestion, placed the snake about her own bed when she attempted to sleep. The "safe" argument eventuated in a changed marital contract for M. and her mate.

Another instance involving S.: It was suggested that she see multiple images of herself, each colored according to its feeling state. This exercise was incorporated with spontaneous dream images, and S. later reported obtaining the first orgasm of her married life when she found herself seeing the various dream figures while she and her husband made love: The "wooden-armed man with a sword seduced the red girl and this left the field free for the lusty girl to experience sex, so I could enjoy my husband."

These mediating figures later become integrated, so that experience is yet more direct and without consciously imagined correlates. S., when she asked to work on her dreams, was first encouraged to "see a film version of your dreams," then to "dream about your dreams." She dreamed of sitting in a chair telling the meaning of her dreams: that she needn't be suicidal or crazy, but could take care of herself. She then said that she was "fighting it," but when I suggested that she image the fight, she said, "It's a giant wooden Easter egg. . . . but I want to tell you this face to face." So she opened her eyes and spoke directly about her mother's death at Easter.

The point of these instances of therapy is that persons will use what is provided as long as they are allowed to choose to use or refuse it, and they will not use the artifices of therapy beyond the time required for their feelings of trust and safety. This is not to say that others doing therapy, who do not share these principles as active beliefs, will have the same sanguine experiences that compel this discussion: they well might not, but these have, for the greatest part, been my experiences with the uses of active imagination.

I might, too, indicate by example what may be expected if the *it* is extremely powerful and frightening and the person feels immensely wary of it, this by way of emphasizing the person's right to refuse to deal with the "unconscious-mind mirror" image and what use may be made of that refusal: A.'s image was a shadowy male figure who at times resembled a judge. Encouraged to go toward him, she found a glass wall standing in the way, and when encouraged to break the wall, she found that "things became unreal, like a cartoon." I said, "Turn completely around and walk in the other direction until you come across something" (a bit of advice that often brings the person around to where the person began).

A. imagined this, then reported coming upon a house in the forest, in which an old man sat bent over a ledger and surrounded by instruments of torture. A. didn't want to enter, and I suggested that she take a deep breath and go in, one step at a time, and, 'I'll go in with you." A. was to talk to the old man while I took an axe and broke up the torture stuff, made a fire with it, brewed some tea, and cleaned up. A. said, "He has no redeeming character." I replied, "I'll string him up by the armpits over this beam, out of the way, so he can think things over while you decide what to do with the house."

A.: I thought of burning it down, letting the forest grow. . . . I don't know what to do.
E.: Well, I'll clean up some more while you listen to his life story.
A.: (*Through tears*) He's my brother. He treated me so very badly I became bitter, I hated him and was afraid of him. . . . I can let him down now.
E.: Perhaps you'll both have some of this tea that's been brewing.

Again, beyond the relational structure of these interchanges, the person's right to refuse or to comply, and the set of mind that allows both persons to make use of what's available in the therapy as long as it's needed, inform the use of the imagination experiences reported. This may be the case even when the person is fearful, shy, or revolts and refuses to speak to the "unconscious-mind image" or to aid it directly.

In Chapter 4, we turn our attention from the exchange of images in therapeutic relationships to ideas about images and their place in the stories we tell to each other and live in our lives.

Chapter 4

A Narrative of Images

Toward an Outdoor Psychology

All culture rests upon representation.

—C. Geertz (1983, p. 173)

Representation itself forms the theme and substance of this chapter. This central theme coordinates with a collage of modern notions that form the basis of a kind of thinking about human relations and psychotherapy. To communicate, we must form representations of the world. Memory, language, mental imagery, dreams, and gestural action are the means for this representation and communication. Since we are basing our psychology on human relationships among persons rather than on "intrapsychic events," we are obliged to consider the interplay of persons through language and the social forms as the stuff of our commentary and of psychotherapy.

How precisely to accomplish this, how to analyze symbol use as social action and write thereby an outdoor psychology is, of course,

> an exceedingly difficult business at which everyone from Kenneth
> Burke, J. L. Austin and Roland Barthes to Gregory Bateson, Jurgen
> Habermas and Erving Goffman has had some sort of pass.
>
> —*Geertz (1983. p. 153)*

The modern sensibility, expressed colloquially or philosophically ("Wag the Dog" or Wittgenstein), is alert to the functions of language in the co-construction of social reality. Epstein (1998) characterizes modernism as "the evolution of the Romantic idea that the objective world is, as Wilde called it, 'fictional,' while reality is created by the 'critical' imagination in its various artistic forms." He describes the "profound revolution in consciousness that continues to shape . . . the modern sensibility: the transformation, or deconstruction, or . . . the criticism of the general culture by one's personal vision" (p. 10). This critical function of the individual informs narrative psychotherapies as it does Erickson's work and the Jungian theory of individuation. The integration of individual and social understandings through the communication media of dreams and trance and social relationships has been a central pillar of the therapies I've described. "The program," as Geertz (1983) puts it, "is seeing thoughts as social things" (p. 15).

Language and Image

> Mimesis is a kind of metaphor of reality. It refers to reality not in
> order to copy it, but in order to give it a new reading.
>
> —*Ricoeur (cited in Bruner, 1990, p. 46)*

I've been puzzling about the happy combination of the "natural-seeming" use of images and the concrete aid given persons in living their lives, a combination that seems to characterize active imagination techniques. How should such images come to affect lives in this way? I'd progressed this far—that English in large part lacks terms to express human relationship (that space "between persons") and lacks as well terms that refer to "experience" or "states of consciousness" with precision. Metaphors, visual or action terms taken whole, as it were, from remembered experience, would provide both the therapist and the person with whom he or she works a sense of understanding of the difficulties of their situation together and of the possible ways through those difficulties.

> *Just in this way we refer by the phrase 'understanding a word' not necessarily to that which happens while we are saying or hearing it, but to the whole environment of the event of saying it. (Wittgenstein, 1958)*

So, the translation into actively imagined scenes of the groping attempts of people to phrase their distress in the barren areas of the English language would lead to more intense experiences, somewhat in the way that dreams are intensely meaningful experiences that slip away when we try to squeeze them into words. An article by B. L. Whorf (1956), "The Relation of Habitual Thought and Behavior to Language," so clarifies this area that I will quote from it extensively, especially since the explanation inherent in it makes the use of active imagination techniques a necessity rather than a happy coincidence or a makeshift when we work therapeutically in the areas of human experience. Whorf's central thesis is this:

> *Concepts. . . . are not given in substantially the same form by experience to all men but depend upon the nature of the language or languages through the use of which they have been developed. They do not depend so much upon any one system (e.g., tense, or nouns) within the grammar as upon ways of analyzing and reporting experience which have become fixed in the language as integrated fashions of speaking.*

In English, our predominant way of reporting experience is to "objectify" it. For example, the experience of duration, or time:

> *Without objectification, it would be a subjective experience of real time, i.e., of the consciousness of "becoming later and later"—simply a cyclic phase similar to an earlier phase in that ever-later-becoming duration. Only by imagination can such a cyclic phase be set beside another and another in the manner of a spatial (i.e., visually perceived) configuration. But such is the power of linguistic analogy that we do so objectify cyclical phasing.*

> It is clear how this condition "fits in." It is part of our whole
> scheme of objectifying—imaginatively spatializing qualities and poten-
> tials that are quite nonspatial (so far as any spatially perceptive senses
> can tell us). . . . Physical shapes move, stop, rise, sink, approach, etc.,
> in perceived space; why not these other referents in their imaginary
> space? This has gone so far that we can hardly refer to the simplest
> nonspatial situation without constant resort to physical metaphors.
> I "grasp" the "thread" of another's arguments, but if its "level" is
> "over my head" my attention may "wander" and "lose touch" with
> the "drift" of it, so that when he "comes" to his "point" we differ
> "widely," our "views" being indeed so "far apart" that the "things"
> he says "appear" "much" too arbitrary, or even "a lot" of nonsense!

Speaking and "experiencing" English, we "refer to nonspatial experiences by terms for spatial ones":

> Nonspatial experience has but one well-organized sense, hear-
> ing—for smell and taste are but little organized. Nonspatial con-
> sciousness is a realm chiefly of thought, feeling, and sound.
> Spatial consciousness is a realm of light, color, sight, touch, and
> presents shapes and dimension. Our metaphorical system, by naming
> nonspatial experiences after spatial ones, imputes to sounds, smells,
> tastes, emotions and thoughts qualities like the colors, luminosities,
> shapes, angles, textures, and motions of spatial experience.

In other words, the language itself, as we ordinarily use it, is so constructed that, if we speak of our "inner experience," feelings, and
thoughts at all, we must do so in terms taken from the rich description
English affords of the world of physical objects apprehended through
sight, kinesthesis, touch. People seeking help with their lives will naturally and persistently use such metaphors to describe their "feelings."
Active imagination provides an excellent way, within the English language, to speak of human experience.

The widespread use of dream materials, practically coextensive with
the practice of the psychotherapies and with shamanism and other pre-
modern therapies, correlates with the general viewpoint presented
through Whorf's work. So, too, does the employment of synesthetic expe-

riences by the therapist, as in the case of S. cited earlier, for, as Whorf claims, synesthesia, or suggestion by certain sense receptors of characteristics belonging to another sense, as of light and color by sounds and vice versa, should be made more conscious by a linguistic metaphorical system that refers to nonspatial experiences by terms for spatial ones.

In therapies based on active imagination, then, we may employ the ready and natural understanding of inner experience that visual metaphor affords. We need not "interpret" the metaphor, although we can and do translate vaguely reported or apprehended human situations into the language of visual imagery, touch, and motion, the English language forms for inner experience. Then, as in any dialogue, we persuade, soothe, aid, and argue with the other and, through our relationship, couched in the language of spatial consciousness, contribute, if we can, to the well-being of the other person. As therapists, we exploit the metaphorical structure to communicate about emotions and experiences and relationships, and to effect changes in these experiences through that same medium of language, for, as Whorf notes, "People act about situations in ways which are like the ways they talk about them."

This is especially, although by no means exclusively, the case when we speak of inner experience, feelings, emotions, and the like, in which the "talk" of active imagination and the experience of states of consciousness or of self is one and the same. I say "by no means exclusively" to remind the reader of real-life effects flowing from these therapies, for example, S.'s sexual satisfaction and M.'s relational acts, as discussed in the "Unconscious-Mind Mirror." It is obvious as well that meeting "parts of the self" and meeting persons external, yet equally unknown to or feared by the conscious "person," are homologous. There are many reasons for employing active imagination in treatment. The individuals' dialogues themselves, their own constructed stories, are the most important aspects of these approaches, and their dramatic metaphors lead the way toward new lives lived.

The Story Metaphor

In psychology we can describe only with the help of comparisons. This is nothing special, it is the same elsewhere. But we are forced

> to change these comparisons over and over again, for none of them
> can serve us for any length of time.
>
> —*Sigmund Freud (cited in Bettelheim, 1983, p. 37)*

A change in metaphorical relationship from that of the therapist as a doctor, treating mental illness with measures that affect mental organs and their libidinal energies, to one in which the therapist collaborates as a stand-in for the star in rehearsals for a play, has already been suggested. In the development of a psychotherapy that is more collaborative and flexible and that encourages humane values of interaction, this metaphorical shift suggests a different arrangement of values. Ezrahi (1995), discussing political change, claims that:

> *Towards the late twentieth century, in the age of mass communications . . . it is the return of a radically modified version of the theater metaphor of society and politics which seems to anachronize and weaken the grip of the machine metaphor in key spheres of social and political life. (p. 298)*

The notion of language as a descriptor of our world, convenient to the scientific imagination, is changed quite dramatically when we begin to discuss ideas about imagination itself, that quality of mind that "bodies forth the forms of things unknown," and gives to them "a local habitation and a name" (Shakespeare, cited in Leary, 1995, p. 269). To place and label our experience of the world is fundamental to thought, and it is the replacement and relabeling of experience that can constitute distress or comfort in conversations.

Leary's (1995) discussion of scientific thinking and metaphor cites the agreement of writers from Aristotle to Thomas Kuhn to support the contention, "Thinking is radically metaphoric" (p. 272). Kuhn (cited in Leary, 1995), describes scientific revolutions as turning on a "central change of model, metaphor or analogy—a change in one's sense of what is similar to what, and of what is different" (p. 273), and suggests that "knowledge of words and knowledge of nature . . . are two faces of a single coinage that language provides," echoing Abrams' (cited in Leary, 1995) observation that "facts are *facta*, things made as much as things found, and made in part by the analogies through which we look at the world as through a lens" (p. 275). Here we consider metaphor as a mode of thinking, a model for theories and investigations, and a style of therapeutic communication.

Kuhn's remarks (cited in Leary, 1995) demonstrate the pragmatics of metaphor and their general use in matters of learning and of human change:

> *Thus, the education of an Aristotelian associates the flight of an arrow with a falling stone and both with the growth of an oak and the return to health. . . . The student learns what categories of things populate the world, what their salient features are and something about the behavior that is and is not permitted to them. (p. 273)*

Students of life, or of their own lives, similarly rely on metaphor to learn their place in the world and to decide upon what is permitted to them. As Leary (1995) says, all metaphors have "a constituative and directive function as well as a rhetorical function" (p. 288). These functions appear with great poignancy in the stories of individual lives:

A master electrician came for hypnotherapy to stop a lifelong habit of smoking. After he had "rewired the system" in trance, he ceased to smoke. His new goal became to pass his contractor's licensing exams. His 30 years on the job had taught him everything he needed to know about the electrician's craft, and yet he looked at the huge stack of study materials—contracts, regulations, laws—with fearful discomfort. Beaten savagely by his mother all through childhood, he had been told repeatedly, "You'll never amount to a hill of beans!" Yet he took and passed the exam the first time.

The electrician's next goal was to leave an oppressive, demeaning boss and start his own business, helped by his wife. He was quite frightened. I told him about an interview I'd read with Reinhold Meissner who had climbed every major peak in the world alone and without oxygen. Meissner had been definite: "The first thing you must know is, you're *always* afraid." The electrician responded with a true story of his own, a story of cleaning 100,000-volt high-power lines while they were still live. A man with a welding wand flies next to the line in a helicopter. He makes an arc to the wire, but isn't grounded, so doesn't carry the current. "Most people think that positive current flows to negative, but really negative flows to positive." He compares this fact with the idea of the useless positive messages on his "affirmation" tapes and says, proudly, "I'm a scientist."

A few weeks later, celebrating one year without smoking, the passing of his exam, and the beginnings of his own business, he says, "Since seeing you I'm teary all the time and more sensitive. It's OK for me to do good!"

The constituitive and directive function of metaphors is as crucial to our investigation of lives as it is to the living of them. Though we have been taught, in the positivist model that passes for method in the social sciences, to value theory for its utility in the prediction and control of variables, there is another approach to theory that has recently become even more compelling to psychologists. The physicist Richard Feynman (1965) characterizes the situation in this way:

> These Newtonian Laws are wrong. There are no forces, it is all a lot of baloney, the particles do not have orbits, and so on. Yet the analogue, the exact transformation of this principle about the areas and the conservation of angular momentum, is true. (p. 49)

As the anthropologist Geertz (1983) says, "It is analogy that informs . . . and it is upon the capacity of theoretical ideas to set up effective analogies that their value depends" (p. 13). Feynman (1965) gives an example from physics:

> Mathematically, each of the three different formulations, Newton's law, the local field method and the minimum principle, gives exactly the same consequences . . . they are equivalent scientifically. But psychologically they are very different in two ways. First, philosophically you like them, or you do not like them . . . Second, psychologically they are different because they are completely unequivalent when you are trying to guess new laws. . . . We must always keep all the alternative ways of looking at things in our heads. . . .
>
> By putting the theory in a certain kind of framework you get an idea of what to change . . . Therefore psychologically we must keep all the theories in our heads, and every theoretical physicist who is any good knows 6 or 7 different theoretical representations for exactly the same physics. . . . (pp. 53, 168)

In a useful compilation of the systematic analogies used to describe human experience, Epston and White (1990, p. 16) discuss figures of speech drawn from physical science, biology, and the social sciences. Positivist scientific analogies characterize social organization as like that of a machine. Problems are constructed as the mechanical or hydraulic break-down of machines and solutions consist of precise causal analysis, repair, and reconstruction. In analogies drown from biological science, human social organization is like a living organism whose problems exist as symptoms of underlying functions. Solutions require identifying pathology, correct diagnosis, and the excising of pathology.

Social scientific analogical systems include: game theory, drama, ritual process, and written texts. Game theorists construct society as a set of serious games with strategies, rules, and moves. Solutions involve countermoves and strategizing. Drama provides an analogy in which human society constructs roles, scripts, and performances, and solutions require the revising of roles and rescripting of dramatic forms. The rite of passage is a powerful anthropological analogy for society conceived as a ritual process. Problems occur during periods of transition and solutions are aided by mapping distinctions between status positions.

Text analogies provide the favored set for the narrative therapists. Here social organization is constructed as a behavioral text whose problems are seen as the performance of oppressive dominant stories or knowledge. Solutions are constructed by questions that open spaces for creating alternative stories.

In the work described in this book, analogies are drawn from esthetics, and especially from the visual image. Social organization is constructed as the exchange of relational forms, and problems as the misutilization of form. Solutions are constructed by the application of creative form to the revisioning of lives. As Erickson (1980) said, "When dealing with a problem of difficulty make an interesting design out of it."

All analogy is and should be taken tongue-in-cheek, seen heuristically and applied flexibly, as Feynman's earlier examples demonstrate. Wittgenstein, in "Philosophical Investigations" (cited in Geertz, 1983), discussing the use of language to describe life says, "In the actual use of expressions we make detours, we go by side roads. We see the straight highway before us, but of course we cannot use it, because it is permanently closed." To which Geertz adds, "One has to proceed instead by the peculiar detour of evoking its generally recognized tone and temper, the untraveled side road that leads through constructing metaphorical predicates . . . to remind people of what they already know" (p. 92).

In the following, we extensively explore the text and image analogies, showing some of their sources and tributaries as they flow toward the sea of lived human experience. Shifting the investigative and theoretical metaphors in use in psychology from those of science to those of story and from fact as object to fact as a construction of meaning is an ongoing theme of contemporary practice. Bruner (1986) describes these two approaches to thinking:

> There are two modes of cognitive functioning, two modes of thought, . . . of constructinhg reality . . . A good story and a well-formed argument are different natural kinds . . . Arguments convince one of their truth, stories of their lifelikeness. The one verifies by eventual appeal to procedures for establishing formal and empirical truth. The other establishes not truth but verisimilitude. (p. 11)

To highlight the differences in these approaches, we can consider a classic in clinical reporting: Freud's (1911) "*Psychoanalytic Notes Upon an Autobiographical Account of a Case of Paranoia*," the Schreber case.

Understanding Human Action

What I propose, therefore, is very simple: it is nothing more than to
think what we are doing.
—*Hannah Arendt (1959, p. vii)*

I'm going to apply a particular conceptual analysis of social science to Freud's investigation of the Schreber case. Using this conception, I hope to explicate both what Freud was doing when he did psychoanalytic explanation, and, in some sense, what it is legitimate to do when we examine human activity according to these criteria.

Notice that I say "human activity" and not "human behavior." This is to suggest that the data of concern to the social sciences are not entirely made up of movements—even very complex movements—describable in mechanical terms and elaborated in terms of space–time coordinates. Rather, human activity is behavior that is meaningful in a way that mechanical behavior cannot be. It makes no sense, obviously, to ask of a sunset, "What does it mean?" We can be satisfied with a sophisticated explanation of its functioning in terms of the laws of physics and optics.

On the other hand, it makes a great deal of sense, it is even, I would argue, necessary to understanding, to ask of a man who moves his feet and hands around, "What does it mean?" Here we cannot be satisfied with a physical explanation, but might be happy to learn that the man was dancing. This is the *meaning* of his activity, and although both dancing and some statement in terms of space–time coordinates are descriptions, one statement cannot be substituted for the other.

This distinction between the data of natural and social science has important consequences for the modes of investigation appropriate to each study. If we wish to explicate the meaning of a human activity or make sense of the mode of discourse, verbal or otherwise, in which it is embedded, we must appeal to certain criteria, for "to give an account of the meaning of a word is to describe how it is used; and to describe how it is used is to describe the social intercourse into which it enters" (Winch, 1958). This is so because, as Winch, following Wittgenstein, makes clear, "What it is for a word to have meaning" is equivalent to "what it is for someone to follow a rule."

I cannot be said to follow a rule of acting unless somebody else can, in principle, at least, discover that rule. Thus, meaning requires a social context, including some sort of interpersonal agreement about what is going on in any human situation. This necessitates the substitution of participant observation for the arbitrary standards of the single observer. "It is not open to him arbitrarily to impose his own standards from without. In so far as he does so, the events he is studying lose altogether their character as *social* events" (Winch, 1958).

In this sense, the question "What's going on here?" that we ask of the verbal and nonverbal discourse that constitute the data of social science is answered by *understanding* the rules governing a particular human activity. We speak of people dancing, fighting, casting a vote, or even of being defensive. The question, "Why are they doing that?" cannot be answered in terms of cause unless we again revert to descriptions of people moving in space–time coordinates, writing on slips of paper, speaking at x words per minute, and so on. But we have already said that we are asking the question of meaning that cannot be answered in causal terms. The alternative answer to the question "Why?" for human activity as opposed to physical behavior is couched in such terms as "reason," "motive," or "intention."

Motives, as Flew (1954) suggests, are insubstantial, intangible, and subject to normative evaluation, whereas causes are substantial and tangible in a crude sense and are only descriptive: "No translation is possible from causal language into motive language. If it were we might learn physiology from logicians who would deduce the efficient causes of our behavior from knowledge of its motives" (p. 144). Moreover, discovering a person's motives is equivalent to discovering the rules that the person follows in living his or her life in the society of persons. These may be as simple as the rules of the dance or as complex as the rules of psychosis. In all cases, we look to the form of human intercourse that is expressed in the particular language of the human activity, and we determine the meaning of the activity by examining, with the participant, informant, or patient, the concepts that express and inform the person's "forms of life."

Elucidating verbal confusions, such as we do in psychoanalytic interpretation, should also elucidate the nature of human interrelationship in society. For the psychoanalytic perception, as I will try to show later, the significance of a human activity lies precisely in the discovery of the rationale or rule that governs human activity—which, so to say, motivates it—and which is capable of avowal by the participant in that activity. And the motive or rule itself has its origin, however obscurely, in some human interaction. This follows quite naturally from the nature of the investigation of human activity. It does *not* follow, nor could it, from the description and causal explication of neural transmission (barring the case, still far in the future, in which thought can be exactly explained by the scientist, "As if a magic lantern threw the nerves in patterns on a screen," as T. S. Eliot [1934, p. 1] says).

Freud (1911/1959), and with him countless social "scientists," attempted to insert between science—biology, neurology, and the like—and psychology, as here conceived, the strange hybrid of scientific psychology: "What we expect from psychoanalytic investigations . . . is precisely that they shall drive us to some conclusions on questions involving the theory of instincts." It is my contention that we cannot expect such conclusions from such investigations, and not, as Freud suggests, because of the "infancy of the science," but simply because social studies are not science.

This view doesn't preclude the possibility of valid prediction and generalization. Certainly, rule-governed behavior is predictable behavior, and we can say with some certainty that a baseball player, having struck a fair ball, will run to first base—this without recourse to scientific causal explanations but with appeal to the rules of the game. Similarly, we might say that our player has difficulty with the manager because the player follows certain rules of action with regard to authority figures. We might even say that the player runs to first because he or she has "baseball sense" or reacts in a certain way to the manager because of a "father complex." This usage is gratuitous, but only mildly misleading. In this view of the matter though, a concept such as "basebido" used in purportedly causal explanations of the player's actions, or libido, used in the same way to explain the cause of the motive, as it were, is destructive of adequate explanation, if not of the common sense itself.

An examination of the way in which social studies, whether history, sociology, or psychology, are pursued should indicate the usefulness of this view even if the argument fails to convince the reader of its truth.

The Schreber Case

I tell you, you don't know what people mean or what your words
mean to them, until you find out.

—*H. S. Sullivan (1954b, p. 168)*

The aim of the Schreber study, says Freud (1911/1959), is to show that "even mental structures so extraordinary as these and so remote from our common modes of thought are nevertheless derived from the most general and comprehensible of human impulses" (p. 397). He proposes to do this by examining the history and details of Schreber's system, hoping by this method to "succeed in tracing back at any rate the nucleus of the delusional structure. . . . to familiar human motives" (p. 420).

Now it seems that Freud refers here to sexual impulse, using the word interchangeably with "motive." I propose to show that although Freud speaks of discovering the roots of the disorder in the patient's instinctual life, he in fact has recourse to human family constellations and to the forms of social–interpersonal life for an explication of the motives of Schreber. I'll claim that this attempt is successful, whereas the attempt to phrase the explanation in terms of libido does not succeed.

Freud begins his attempt to explicate motives by setting forth the factual history and source of the data. Then follows (p. 397 ff) an internal analysis of the material to establish that sexual persecution is the "primary delusion" and the core of the delusional structure. He does this by showing that the idea of persecution historically precedes the fully developed system and that it remains after the process of returning to society has begun. He then begins to resolve internal contradictions in the material in an "endeavor to arrive at a more exact view of (Schreber's) theological–psychological system." The assumption, later borne out, is that clarification of this sort will also elucidate the nature of Schreber's reality, and through that, the matrix of human relations that gave rise to his particular system of rules of action and thought.

How is this to be done? Freud says, "The psychoanalytic investigation of paranoia would be altogether impossible if the patients themselves did not (betray). . . . precisely those things which other neurotics keep hidden as a secret" (p. 387). This would not be the case if causal analysis based on observation and generalization were enough to explain human action. "Indeed," says Freud, "our only concern is with the meaning and origin (of the ideas)" (p. 427). This is ascertained, not through independent observation of some behaviors, but by some sort of participant observation. Freud's explanation of the equation "birds = girls" (p. 418 ff.) is of this order, as is most psychoanalytic interpretation rendered in clinical practice. It corresponds to translation—in this case, the translation of the paranoiac mode into the "normal" one.

Yet this is only the beginning of Freud's attempt to penetrate the meaning of the history, to "lay bare in it the familiar complexes and motive forces of mental life." Here he begins with the patient's own delusional utterances and applies the usual psychoanalytic rules of translation: strip the sentence of its negative form, take the example as being the actual, take the quote or gloss as the original source. This is because, as Freud shows, especially in his work on dreams and the psychopathology of everyday life, "It not infrequently happens that an incidental note upon some piece of delusional theory gives us the desired indication of the *genesis* of the delusion, and so of its *meaning* (italics added)" (p. 402).

Freud recognizes that the meaning of human action is to be sought in its genesis in human relations and so seeks after the "exciting causes of the illness," finding the appearance in Schreber of a feminine wish fantasy that took Dr. Flechsig as its object. In other words, Freud first takes the two principal elements in the delusion—Schreber's transformation into a woman and his favored relationship with God—and then translates them into the human terms of his life with other people. He shows how Schreber's delusion can be explained as a reflection of a change in emotional attitude between Schreber and Flechsig: "The main purpose of the persecution constructed by the patient's delusion is to serve as a justification for the change" (p. 424). Note: not the "cause" of the delusion, but the "purpose." Freud is discussing motives, not causes, and the way of validating hypotheses about motives is radically different from that germane to causes.

Freud does write as though he is also attempting to discover causes in the scientific sense: "Paranoia decomposes. . . . resolves once more into their elements the products of the condensations and identifications which are effected in the unconscious" (p. 434). But to do this, he would require evidence of a sort he cannot possibly get with psychoanalysis, evidence regarding "elements" that lawfully "decompose" and that do so "in the unconscious." Wisely, Freud attempts no experiments, utilizes no mathematics, observes no entities, for he is really interested in meaning and motive. That is all that is accessible to his method. He concludes this same passage by noting, "They would all be duplications of one and the same important relationship."

To find the situation at the base of Schreber's delusions, Freud looks into the history of Schreber's relationships and into the syntax of his peculiar logic, his rules, his reality: "We shall not feel justified in thus introducing Schreber's father into his delusions until the new hypothesis has shown itself of some use to us in *understanding the case* (and in) *"elucidating details which are as yet unintelligible"* (p. 435, italics added).

The validity of the hypothesis is established on the basis of the aid it gives in the process of understanding meaning. Notice that the prediction, "They would all be duplications of one and the same important relationship," can coexist with the method of social studies, as well as with that of science. The methods, however, differ. Here, Freud's method involves detailing the rules of thought of paranoia and deducing the system from these rules applied to the matrix of Schreber's fantasied and real human relations with other men. Thus: "If the persecutor Flechsig was originally a person whom Schreber loved, then God must also simply be the reappearance of someone else whom he loved, and probably of someone of greater importance" (p. 437).

Freud finally decides that the form of life shown here is the familiar one of the "father complex":

> *Just as to the patient his struggle with Flechsig becomes revealed as a conflict with God, so we must construe the latter as an infantile conflict with the father whom he loved; the details of that conflict (of which we know nothing) are what determined the content of his delusions. (p. 440)*

It is the human motive that determines the content of the delusion— the details of Schreber's conflict with his father and the fact of Schreber's childlessness (cf. p. 469).

On one side, then, we have historical material dependent on the participant-observer's cooperation, through either manuscript or some other form of avowal. This is of the sort of Schreber's relations with Flechsig, his fantasies regarding this relationship, and so on. On the other side is the paranoid delusional system with its concomitant symptoms and actions. Between them, Freud has been seen to interpose a series of translations based on the rules of human discourse—symbolism, the defenses, unconscious "paralogic." He brilliantly exploits the "remarkable fact that the familiar principal forms of paranoia can all be represented as contradictions of a single proposition" (p. 448 ff.). The rules of transformation Freud proposes for the statement "I (a man) love him" are, to my mind, adequate explanations of human motives as here conceived.

Freud, after explicating in this manner, inserts a different sort of theory to account for the transformation. This is the theory of normal psychosexual development, including such concepts as sexual instincts, cathexis, fixation, and sublimation. According to this presentation, if libido increases with no available outlet, sublimation may be undone at the point of fixation. The frustration thus produces regression (and a more primitive order of conceptualization of the world).

This theory is certainly worth consideration, but the means for its verification do not lie anywhere near the psychoanalytic method that Freud hopes to employ. Indeed, psychoanalysis cannot produce theories of causality. It can produce maps of the rules of human action; and often this is done under the guise of scientific theory, but I would ask whether anything is gained by saying, "The patient has withdrawn from the persons in his environment and from the external world generally the libidinal cathexes which he has hitherto directed on to them" (p. 456)? Can we not as easily say as Freud later does, "... for his subjective world has come to an end since he has withdrawn his love from it" (p. 457)?

Now there is no a priori reason suggesting that a causal explanation of mental processes based in neurophysiology cannot explain why we think the thoughts we think and follow the rules we follow. But no one has yet provided such a neurophysiology. "Are we to suppose that a general detachment of libido from the external world would be an effective enough agent to account for the idea of the 'end of the world' " (p. 461)? We may suppose this, but there is as yet no way of testing this statement as though it were a scientific hypothesis; nor *can* it be tested using psychoanalytic methods.

"These are problems with which we are still quite unaccustomed to deal, and before which we stand helpless. It would be otherwise if we could start out from some well-grounded theory of instincts; but in fact we have nothing of the kind at our disposal." In short, we have no "term situated on the frontier line between the somatic and the mental" (p. 461). And if we could somehow resolve these issues, we would still have to deal with meaning: the study of the larynx has yet to eliminate linguistics.

The Narrative Turn

The first sign that a baby is going to be a human being and not a noisy pet comes when he begins naming the world and demanding the stories that connect its parts. Once he knows the first of these he will instruct his teddy bear, enforce his worldview on victims in the sandlot, tell himself stories of what he is doing as he plays and forecast stories of what he will do when he grows up. He will keep track of the actions of others and report deviations to the person in charge. He will want a story at bedtime—K. Morton (cited in Calvin, 1994, p. 103)

The modern day of psychology, after a long, dark night cohabited by behaviorism and psychoanalysis, has been called the "cognitive revolution." This revolution has two heads, one represented by computational metaphors, the other by the metaphor of narrative, or story. Jerome Bruner (1990), a signer of the Declaration of Cognitive Independence from behaviorism, holds the conviction, "The central concept of a human psychology is meaning and the processes and transactions involved in the construction of meanings." He advances two connected arguments, "To understand (people) you must understand how (their) experiences and acts are shaped by intentional states," and "the form of these intentional states is realized in the symbolic systems of the culture" (p. 33).

Here Bruner, while preparing the narrative turn in psychology, brushes against anthropology and presents a view of culture with radical implications for psychology:

> But culture is also constitutive of mind. By virtue of this actualization in culture, meaning achieves a form that is public and communal rather than private and autistic . . . Action requires for its explication that it be situated, that it be conceived of as continuous with a cultural world. The realities that people (construct are) social realities, negotiated with others, distributed between them. (pp. 33, 105)

The representation of life experience, its communication, even those *selves* that represent and communicate, come to be seen in their interpersonal aspect. Bruner quotes with approval David Perkins' notion, "The proper person is conceived, not as the pure and enduring nucleus but as the sum and swarm of participations" (p. 106). Anthropologists are comfortable with this notion of self, easily seen in other cultures, and, as Geertz (1983) says with some glee:

> If (social scientists) are going to develop systems of analysis in which such conceptions as following a rule, constructing a representation, expressing an attitude and forming an intention are going to play central roles—rather than such conceptions as isolating a cause, determining a variable, measuring a force or defining a function— they are going to need all the help they can get from people who are more at home among such notions than they are. (p. 23)

Modern social scientists within psychology, represented by situative theorists (Greeno et al., 1998), suggest a perspective that "shifts the focus of analysis from individual behavior and cognition to larger systems that include behaving cognitive agents interacting with each other and with other subsystems in the environment" (p. 5).

Greeno notes that cognitive psychology models processes of constructing, storing, and modifying representations of *information*. Interactional studies, based on ethnographic and discourse analyses, focus on *systems of activity*. Activity is conceived of as "a continual *negotiation* of people with each other and with the resources of their environments." Individuals participate in these systems to achieve objectives that are *meaningful* and that relate to their *identities* as constructed in *communities of practice*. Meaning, in a situative theory, refers to analyses of mental representations that "include hypotheses about what they refer to in activity, rather than merely what their properties are and how they are modified by symbol-manipulating procedures" (p. 11).

The italicized terms in this discussion will appear again in our depiction of the work of the narrative therapists and in Bruner's discourses, as well as in my discussions of practice and action in psychotherapy. Thirty years ago (Greenleaf, 1969a), I proposed a situative view of psychological research and information:

For studies in psychology, one might argue that the terms used to delimit phenomenal areas are tied rather directly to the social situations in which they exist, rather than to phenomena embedded in some social structure, which is then reduced in the laboratory to lay bare the phenomena. We have begun to ask, for example, "How does a person come to be labeled 'schizophrenic' "? rather than the more traditional questions, "What are the characteristics of schizophrenics?" or, "What causes schizophrenia?"

The strategy is clear in cases where the common language provides such terms as "criminal" or "crazy." Certain forms of social intercourse give rise to the labels in specific situations, and social labeling, as opposed to the labeling of social scientists, requires, almost without fail, considerations of social context and appropriateness and often considerations of internal state, before applying terms. Compare, among numerous examples, the rules for "crazy" and "crazy like a fox."

For technical terms of social science, such as "regression" or "hypnosis," the community of psychologists structures a language from forms of social interaction developed in the laboratory or other artificial situations. Orne (1962) has written about the social psychology of the psychological experiment. Within the causal model of psychological research, such revelations have some of the status of the Uncertainty Principle in physics, which sets limits on observation of the electron. I'll argue that the data of social studies not only are limited but are *defined* by a sort of uncertainty. That is, our observations and the conditions under which they are made not only change but define the phenomena we wish to study. Radically, we might propose that experimental instructions produce, rather than simply control, the phenomena of the social sciences, and that what have seemed an inconvenience, at times an obstruction to research—subjective report, verbal behavior, the demand characteristics of experiments—are in fact the central stuff of psychology.

Greeno and colleagues (1998) make the point this way:

> *Without analyzing the larger systems thoroughly, we risk arriving at conclusions that depend on specific features of activities that occur in the special circumstances that we arrange and these specific features will prevent generalization to the domains of activity that we hope to understand. (p. 7)*

In psychotherapy, the shift from intrapsychic structures of information to communities of practice as explanatory ideas changes our understandings of problem spaces in lives, and also of the possibilities of solution. Erickson pioneered the therapeutic uses of the social environment to effect changes in personally conceived problems. Bateson termed his view of individuals as aspects of their social contexts, "natural history." The development of the family therapies has rested on versions of the idea that "symptomatic behavior, by metaphorically transforming aspects of the social context into the self, validates the basic dissonances of the system" (Schwartzman, 1982, p. 123).

A corollary of the shift in ideas is, as Greeno says (Greeno et al., 1998), "Reference is an achievement of joint action, rather than being a property of a symbol itself" (p. 8). And, by extension, personal identity, its scope, meaning, and valuation, is also an achievement of joint action. Joseph P. Gone (1998), a Native American, in describing the idea of "an authentic Indian identity," complains about psychologists' linear models:

> *The problem with them, of course, is that they represent Indian identity as a relatively stable quality of individual Indian persons that depends too heavily upon the simplistic reduction of complex life experience into the pre-ordained criteria and categories deemed important by social scientists.*
>
> *These perspectives situate Indian identity primarily in the psyches or minds of the people in question . . . As a result, they posit a core or*

essence of Indianness, usually a laundry list of certain qualities that a
person either has or does not have, independent of the social
processes through which Indian identity is regularly asserted and
contested. (pp. 5–6)

Ethnographic understandings provide an interesting guide to this territory. Consider White's description of the concept of "person" in Papua
New Guinea (cited in Errington & Gewertz, 1995):

In the tightly interwoven and constantly public arenas of village
life, where persons are conceptualized as enmeshed in interdependent
relations of all sorts, social and moral thought frequently de-empha-
size the individual as the primary locus of experience. (p. 116)

Errington and Gewertz (1990) note that "Chambri men and women . . .
define themselves *positionally* as members of social networks" (p. 111),
and, in phrases reminiscent of our discussion of psychotherapy in the
section on "Locus, Structure, and Meaning," describe the reformulation
of social power and position through ritual performance:

The object of both performances was to catch actors and audience
up in the action so that they could forget their habitual patterns of
interaction. In other words, the object was to reconfigure existing
lines of cleavage, fragmentation and distinction . . . (Errington &
Gewertz, 1995, p. 103)

Geertz (1983), in studying Moroccan culture, also sees the self as social:

Indeed, the social pattern would seem virtually to create this con-
cept of selfhood, for it produces a situation where people interact
with one another in terms of categories whose meaning is almost
purely positional, location in the general mosaic, leaving the substan-
tive content of the categories, what they mean subjectively as experi-
enced forms of life, aside as something properly concealed in
apartments, temples and tents. (pp. 67–68)

Psychologists, too, have shared this view of the person as social, and
have seen even the experiences of pain and of the emotions in this light.

Melzack, one of the originators of the gate-control theory of pain, remarks:

> *Pain is a symphony—a complex response that includes not just a distinct sensation but also motor activity, a change in emotion, a focussing of attention, a brand-new memory.*
>
> *In fact, some forms of chronic pain behave astonishingly like social epidemics. . . . Studies have shown that social conditions play a dominant role in many chronic pain syndromes, including chronic pelvic pain, tmj disorder and chronic tension headache, to name just a few. . . . And so a compassionate approach to chronic pain means investigating its social coordinates, not just its physical ones. For the solution to chronic pain may lie more in what goes on around us than in what is going on inside. (Cited in Gawande, 1998, p. 93)*

Goleman (1991, October), citing Jung's observation that "emotions are contagious," discusses studies demonstrating that "the transmission of moods between persons seems to occur . . . as one person mimics . . . another's facial expressions" (p. D1). Nonverbal markers, nods, postural shifts, and breathing changes punctuate and orchestrate such moods as emotional rapport. The autonomic nervous system responds rapidly and unconsciously to this "dance of moods" (p. D7).

Even the individual's sense of his or her own body may be constructed as a series of interpersonal events. A registered nurse in her 30s had suffered for 10 years from anxiety, migraines, and facial herpes. She had severe test anxiety. To become a nurse-anesthetist, she had had to pass organic chemistry, mathematics, and the GREs. Yet she had been told by a third-grade teacher, "You'll never go to college." She also felt ashamed of her "failure to marry, have kids."

In our first meeting, I asked her to describe her work. She said that she enjoyed helping postoperative patients to achieve "a state of gradual equilibrium . . . followed by rapid recovery." She was introduced to hypnosis by being invited to achieve this state for herself, by quieting her body's interior.

She was encouraged to tell her mother and stepfather about her feelings concerning marriage. After speaking with them, she told me the outcome at our next meeting. Surprisingly, her mother had said, "You are doing the right thing. Don't end up in my position." About the exam, the nurse said, "I want to eat it like a big piece of pie!" We discussed staying emotionally close to others and being different from them. When discussing her married lover, she noticed a kink in her neck. Imagining the lavender flowers of her self, she exclaimed, "Wow, this is really cool. The kink is going away!" In our third and final hour, she reported, "I can and have been talking nicely to myself. I can hear your voice. I fall asleep and I sleep very soundly. I pushed my boyfriend out of my life."

The stories people tell to express and participate in the social world, and to come to a sense of themselves, form a portal to therapeutic discussion and the resolution of problems in living. Modern narrative therapies construct powerful ways of entering these discussions.

Narrative Therapy

Bartlett, in his 1932 book, *Remembering*, writes:

> *Every social group provides that setting of interest, excitement and emotion which favors the development of specific images and . . . a persistent framework of institutions and customs which acts as a schematic basis for constructive memory. (Cited in Bruner, 1990, p. 58)*

The therapeutic utilization of specific images is, of course, the means and matter of our discussion. The framework of institutions and customs that co-constructs these images, informing power relations, judgments, self-identity, and patterns of action, is scrutinized in the work of modern feminist and narrative thinkers. Their consideration of experiences of power, freedom, and originality adds a social politics to what had been, save for the family therapists, a psychology of internalized psychodynamic struggle and explanation. White and Epston (1990), gathering from the work of Bruner (1986), the sociologist Goffman (1967), the philosopher Foucault (1980), and Epston's training as an anthropologist and hypnotherapist, have developed a storied, playful, and effective psychotherapy styled "narrative therapy."

The hinge between Erickson's hypnotherapy and modern narrative therapy is shown in David Epston's (White & Epston, 1992) earlier work, "Hayden Barlow Regains His Appetite." Eleven year-old Hayden's complete loss of appetite followed several rounds of surgery, chemotherapy, and radiation for a malignancy diagnosed when he was 3.

Epston encouraged Hayden to display his "strong emotions" as a test of his parents' strength "to stand up to his worries." The playful test of a serious subject derives from everyone's work with children and is exemplified over and over in Erickson's active directives, challenges, riddles, and games. (Use of the "test" in therapy with a young woman was described earlier in Chapter 3.)

Hayden tells several terrible nightmares in which people scream at him, "It's your fault!" He tells Epston that, while caring for a disabled uncle, he and the uncle crossed a road and the uncle walked in front of an oncoming truck. Hospitalized, he later died. Hayden was tortured by guilt. Epston's narrative continues:

> I then asked his parents . . . for permission to hypnotize Hayden. . . .
> I guided us all into a trance by inviting Hayden to close his eyes and
> then asked him if he could see a TV set in his mind. "Is it black and
> white, or color? Is it a big one or a small one?"

While Hayden's hand is levitated by imagining a balloon tied to his wrist with string, Epston tells him a story:

> A long time ago and at another faraway place, I was doing the job
> I'm doing now. A man came to see me. He told me he copuldn't eat
> anymore, and that he used to really like his grub. "Why not? I asked."

Epston's story concerns a truck driver who kills a man accidentally and then is unable to eat. As a young boy crossed in front of his truck, a bee stung him in the face. He lost control and ran over a man who had been following the boy. Then, in a fine twist, Epston says that the driver "is worried sick about the boy," who will surely blame himself although it wasn't his fault.

> Now I knew I was getting somewhere. I told him, "Look, I've
> been doing this job for nine years and I know what I'm talking about.
> I want you to know that no boy would believe such a crazy idea. . . ."

*And you know, he went home again that day, regained his appetite
and started eating again. He let me know later that his life improved
in many other ways, although to this day he doesn't like bees much.
But I guess that is easy to understand.*

Hayden did regain his appetite, and he used self-hypnosis successfully
for problems of temper, stealing, studying and the nausea associated with
chemotherapy. At his death a few years later, his mother wrote: "Hayden
has left us with the gift of love, and patience, how to endure suffering and
understand each other."

In their therapeutic practices, Epston and White attempt to turn from
"internalizing" to "externalizing" conversations. These are converse
ideas, with internalizing characterized as:

> *Those conversations that people engage in with the "self" and
> with others that: erase context, split personal experience from the
> politics of relationship, objectify peoples lives by fixing problems at
> sites that are considered to be at the center of identity or at sites that
> are considered to be at the "heart" of relationship, are totalizing and
> pathologizing of persons' lives and of their relationships through the
> fabrication of the "disorders," the "psychopathologies," the "dys-
> functions," and through the production of relationship "dynamics"
> that speak to the "truth" of a person's identity and of the "nature" of
> their relationships. (White, 1998)*

White continues with a description of the "technologies for the gov-
ernment of persons" based in these internalizing practices, and contrasts
them with the externalizing conversations of narrative therapy.

An example from my practice shows a simple form of this intellectually
rich approach: A highly intelligent woman, given to rather thorough
analyses of the morality of interpersonal life, had suffered bitterly from
the lies of others about her. Self-reliant and proud of her work, she was
troubled by "inefficient production." After she became acquainted with
the locus of the trouble in an "externalizing conversation," she found that:

> *I got home, took a nap to let our session register, and woke up
> suddenly able to function. I neither feel blocked nor wince when I
> think of an undone task. I am having fun and I am getting more done*

*this afternoon than I have all week—a great relief. I simply tell myself
that the problem is outside of me, and then I refrain from analyzing
further. Thank you!*

Externalizing conversations can be seen as a shift in locus of the entire problem. White and Epston (1990) extend this notion in their inquiries about the life of the problem:

> *In contrast to some family therapy theories, rather than consider-
> ing the problem as being required in any way by persons or by the
> "system," I have been interested in the requirements of the problem
> for its survival and in the effect of those requirements on the lives and
> relationships of persons.*
>
> *These requirements include specific arrangements of persons and
> particular relationships to oneself and others and can be identified
> through an exploration of the way that the problem appears to com-
> pel persons to treat themselves and others. This provides the details
> of the techniques of power that persons are being subjected to, sub-
> jecting themselves to and subjecting others to. (pp. 14, 34)*

Often problems are held as an invisible, inner experience, originating in unconscious conflict and constitutive of a person's moral burden. When, as White and Epston (1990) say, we "introduce ways of speaking about life that emphasize context," problems are held to be in the interpersonal field, responsibility is shared, and the problem is made visible. Often, in their work, as in ours, a problem is personified, as when they speak of a child's encopresis as "Sneaky-poo," and devise family strategies to thwart "him." To personify the problem repersonalizes the person, allowing him or her to act and decide and to collaborate in recovery from trouble.

The shift that is accomplished interpersonally by movements in the locus of emotion, action, or responsibility is worked in hypnotic therapies by dissociative strategies. In one of Erickson's (cited in Haley, 1981) cases, he persuaded a woman to keep her delusions locked in the closet of his office where they would be secure and not interfere with her life. Later, when she moved to another city, she said she didn't know what to do. Erickson said to her, "If you have a psychotic episode, why not put it in a Manila envelope and mail it to me" (p. 165). She did, and Erickson kept the envelopes for her return.

Erickson's approach to this problem, like so many in hypnotherapy, rested on a utilization of natural social forms and ordinary language to effect both a shift in locus of the problem and what White and Epston (1990) call "a deconstruction of the 'truths' of identity and relationship that are objectifying people's lives." The ideas of deconstruction and objectification have both philosophical and political correlates of great importance. In White's (1992) definition:

> *Deconstruction has to do with procedures that subvert taken-for-granted realities and practices; those so-called "truths" that are split off from the conditions and the context of their production, those disembodied ways of speaking . . . and those familiar practices of self and relationship that are subjugating of persons' lives. (p. 121)*

The depiction of these terms in the lives of persons is moving, funny, and dramatic, as in this transcript recorded by a woman of her interview by a caseworker (CW) at the Social Security office. She represents herself as "I" (Dart, personal communication, 1995):

I: What I would really like to know is how to phase out the SSI payments, now that I have control of the drinking and am working part-time. At what point am I legally obligated to cut myself off, and can the MediCal be separated from the cash payments?
CW: I don't know about any of that. My job as your caseworker is to get you into treatment for alcoholism.
I: I have been and am still in treatment. What I need to know is how to phase out the SSI.
CW: Where are you in treatment?
I: I see a psychotherapist in Berkeley.
CW: That isn't treatment. Do you attend AA?
I: No. But as a consequence of the therapy, I have not had a drink or wanted one for a year and eight months.
CW: That is not possible unless you attend AA or one of the programs I have listed here that include AA. Are you sure you don't attend AA?
I: Very sure.
CW: (*Looks at his notes.*) Then the length of sobriety you are talking about can't apply here.
I: But here I am.

CW: You can't be.

I: I have found a way to address strong emotion before it becomes so overwhelming that I think of drinking.

CW: Then clearly you don't attend AA, because AA members report thinking often about drinking. You need to get into treatment, and I'll refer you to a program. Now, I am going to ask you a series of questions, and I would like you to answer according to the range of responses listed here. (*Hands her a paper containing the list*: "Not At All/Slightly/Somewhat/Considerably/Extremely.") Here is the first question: During the last 30 days, to what extent have you been bothered bv alcohol consumption'?

I: Not at all.

CW: To what extent have you been bothered by the wish to drink alcohol?

I: Not at all.

CW: To what extent have you been bothered by ill health?

I: Not at all.

CW: To what extent have you been bothered by thoughts of suicide?

I: Not at all

CW: To what extent would you describe yourself as depressed?

I: Not at all.

CW: To what extent would you describe yourself as unhappy?

I: Not at all.

CW: Wait a minute. You see this therapist. Therefore, you must be unhappy about something. You can't just say "Not at all" if you also say you see a therapist.

I: That's interesting. I haven't taken that view of seeing my therapist for a long time. It's more of a rounding-out process. I can come out of a therapy session feeling happier and stronger than I had ever thought possible, without having gone in unhappy. I don't need to be unhappy before growing and exploring and enjoying. The therapy is more like cultivating a flower to ensure the process of blooming.

CW: So you are never unhappy or stressed'?

I: Okay, we can put down "Slightly" for that one.

CW: Good. Now, to what extent is it important to you to continue the therapy?

I: Considerably. Now we have some variety.

As White and Epston (1990) say, "The narrative structures we construct are not secondary narratives about data but primary narratives that establish what is to count as data" (p. 20). "Expert knowledge," but forth by the caseworker, struggles with "I's" narrative of her own lived experience. A narrative therapy "privileges the person's lived experience, encourages the use of ordinary, poetic and picturesque language, encourages a perception of a changing world and encourages a sense of authorship of one's lives and relationships in telling and retelling one's story" (p. 49). While holding that "the personal story or self-narrative structures our experience," they emphasize that "the personal story or self-narrative is not radically invented inside our heads. Rather, it is something that is negotiated and distributed within various communities of persons and in the institutions of our culture" (White, 1998).

Examples of the co-construction of life stories are found throughout this book, and the restorying of life identities is a common theme of these stories, discussed again under "Knowledge Through Action" and "Developing Alternative Knowledge Through Imagery," which follow "A Therapy of Ignorance."

The narrative therapists join Erickson in noting that "storytelling is just an ordinary thing, something they do every day of their lives." The use of inquiry to develop "secret" or "virtual" stories of resistance, knowledge, and skills of living, and the histories of these stories, is reminiscent both of Erickson's work and of the natural courage of homemakers in the concentration camps reciting their favorite recipes to each other to remember who they were. White and Epston (1990) connect the newly developed stories of persons to their social groups, families, schools, and workplaces by encouraging the practices of witness groups, networks of conversation, and the telling and retelling of stories in communities. They say that:

> The identification of unique outcomes can be facilitated by the externalization of the dominant "problem-saturated" description or story of a person's life and of their relationships. . . . When unique outsomes are identified, persons can be invited to ascribe meaning to them (by plotting them into) an alternative story or narrative. . . . And in this process . . . "imagining" plays a very significant role. (p. 23)

Bruner (1986) beautifully renders the case for the use of story in change, using "subjunctive" in its dictionary meaning of "a verb used in expressing what is imagined or wished, or possible":

> I have tried to make the case that the function of literature as art is to open us to dilemmas, to the hypothetical, to the range of possible worlds that a text can refer to. I have used the term "to subjunctivize" to render the world less fixed, less banal, more susceptible to recreation. Literature subjunctivizes, makes strange, renders the obvious less so, the unknowable less so as well, matters of value more open to reason and intuition. (p. 159)

A Therapy of Ignorance

I didn't know what her problem was. She didn't know what her
problem was. I didn't know what kind of psychotherapy I was doing.
All I was was as a source of weather or a garden in which her
thoughts could grow and mature and do so without her knowledge.

—Milton H. Erickson (cited in Havens, 1996, p. 143)

Another use of storied forms in therapy is one I've styled "A Therapy of Ignorance." Narrative therapies center on the *question* as an instrument for the collaborative construction of original stories recounting unique outcomes and "sparkling events" (White, 1998). White and Epston (1990) lavish exceptional ingenuity and care on the formulation of interesting and original questions. At times, though, even the most democratic manner, casual dress, and absence of expert trappings can run into a fact of interpersonal power relations: The one who asks the question acts with implicit authority toward the one questioned.

When we work in the language of imagery, we communicate "experience-near descriptions" and conduct "externalizing conversations" in a naturalistic manner, and largely avoid the technical language in which even the narrative therapists converse about their work and its presumptions.

Hypnotherapists assume the directional element in all statements, including questions. Their aim is to craft communication toward the accomplishment of the patient's goals. In this form of metaphorical communication, it may be important for the therapist to cut against presumptions of expertise and the notions of hypnotic control. True statements of *in*ability to fully understand the other are helpful in this way. An example of this approach was developed in a workshop experience in which the therapists, who were body workers, engaged the dilemmas posed by assertions of physical beauty.

Beautiful Brown Eyes

Lou: I can just feel when something is presented as a story or as a curious question or as a direct observation, that something is really actually there, observable, and I have no resistance. I can accept it even if I don't even know where the story is going or how it relates to me. It just comes in, and I don't stop it.

   I learned something about this yesterday when I was the practitioner and Frank was my client. I was saying, "Just experience how relaxed you feel," and later he said that he hated to be told how he felt. It was like the authoritarian school of hypnosis, He suggested that I could have said, "When I was sitting on the beach, I always felt so relaxed." I saw how there is a resistance when you start imposing something that you either want or are thinking but of which you have no evidence.

Eric: And you can think of a natural model for this "resistance." Think about being a kid and playing. You play and play, and then you are interrupted. The natural thing is to play until you drop, until you get hungry. I think that in therapy, if someone comments about you while you are experiencing things, it can have that same effect: It can interrupt something you don't know about because you are just about to get to it. It is just about to happen.

Ellen: This is very helpful for me. I have been working with a couple of people in therapy who have very, very low self-esteem, who are very beautiful women, and I naturally praise them and tell them how beautiful they are and how wonderful they look. And I realize that they don't get it, they don't believe it themselves. This "resistance" is absolutely what I mean.

Eric: You could talk directly to the women about their difficulty in accepting their beauty or talk indirectly and tell a story. Remember that this experience is interpersonal, not entirely within the women: Beauty is in the eye of the beholder, but it's even more between the beholder and the beheld. It's not indirect to talk about things in general: It points to the space in between—to the interpersonal, and if you think about these women's troubles, you will be led to considerations of how women discuss each other and look at each other and feel toward each other, and of the place of women in the culture, and people will speak rather generally. Otherwise, you'll have a discussion with one of these beautiful women in which she'll tell you that one side of her mouth is a bit crooked. You may be sitting there thinking, "What a beautiful woman, it's a pleasure to sit in the room and look at her eyes." It's good to speak in the middle of things.

Ellen: So you are saying not to think of that as indirect?

Eric: It is not indirect. It directly points to the thing that cannot be spoken about: the way her father looked at her when she was 12 and beginning to develop into a woman, and he took her for a walk in the street, and all these boys followed her, and how strange she felt, but how nobody talked with her about this, nobody put it into words. She may not even remember it, and she may have experienced it thousands of times since in other ways. Then she comes into therapy, and the therapist doesn't say anything and stares at her. There she is again with those same feelings that she cannot articulate, except to say, "There must be something wrong with me: It must be this, it must be that." You go through all the negative things you can think of that might have influenced you, put the blame on yourself, and so on.

I want to suggest something that the therapist can do, confronted with these kinds of problems. I would include physical problems, or physical expressions of problems that you just don't know what to do about but that you'd like to help with, or imponderables, like death. You can help someone breathe more easily, and people know how to do that, but how in the world can you solve the problem of the death of a loved one? That's impossible, yet people want to be comforting and to comfort.

Similarly, how could I, as a man who appreciates beautiful women, ever talk to this beautiful woman in a way that will make sense to her? It's not going to be easy for me. So I want to suggest a trance induction of ignorance as a way of talking to patients about this. That's the way I think about it. I could say, "I don't really know what it is like to be a beautiful woman. I only know such, such and such, but I don't really know. I don't know what you feel like."

Molly: When he says, "I don't know what it is like to be a beautiful woman," in order for the listener to hear that, she has to accept on one level that she *is* a beautiful woman. He would just be telling the absolute truth, and she must accept that she is beautiful, simply by hearing the truism. It opens the door just a tiny crack. If I say I don't know what it's like to have beautiful brown eyes; you may not think your eyes are beautiful brown, but the door is open because you've accepted half of the sentence, and the tendency in our language is that when you accept half of the sentence, you accept the other half.

Eric: It's at least in the conversation now, without any negatives attached. I could say, "I'm so curious about that because I have brown eyes too, and I don't really know what it's like to have such beautiful brown eyes." You can leave it and come back to it again, because we are going to learn how to have beautiful brown eyes before too long. What can people say about that? I'm very curious, and I really don't know. What would you say to a beautiful woman who does not know about her beauty, which is true of many beautiful women . . .

Ellen: I'm reminded of how many books there are about children—you know, like "The Ugly Duckling," and "Dumbo" with big ears—and about different aspects of beauty and what we consider to be beauty internally.

Eric: How can I begin to experience something that I've never felt before? It's such an odd thing even to talk about.

Sally: I would probably say . . . I would use . . . Maybe I could make up a story and just ask this person what she felt as I talked about the story, and just use that.

Eric: What story—I'm curious—would you tell?

Sally: I don't know. I just think I'd make one up.

Eric: Could you make up a story about a woman who realizes how beautiful her brown eyes are?

Sally: Oh gosh, how much time do we have? All right: Once upon a time, there was a woman. And this woman didn't like to look at herself, at her reflection in the mirror, because when she looked into the mirror and looked into her big brown eyes, she didn't like what she saw, and she turned away in fear and told herself she would never look into a mirror again. (I am going to cry.) One day, she was walking through the woods, and she came upon a little boy who was playing. She walked very, very quietly up to the child, careful not to scare the little one, and as she approached, she noticed that the child was blind. So she was very careful to let the little child know that she was coming toward him. She chose to sing a little tune so that the child would hear an approach. And as she sang this beautiful little song, she saw the child lift his head to one side, and she was aware that he knew that she was there. He had a curious look on his face, and so she felt safe to keep approaching. As she got closer to the child, he asked, "What is that song you are singing?" And she said, "This is a song about beauty and about wonder. This is a song about joy." And the child started beaming as the woman continued singing this song. And then and there, between the two of them a beautiful, beautiful dance took place, where the woman sang and the child moved and danced, and the wind blew, and the trees and the leaves on the trees fluttered. And it was in this suspended time that there was a moment of grace.

And after a spell, it was time for them to part. So they said their goodbyes, and they went their separate ways. And when the woman got back to her home, she felt a sense—a shift—inside of her that compelled her to look into the mirror, even though this was something she had decided she would never do again. As she glanced at her reflection in the mirror, she saw beyond the eyes from which she used to turn away and what she sensed instead was a sense of her soul. And in this day, she had touched in her heart an acceptance that she had never known before. And from this day on, she knew that she could always look at herself in this mirror, and that if she stayed there long enough, stayed and breathed and just kept looking at her eyes in the mirror, she could go beyond the fear and come to find the inside place of peace and acceptance.

Eric: That's beautiful, beautiful. The goal of the therapy is to help the patient resolve some difficulty, whether or not you know what the difficulty is. This story will be a way of making contact with the person who's experiencing the troubles of being a beautiful woman and of talking about it, even though you don't know the solution to the problem.

There is another thing you could show that is so beautiful. When you start to speak and you don't know what you are going to say, or when you start to move and you don't know what step you are going to do, or when you start to touch and you don't know what is going to happen, all this emotion arrives, from where I don't know.

This story affects many people differently: That is another of its beauties. You don't know tomorrow what will happen with this beautiful story. I don't know what will happen when I look in the mirror tonight—I just don't know. Thank you very much for that beautiful story.

Knowledge Through Action

The way to solve the problem you see in life is to live in a way that
makes the problem disappear.

—*L. Wittgenstein (cited in Phillips, 1993, p. 79)*

Every evening after dinner, my father would leave our big, old kitchen and lie on the living room couch to nap between his day job and his evening job. My mother would wash and dry the dishes, complaining that he never helped. One time my father left the table and headed for the sink, picking up a dish towel on the way. My mother intercepted him, snatched the towel, and said, "What do you think you're doing?" and pushed him toward the living room.

The next evening, my father said to my mother, "Why don't you sit and rest. Eric and I will do the dishes." She agreed and my father stationed himself by the sink and motioned me to stand near the open dish cupboard, some 10 feet away. Then, he washed and dried each dish before flinging it across the room for me to catch and put away, while my mother watched, open mouthed. I didn't drop a single dish.

Perhaps this experience helped me to understand the Delphic response of a physician studying hypnosis, when she was asked whether the conversation about her problems over lunch had cleared them up: "Not the discussion. The solution was the lunch." This may serve to remind us that the Socratic injunction to "know thyself" as exemplified, say, by Rogers and the analytic therapists, is accompanied by an equally ancient tradition in which the ideal is *arete*, a sort of virtue in performance. I think it is fair to say that modern forms of psychotherapy are concerned with the performance of new stories rather than the contemplation of existing ones.

Haley (1981) characterizes Erickson's approach to therapy as focusing on the practical skills needed in the real world to solve real problems, and discarding methods that don't work in favor of those that do. "These ideas are considered characteristic of American pragmatism, just as is Erickson's emphasis upon taking action rather than being an observer and waiting for change" (p. 166). Many of Erickson's (1980) treatments begin with his promoting small changes in action with his patients, such as entering a room backwards, or walking up a mountain trail. The effect of the hypnotist's expectant attitude and focused attentiveness by itself signals a readiness to engage and to act.

A computer programmer asked me to use hypnosis in order to help him reach his goal of programming more efficiently. I obliged him with a lengthy description of hypnosis and then asked about his experience of my talk. He said, "I just drifted away into doing it. As you were saying things, I was doing it. I didn't hear what you said. I just translated it into doing it." This experience depicts what William James (1975) framed in his American pragmatism: "Beliefs, in short, are really rules for action; and the whole function of thinking is but one step in the production of habits of action" (p. 259). James expressed the epistemology of pragmatism in the same work, along with a notion about the relationship of truth, action, and value:

> *Pragmatism gets her general notion of the truth as something essentially bound up with the way in which one moment of our experience may lead us towards other moments which it will be worthwhile to have been led to. Primarily, and on the common-sense level, the truth of a state of mind means this function of a leading which is worthwhile.*

I find it striking that this notion of truth allows that value—what is worthwhile—is determined by that to which we *will have* been led. It is not a function of where we think ourselves to be going, or, I think, of where, on reflection, we decide we have been. Wittgenstein (cited in Brand, 1979), with a lovely economy of language, expresses this notion and ties it with the metaphor of story or text:

> *What is given, what is to be accepted, leads us. Let us study the use of the expression "to be guided" by studying the use of the word "reading." First of all, we can say . . . that we read reality, we read the world. Secondly, the given leads us when we reduplicate it with itself and represent it in language. (p. 153)*

Wittgenstein's (1958) idea of explanation echoes the pragmatic turn:

> *Giving a reason for something one did or said means showing a way which leads to this action. In some cases it means telling the way in which one has gone oneself; in others it means describing a way which leads there and is in accordance with certain rules.*

Bruner associates his ideas with those of pragmatism and with Richard Rorty (cited in Bruner, 1990), who argues that pragmatism is part of a "deep, slow movement to strip philosophy of its 'foundational' status." Ideas like "truth," "knowledge," and "language" are treated to "antiessentialism." We want truth to have an essence, to be true absolutely, "but to say something useful about truth is to explore practice rather than theory, action rather than contemplation" (p. 25).

The type of action most crucial for humans, after the coordination of the body in physical space, is social interaction. No human survives infancy without the care, feeding, and affection provided by others in the social environment. Bruner (1990) argues that these crucial social interactions give rise to the forms of narrative representation of life, that young children's linguistic interest centers on "human action and its outcomes, particularly human interaction," and that "narrative structure is even inherent in the praxis of social interaction before it achieves linguistic expression" (p. 77):

> *What then is this prelinguistic readiness for selective classes of meaning? We have characterized it as a form of mental representation. But what is it a representation of? I believe it is a highly mal-*

leable yet innate representation that is triggered by the acts and expressions of others and by certain basic social contexts in which human beings interact. (p. 73)

Bruner's (1990) discussion of narratives emphasizes a basket of grammatical constituents that stories require. The collection is interesting and unusual and provides a recipe for both the telling of human life and the restructuring of that telling in therapy. Narrative requires agency, sequence, sensitivity to the unusual, a narrator. Human action is seen as directed toward goals along a sequential order of actions in which the protagonist is sensitive to the unusual rather than to the canonical event. Narrative can be "real" or "imaginary" without losing its power as a story. This feature of narrative, that it allows for and highlights "subjective states, attenuating circumstances, alternative possibilities," that "to make a story good . . . you must make it somewhat uncertain, somehow open to variant readings . . . undetermined" (p. 49), provides a guide for social and individual change and invention through the exchange of story, dream, imagining, and meaningful action.

I'd Like to Steal That Desk

Arguments of action organize our experience.

—*J. Bruner (1990 p. 77)*

Throughout these discussions, I've emphasized the place of dream images and the stories woven from them in recovering people's lives. I've also noted the ancient origins of these ways of healing and the social or interpersonal nature of the therapy. As Freud (cited in Bettelheim, 1983) said in *The Question of Lay Analysis*, "We base ourselves on common knowledge" (p. 61). In his original method, described in *On Beginning the Treatment* (Freud, 1913), he asked patients to imagine themselves seated comfortably in a railway carriage, reporting on anything they might see outside the window of the moving car. The method was both common and imaginative. Freud soon focused on childhood, reasonably, as the origin of one's ways of life.

A solution-focused, forward-looking, or reconstructive therapy, such as we practice today, also can look to childhood. Here what is important is the combination of dramatic, exploratory play; metaphorical language; and the rapid assumption of different social and archetypal roles that characterize children's imagination. These practices form the many notions of self. Psychotherapy can be based in these same approaches in the reconstruction of image, story, and self through playful action, as with Ozma:

Ozma, a woman in her 60s, as a child was tormented by her mother as a source of enjoyment and was isolated from other children. When grown, she was abused by her husband, a sadistic physician. During a long, successful struggle to avoid institutionalization, she has been "considered" schizoid, schizophrenic, and borderline. She came to therapy because she had finally separated from an abusive boyfriend and was terrified to stay alone in her house at night. She commented after the second session, "I haven't had those terrors since we talked. I have not wakened in terror. I am surprised that it's helpful."

One thing I want to look for and ask about is, "What surprised you? What did you notice?" Rather than looking for constancy of understanding or familiarity of belief, or accession to the therapist's way of thinking, what I would like to think about is what is surprising or novel. Like the narrative therapists, I am looking for surprising or novel outcomes from which to construct alternative histories of the person—real histories based on real events forgotten or slighted.

Two months later (I saw her about once a month), she said: "The night is friendly. Something is happening here in therapy. I was alone for three nights. I managed." Three months later, she said, "I am fairly well centered." The next month she had a dream that someone had broken into her house. After the dream she woke up and called the police. They came, checked out her house. Things were safe. "It's okay," an officer reassured her. "Whoever it was has gone away." She said: "I haven't felt stuck. I feel confident. There is something to be honored in myself. I feel different about my space, about using it. In a real sense I am facing my problems." A month later, she said, "We have done it together." This is another feature of this kind of work. It's felt to be collaborative:

> We've done it together. I can wake at any time. And a feeling of quiet is there, a feeling of contentment and order, a feeling for the first time that things are all right in the world. Now out there is out there. I don't have any chaotic confusion.

These were issues never discussed in the therapy. There was no talk of boundaries, and no talk of the inside and outside, and no talk of the sort, "You know it would be a good thing if you could face your problems."

In September, we did talk about a guilty feeling that has carried through her life because her father was a drunk. I said to her, "It cannot be true that the baby causes the drunkenness of the father." We had a talk about babies and what babies are, what they know and what they can do, how helpless they are. A month later, she said:

> I think I am improving in every way I hope to. I have a place to stand. I am more confident, more comfortable at night, more like I am here, with the others outside. The dialogue continues inside me. I have been dislodged from my utter certainty of feeling responsible for the bad as a child. There is no gnashing, no gnawing.

Remember that gesture is a way of talking unconsciously, but action is, as well. Among my many prejudices in language, I dislike the term "acting out." I like the term acting up and I like the term "acting." It's action, and you can treat by action. You hug your friend in compassion, take over a shift at work for somebody—pretty therapeutic. The typical thing people do if someone dies is to bring food to the house, help out with phone calls. We say, "I wish I could do something. Tell me what to do."

One day, Ozma showed me a piece of wood, a scrap from her woodworking class. She said, "I stole this. I steal things. I don't know why I do this. I go to the bin when Harry's gone and I take the scraps from his work. I don't even know if he needs them, but I take them and bring them home." And then, looking guilty and wrong, she said, "And I like your desk. I'd like to steal that desk."

In the drawer of the desk, I keep a Polaroid camera. I reached for the camera and took a picture of the desk. I gave her the picture. I said, "Here, this is for you." That was the therapy: I gave her the picture. At the next session, a month later, she said, "You gave me the desk . . . and there's so much humor on the other side of that thievery. The chains (of guilt) don't lie heavy on me. I carry the picture with me and it means so much. My stealing urge has quieted down." Another month later, she said:

> The last session is still there, but I don't have words for it at all. Things are making a difference these days. They are closer to me,

assimilable. What we do here in therapy is mine. They are not only hard to put into words, they are felt, they are somewhere else. They are something outside the realm of my usual language. Where is that, "beyond language?" The theft matter has removed itself from my urges. It was your picture: It was funny and magical. It moved into the space where the urge was.

Another month passed:

I feel more human. The feeling is really new. The thievery is socialized by sharing it with you. What makes this work when other things don't work? Everything is green lights, open and spacious. I am weary of years and years of therapy. I like that you gave me the picture. I carry it with me in my purse, and the story of it, too.

This story became the beginning of Ozma's continuing effort to know the story of her own life, and to tell it and to write it, a story we'll return to in "Developing Alternative Knowledge Through Imagery."

Solving the Unknown Problem

The therapy described in this book may be thought of as public conversations in the language of dream images, the language of the unconscious. The conversation concludes as the problem resolves. "Passing the trance" is a hypnotic simile for the discussion that obtains in a reflecting team or consultation. Hypnosis, as a prime metaphor for unforeseen solutions and for the utilization of the unconscious mind, can be applied to an "unknown problem." The practice of hypnotherapy has always been solution oriented, from the work of hypnoanesthesia in surgery and pain control through the early work of Freud.

In my hypnotherapy classes, we practice passing the trance to each other, as the first experience most have had in hypnotizing another person. The form of the trance is to focus attention on a faceted crystal, close the eyes comfortably, and allow the hypnotist to lift the subject's hand lightly. Then the subject hypnotizes the next person in a like manner.

After this first practice, we posed a challenge for the following class meeting: to consider solving an unknown problem that had been interfering in life. We discussed some metaphorical expressions of the "unknown" in solving human problems: the engineer's black box and the photographer's darkroom. In the former, inputs and outputs can be described, but the workings of the connections between them remain obscure. In the latter, a negative is placed in a series of solutions in a darkroom. After it is passed through these solutions, developed, and fixed, it emerges as a positive image.

Therapists wishing to play these themes in their work ought to listen to the music of images and to practice developing them in cooperative conversations. An excellent first book of practice is Furman and Ahola's (1992) *Solution Talk*. The Beethoven quartets of the genre are represented by the work of Milton Erickson. In the class described below, we began with a discussion of women and power and the feelings that were developed in the course of inducing a trance, of "being the hypnotist." Then we returned to the unknown problem.

The Lady of the Lake

Eric: I want to catch up with what people's experiences were last week and then go on from there to be on the track of this unknown problem. What do you recall that was of interest?

Holly: I felt very anxious about being first in line and turning to Cole and hypnotizing him and passing the trance around and wondering if I could do that. It was such a strange experience, because I thought I was in trance, but I could still feel the anxiety. I did get calmer and more trusting that I could do my task of being a hypnotist, and when I turned to Cole, I felt like I was bringing some of that trance with me and not being so worried or so self-conscious about it . . . I felt that I shared that induction around the room, and what I noticed was a more intense kind of curiosity and noticing, as people did the inductions and went into trance. I had this sense of more freely and openly looking at people and really looking and taking it in. . . . and then I really listened—this kind of quiet, open nonintrusive listening which is really being aware, and I really liked that. It seemed kind of like a surprise to me.

The other thing I noticed during the week—I just wondered the other day if it was related to that unknown problem—was that I took care of a lot of little personal details that were just hanging. Even today I remembered to bring that tape back here. I'll think of little things and feel like I don't have time to do them. But I just did them.

When we left here last week, Carol and Melinda and Jan were walking in front of me and I said, "Hey, you guys! We did it. We hypnotized them!"

Melinda: We assured one another that we hadn't been pretending.

Eric: Really?

Holly: So that was really helpful to me too. I think that really put me over into the camp of believing that I can do it.

Eric: How about you, Jan? What was it like for you?

Jan: Well, I felt the experience was cumulative. (*General laughter.*) I couldn't see straight. I really felt from the very first as we passed it around that I had to stop listening, otherwise I would be really uptight when it came to Carol's turn to do it to me. I was very anxious too about passing it on: I didn't know what would happen—what would actually happen. I had lots of doubts. But what I recall during the experiencing was actually going back to the beaches of Hawaii, actually being there. It was just very, very clear, and that's where I was. I figured it was a cumulative experience with everybody talking about it and it became more and more crystallized and refined until it was just an absolutely clear picture.

What I was thinking about during the week as well was that solution to an unknown problem, and not knowing where the picture will bridge that unknown problem. Where will it meet? Where is it in that picture, that crystal-clear picture that I have in my head of the beach? The unknown problem: Where will it meet? It actually pops into my head almost every day. I find it so interesting, the unknown problem.

I have been talking a lot about all these problems that I have, wondering if maybe I shouldn't be talking about them, and hoping that somehow a solution would emerge. Maybe I shouldn't be so interested in problems because if I'm not maybe I'll forget they are problems and maybe they will become unknown problems and be duly addressed. It's really crazy.

Eric: I like this idea of the unknown problem so much partly because it's another way of talking about the metaphor of unconscious mind or unconsciousness. Remember the psycho-analytic version of things in which you get a problem because something falls into your unconscious. You repress information or feelings or desires or memories, or your whole childhood is unknown to you. Thereby you get an unknown problem. But if you think about the way we've been working hypnotically, with the unconscious as a kind of resource, you could drop something like your problems into the unconscious and get them solved in just that same way. You could say, "Well, this isn't too bad, I'll just drop that in." It's like a stock pot: "This looks like leavings, but I don't want to throw it away; I'll just toss it in," and pretty soon it develops its own flavor and you can use it to make sauce.

Holly: In the 12-step programs, that's what they call "letting go."

Eric: Yes. You give it up to the Higher Power, or you drop it into the unconscious mind. That's kind of the approach Ann is taking with this; I think it's a very interesting one. Now, "unconscious" is usually thought of in a personal way, but here is another way of thinking: Things that are unconscious are also impersonal, social, and interpersonal things. Your family feeling when you were a child may qualify as something unconscious: You know what it feels like; if you were there again, you would recognize it; but it would be very hard to put into words. So this business of an unknown problem can be a simile for or similar to an idea of the whole background you come from. I like the notion of an unconscious solution even better than I like the one of an unknown problem.

Jan: Yes, finding an unconscious solution—solving the unknown problem.

Eric: Carol, what was it like for you this last week?

Carol: It was interesting, Jan, when you said that it seemed cumulative, because by the time it got to Cole, I was gone. I felt so deep into something that I don't even remember what Jim said to me. And when Eric first said, "This is what we are going to do," at first I felt nervous, because, like you, I felt, "Oh my God! I've got to perform. . . . Instead of the one who is learning I've got to be the one who has to accept some sort of responsibility." So I felt nervous, but as we went along I just let it go, and as I sat there I just went under and under and under, and I just had that soft gaze, and I was here but not in any specific way, and by the time Jim got to me, it was very strange.

It was like I was in this meditative trance and I didn't want to come out of it. It felt like being asleep but being awake. I recalled a lot of physical energy, and he must have been saying something about my hand, because my hand got so tingly with energy, and heavy. I don't remember what I said to you. I just felt like I needed to talk. I completely forgot that there was a purpose, and I didn't remember until you just said that there was this undefined problem. All of a sudden: "Oh yeah, that's right." I forgot there was a beach. I just was out of it. I couldn't tell you what Jim said to me, other than that I remember something about my hand. There was some focus that brought my energy into my hand and that crystal. It was a very intense experience that I don't really know how to describe.

Eric: You are doing a good job. The soft gaze is like what Holly talked about: being able to watch without being so intent, and then that feeling of going under, under, under—of doing that thing that Jan's been fooling with all week, which is kind of the boundary between consciousness and unconsciousness. "Where does the beach apply to something unknown?" is a story about going under, and at some point, it's like where your eyes are closing, where you're hitting the water, and then where you're under, and then you go way under. It can feel that way or it can feel like trying to approximate a boundary—to come close or to let something "go into" that. Those are all similar experiences.

Carol: That soft gaze . . . It was almost as if the soft gaze were turned inward. I felt like I left my body, except for my hand—like the only energy that was left was in my hand . . .

Holly: I noticed, though, that your words just flowed. You were very articulate. I was very moved and impressed. I thought you were probably in trance. . . .

Carol: That's interesting. That really surprises me because I felt like I just let go. I really don't know what I said; I really don't.

Holly: You'll enjoy watching the tape.

Carol: I felt this to be a very, very profound something. I checked out. It was a different experience. And it's really interesting because I came to this class with all this uncertainty about whether I could even experience this stuff and it seems like each time it's gotten more and more profound in terms of my experience. Remember that you and I had a similar experience in one induction where we thought we went to sleep? Well in some ways, I think I am going that deeply under but I'm staying conscious— there is a part of me that is staying conscious—whereas before I was completely unconscious. Now, it's like having a foot in both worlds.

Eric: Yes, that's exactly what it is like. It's very pleasing, it's a very powerful sensation, and that's the one you're aiming at. Then what developed in you was individual. Melinda, what happened with you?

Melinda: I also felt a cumulative effect, being the last person, and I did my various trips—I just did my various Melinda things. I was also nervous; I got to be nervous the whole time. (*General laughter.*) I also had this dual sense of feeling the cumulative trance, but also the nervousness. That was very strange for me: To feel that experience of being in trance and being nervous at the same time was novel. And I was also observing, watching. It seemed to me that everyone added their own little flavor when they did it: How they do stuff, how their minds work, how the words of each of us come through. And I was trying to say to myself, "Stop observing so much. Just stop worrying." There was all this chatter, all those committee members in there chattering away, and my back was really hurting me at the time.

      There was also this awareness that at some point I was going to have to turn to you and I was going to have to perform and put the teacher in trance. (*General laughter.*) But you approached me with such purity of intent—and you were just you, being here with me—that the rest just kind of dropped away. And I got very entranced with the different facets of the crystal, looking at the colors. I really wanted to look at all the objects in the room through them. That was mostly what I was fixated on.

Eric: What you just described is what's meant by "utilization" in hypnotherapy. You sit there before you hypnotize, looking at things every different possible way, being like Melinda. Your mind works that way. You look at the different possible situations and sensations and what went before and what will go next, and you're looking at things from different angles.

Jan gives you a hypnotic induction that allows you to use that style as a skill instead of feeling it as a symptom, because then you start looking at the different facets of everything in order to help you meet your goals. (In this case, they are sort of unknown goals.) That enables you to utilize the thing that was bothering you without your having to change: You don't have to become single-minded. Instead you can use this ability to look at all the different angles and facets and enjoy it. It's a great talent.

Melinda: Yes, it was very enjoyable. I don't really remember, things got lifted and all, but there wasn't much more to it than that. Still there was a sense of well-being, and that was very pleasurable, and then it was my turn to pass to you. I was just aware of the fear (*expressive gesture, general laughter*), and at one point when I went to lift your wrist my hand was so icy cold in comparison.

Holly: There was this really nice sort of duet where he dropped his hand and you held your hand out and he dropped the crystal in it.

Eric: Everybody did splendidly. Oh, what about the unknown problem?

Melinda: I have no idea. Another part of me was realizing I always come to this class after couple's therapy, and we have some very known problems that are taking up a lot of space in my life. Again, when we were going around the room I was thinking, "How can I do this paradoxical thing, to make this

	known problem become an unknown problem, because I want to find a solution?"
Jan:	You could get me into this dream.
Carol:	I kept a dream journal while I was studying with Eric. I never do that, but what was very interesting was that all of the dreams somehow tied together as one long all-encompassing story, which I didn't anticipate at all. Sort of like the image that you talked about, Holly: the whirlpool. Somehow it all connects because it's all down this same funnel, surrounding this central issue. It's just a powerful way to work with metaphors and ways to just hook right in immediately to a person's personal image, without the person having to know what it means.
Holly:	You didn't have to know what it meant?
Carol:	Yes, and I kept thinking, "Okay, all right, fine, but what does that mean?" And what I got, but not until the very end, was this sensation of understanding without the language, the experience of knowing, resolution, and letting go of my need to intellectualize it, rationalize it, put it into little categories and boxes, and file it away. It was a very different sort of experience.
Holly:	That makes me think: I said I don't remember dreams, but I wake up, and I'm not quite awake, and I have this knowing about this dream and I go back to sleep. I never remember the next day. I vaguely remember the dream. I never remember what that knowing was.
Eric:	You don't remember what you knew, but you remember knowing it. That is what you're both describing. That's the experience that I'm referring to by those words, "solving the unknown problem." You feel something's solved or resolved but you don't know what it was.
Holly:	It's like a new knowing or a surprise? It seems right. I go back to sleep.
Eric:	That's right, you were reorganizing unconsciously, you might say. You don't know what you were doing wrong, but now you are not doing it wrong any more. In a physical analogy to this, the ball gets where you throw it, or you keep the beat while you're drumming. You didn't know what was wrong. So

you have to figure it out without the language for it, usually by trial and error, until it feels right. I think that's the way that many many important problems are solved.

Melinda: I had a dance teacher who taught metaphorically, and we had common metaphors, but when I look back, the language seems so imprecise. What did it mean to "lift" or to "get lighter" or imagine this happening with the front and that happening with the back? . . .

Holly: I had that experience with a friend coaching me in my ever-failing golf game. He kept telling me I was picking the club up, and I didn't know what he meant until I saw it on video; then "Oh!" I could see it immediately.

Eric: What was the difference? It's imprecise, it's allusive: It points to but it does not define. So a lot of the words that are metaphorical in that sense we use as though they were technical. "Hypnosis," which is a technical-sounding term, only means "pertaining to sleep"; that's all it means.

Jan: As you were talking, I was thinking about what you said earlier: If you could talk about it, it becomes more conscious. But if words are so imprecise, then you really are unconscious. I'm thinking of clients who insist on talking about their understanding of an experience, and they beat it to death. I thought, well, maybe they need clearer understanding of it, but when you talk about words being imprecise anyway, well, we know very little.

Eric: It's interesting that people have a faith in explanations as though giving the reason for something were a solution to a problem, and I've always been very puzzled by that, as though if you could give words to it, you could solve it. I think you can resolve it—you can feel okay about it and not question it any more. Now, this known problem of yours: Could I say, "The known part of the problem has something to do with the way two people get along?" (*Pause.*) Maybe it doesn't.

Melinda: No, it doesn't. It has to do with when two people choose to be together, then what? That's my formulation.

Eric: Okay, let's suppose that that's the way the problem is expressed and let's say that we have the odd faith that the solution is somewhere within the problem. Somewhere within the body of the dancer is the solution to the matter of putting her feet right, assuming that there is a way this dance can be done. We'll assume we have a solvable problem, a resolvable problem, okay so far?

We don't know quite what the problem looks like. Four of us don't know very much about the problem at all, and the fifth person may or may not know a lot about it. So let's say that there's this problem but we don't exactly know what it's like. If you dreamed about a problem and you didn't know what it was, what would it look like? What's an image of an unknown problem? You can see that it's there, but you cannot see what's in it.

Holly: A lake. I imagined a lake, a body of water. I couldn't see the fish or the rocks.

Melinda: I had an image of a fog, also over a body of water. So it was both the water and the fog, and things sort of dimly emerging, but I couldn't make out what they were; there were things behind the cloud.

Jan: I had a cloud like a black fire creating smoke. I couldn't see through it. It was framed by white but it was black.

Carol: I saw this thing that you can't tell which one's the black side and which one's the white side. Is it a woman? Is it a vase? And you can't tell. That was my image of the problem.

Eric: Very nice. I think, because it's Melinda's image, let's say it's a lake. . . . It's a lake. Now suppose that the solution to this problem comes out of the lake and appears when the fog clears. Suppose you take a look and see what it looks like.

Holly: Well, I had an instant image when you said "the solution." It was the image of a woman—a woman's body—this very classical, statuesque, tall woman's body coming up out of the lake. I couldn't tell if it was a statue or if it was a woman. There's the sense of nudity, but she is draped in something gauzy, something around her. You can't see her features. Long hair. Dark or light? I really can't tell. I really can't see. It's sort of misty, sort of pale, light.

Eric: Is she carrying anything, or is she unadorned and unencumbered?

Holly: She's not carrying anything. She's unadorned and unencumbered. It's a very powerful figure, a very strong . . . horrible woman. Turned sort of and looking straight ahead.

Eric: And the mood about her beside her power: Is there another feeling you sense?

Holly: Light. There's a sense of light, light coming from her.

Eric: Now suppose that you pass that image of her to Jan and see what happens with it. You can do that by handing it to her if you like. And suppose you say what you see or feel when you look at this woman, and what she does.

Jan: I also see a sword in the lake, and this jewel. Everything is glistening as though there's a bright light behind it. She is immersed in the lake as if she's just standing there.

Eric: And what's the feeling that she conveys to you now?

Jan: It's kind of . . . a feeling of comfort.

Eric: So there's power and brilliance and comfort too. Go on.

Jan: Yes, as if all the answers were contained. I feel comforted by the image.

Eric: And do you see her face, her hair, or her gestures?

Jan: Brilliant yellow hair and kind of wavy; kind of serene; no striking features of any kind; no strong feeling, emotion, or anything like that. It's more . . . presence. Her eyes are open. Her features are delicate. Her skin is very smooth . . . pretty, very pretty.

Eric: And what is she doing with the sword? Is she holding it or looking at it, or . . .

Jan: No, she's not doing anything with it. It is just there beside her. Light's really reflecting off it. It's sort of part of her and sort of there with her.

Eric: Now suppose you hand the image to Carol and see what she says.

Carol: I can see this woman's statuesque figure coming marching out of this lake. Actually, I can't see the boundaries of the lake, so it feels like an expansive body of water. I have no sense about where it ends or where it begins. I see the sword lying across the top of the water within her reach. I see the way the light from the sky glitters off of it. I can't see her yellow hair as clearly. It's very interesting because when she looks out across the horizon, there are beautiful golden lights in the distance.

They're not necessarily lights from a city or anything, but there is just some beautiful light from a distance. Light from the horizon casts a glow on the water.

The image of the woman when I looked more closely at her was very odd. She was made of this substance that was very hard, like cement, but she didn't feel rigid. It was just solid and the temperature of it was almost cold, but not cold in an emotional sense, not detachment. I get a feeling of a very strong presence on this horizon or on this area. It is literally like a statue and yet there is movement. You get a sense of softness here. There is grace, there is serenity, there is incredible wisdom and a very strong caretaking sense.

Eric: And suppose you convey that to Melinda.

Melinda :   I'm having a little trouble with this, because as soon as you began talking, I also got the "Lady of the Lake" and I had my own image of that, so it's a bit hard to let that one go and fit in your images.

Eric: You can have them both.

Melinda :   I also see a lot of glistening and shimmering light off of her; also that sense of being a statue, so ideal, almost inhuman. I don't feel the nurturing part as much as the truth part. So there is water that's running off of her. She comes up with all that power, and there's water running off of her, and everything is glistening, as well as the jewels and the sword. Actually, I saw a chalice; she came up with this chalice.

Eric: Do you swim?

Melinda :   Do I? Yes, sort of.

Eric: Suppose you swim out to the middle.

Melinda :   To her?

Eric: Yes, unless she will stroll over to you.

Melinda :   No, she's set out there. She sort of comes up like on a dolly or something and down again. (*Pause.*) Okay, I'm about there . . . Okay . . . She is a little bit scary to get close to. She is a very imposing figure, so I want to keep my distance. I want to get close enough to experience her, but not too close—just a little bit farther out.

Eric: Suppose you go a little bit closer than you think is prudent, just a little bit, just a little bit closer if that's okay. It's like making a movement that's a little bit like reaching toward imbalance, but you know you can sustain it—sort of like being *en pointe.*

Melinda : I start to have a feeling of sharing in her power. It's frightening, but also it's like a movement to her or something of which I'm partaking. I'm too frightened by her to get closer. She's got a chalice in one hand and a sword in the other. These are heavy objects, and she is no one to mess with. She brooks—I don't know what that word means—she brooks, she allows, no hesitation.

Eric: That's like a truth function, so you are safer with her if you move directly.

Melinda : If I move directly, then I have to move either toward her or away from her.

Eric: Toward her is a good idea. Breathe deeply and use everything you know.

Melinda : (*Weeps for a while, then laughs.*) I want to get the hell out of here.

Eric: I appreciate your honesty. That is the truth, isn't it?

Melinda : That is the truth.

Eric: But since you've come this far . . .

Melinda : I was going to say before, because she'll permit no lies: That's the truth. (*Pause.*) I'm done.

Eric: Oh no, I don't think so. Not quite yet. You have to remember: You're out in the middle of a lake and it's a long swim back. You'll need all your strength to go back, so in that way you are compelled to go a little closer.

Melinda : There are ripples moving out from her still from that powerful entrance, and they are pushing me a little bit away, and I have to stroke over to get closer; I have to use my own energy to get closer. (*Long pause.*) So I am very close to her, a couple of feet away from her. She's just waiting. I'm supposed to do something, but I don't know what. And she's going to disappear; I only have a short period of time.

Eric: What would you like to do?

Melinda : Nothing that I can think of.

Eric: Suppose you get close enough to get up out of the water. You could put your hand on the sword and pull yourself up, or hold onto the cup and pull yourself up.

Melinda: Okay, I'm standing in the water. Everything's very crystalline and clear.

Eric: Can you see into the chalice? What does it look like?

Melinda: It's glazed . . . red, something gold in the bottom. It could go on forever. I feel awe and curiosity and a desire to find something.

Eric: And when you put your hand on the sword?

Melinda: It felt like all the energy that Carol was talking about—tremendous energy. It's sort of hard to get a grip on it with all the jewels and stuff—nubbly little sharp things—they hurt. At the same time, there is so much energy, almost too much energy.

Eric: And when you hold the chalice in your other hand, how does that feel?

Melinda: (*Long pause.*) It's like my conundrum: It's wisdom and love, how to hold them both.

Eric: Hold them both. Just breathe easily and slowly and keep your head up. Breathe nice and slowly and just wait.

Melinda: (*Long pause.*)

Eric: What do you notice?

Melinda: There's some sense of circuitry. I connect these two disparate pieces. I feel calm and powerful.

Eric: And your body feels how?

Melinda: Solid. A little bit upset, but mostly at peace. I just had a thought. Somebody was talking about how one of my difficulties in working with groups was that I was such an absolutist, that I talk of cooperation, but absolutely, and that I was always looking at people critically. I just seemed to be able to apply those thoughts to what is happening in this relationship: I'm absolutist in my conceptualization of how everything has to be.

Eric: Now what do you feel like doing?

Melinda: Like opening my eyes and getting the attention off me.

Eric: Do you want to swim back or stay out there?

Melinda: I want to acknowledge the lady somehow. She is just the "Lady of the Lake."

Eric: As long as you know the way to contact her.

Melinda: Thank you. I don't know what to do with it now.

Holly: I feel excited and lots of feelings. Most amazing to me was that our images of this woman were similar, because as you described it, that's what I saw too. I didn't see a sword and a chalice, but I saw her right hand out like this (*holds hand out straight*) and her left arm (*holds it at her side*) with sort of the functions of a sword and a chalice.

Eric: The one hand pointing to truth?

Holly: With light coming out.

Eric: And the other by her side?

Holly: Yes. When I swam I wasn't really afraid. I was curious, and I swam out in front. It felt kind of powerful pointing at me, so I moved to the nurturing side. There was a little platform, and I climbed up and sat there and felt pretty good right there.

    The other thing that kept coming forward for me was a powerful, powerful dream I had about 20 years ago: I was standing on top of a mountain or hill looking at this huge yellow moon. I stretched my arms out to the moon and to the light and I got filled up with the light of the moon. It's the most wonderful . . . I can't describe this feeling of total fullness of light. Then I turned around and looked over a vast dark landscape, like a desert. I couldn't see anything out there, but I was just glowing. I could hear voices out there, people saying, "Look at her! There she is!" and coming toward me. In my dream, I got very scared and I ran, and it was sort of like hiding my light under a bushel. I felt such a terribly sad feeling to run away from that, but it was so terrifying to me to be the beacon, to be the light. And yet there is this sense of being more able and more willing to be full of light, or to be the power.

Eric: And you can see the courage it took to move that little bit in the water, because it is so terrifying when you approach that. It takes enormous courage. You were just sitting in a living room, but the interior of that dream is so powerful and there is the awesome feeling that everyone described, where you are stunned by her power.

Carol: Melinda, I really felt very moved by sharing the experience. I participated with you and felt the struggles and it felt very intense, very personal, very intimate, and I felt that I went there with you, I shared something with you. I felt awed by your willingness to participate in it and your strength to be able to accept the challenge when you were cautious and hesitant. You allowed yourself to be coaxed by Eric, encouraging you to go a little closer, to check things out, and it was just a wonderful experience to witness this. Even though it was in my mind, witnessing your experience, even though you were just sitting in a room and I was just sitting across from you, there was a very real journey that you were going on and going through and it felt powerful.

Eric: Side by side with that you had some other experience of your own too. What was that?

Carol: It was very powerful and personal, and it was me. In fact, here it is: it was me. When I was envisioning the statue, I was the statue. It felt like this (*touches the wall*), and cool like this, not cold.

          I felt very powerful; I felt very wise. I felt very knowing, very tolerant, nurturing too, but tolerant, as though I could look off at anything, and even if I felt that what was happening was not what I thought was optimal, there was a knowing that it would work itself out. There was just something wise and tolerant and at peace, and contemplative but not intense. Just that soft focus, but all-encompassing, as though I were observing the world.

Eric: Like that brightness that you both described at the horizon. And the fog was very bright. Jan?

Jan: I was very much into the image, and when you started to tear up, I did too. It was as if we shared the experience. It was really incredible. As Eric said to approach her because she wasn't going to stroll over to meet you, I walked on water too, to meet her. You went swimming, I walked on water to meet her, and it surprised me. As you approached her, there was this fear of feeling strong emotion. I felt a strong emotion with you, and I did cry.

As you tried to find a way to approach her, to get closer to her, to experience her, my experience drifted off to focus on the sword, because when you talked about the sword and the jewels and how difficult it was to climb out because it was difficult to grab because it was so bumpy with the jewels, I saw that. And for me the sword was the most striking thing, not the woman. And when you talked about the chalice, looking into the chalice, the chalice was very heavy, so I took the sword and I brought it inside me and I saw it inside me. And as I thought about it, what I felt more symbolically, was wisdom. Yes, her face was beautiful, but it was perfect, and that's not real to me, and so I couldn't take it in. But I could take in the sword, and maybe that is a solution for me; my solution to the unknown problem. . . . whatever that means.

When I'm the woman capable of connecting, it's the sword. I don't know whether or not there's a name for it, but I can see the jewel and the tapering. It's the experience that is called the solution, whatever that is. Very powerful. I felt the sharing and going with you, being frightened with you and being awed, but for myself, I was being overwhelmed by the image. I could focus on the sword and take that with me. The chalice was too gaudy, too ornate, too heavy, but the sword felt right. Interesting.

Carol: I forgot that we had an unknown problem again. (*General laughter.*)

Eric: I don't know what it is.

Jan: We all have a solution now; what are we going to do with it?

Melinda: We can't find a problem.

Carol: At the end, part of me wanted to talk about it and figure it out and come to some sort of resolution or conclusion, but there was something that had just happened that I needed to just let sit. You can deal with issues without having to identify them, and in a very powerful, personal, impacting way; that's what it felt like for me, and this seems like something that I could use in my own work.

Eric: An interesting thing to me is that the standing of the person with the troubles is very elevated here. Everyone feels the bravery of the person who is troubled, the inventiveness, the beauty of the feeling of that person.

                (*To Melinda*): You had many different emotions in a short span of time, and everyone was there with you in her or his own particular way. It was a very equal sort of experience among us, so that you weren't the identified patient. You were somebody heroically pursuing something very difficult. It's a whole different sense. And so everyone got to remember heroic instances (*Looking around the room.*) You've taken the sword. You became the woman. You remembered that marvelous dream and the courage it took to stand in the full moon and be seen doing that.

                We talked about this at the beginning today: the difficulty felt, especially as a woman, being seen as powerful, or decisive, or as telling the interior truth, or as offering an unfathomable mystery. These are very powerful experiences that you share very naturally if you are in the dream together, or passing around the crystal.

                By your expression of feeling and by agreeing to go further, you have a powerful and positive effect on everyone. Everyone is equally and gracefully moved. And yet, each person is individual in experience. Yours is clearly Holly's way and yours is clearly Melinda's.

Melinda: I am trying to remember what you (Eric) suggested or asked, when you (Holly) first came up with the lady and with the female figure. Do you remember?

Holly: What do you see? You are looking at the lake, and what do you see?

Eric: Yes, what do you see? You'll see the solution.

Holly: Did you see a woman as a solution?

Melinda: Yes.

Jan: I saw just a parting of my cloud as a bright light and then put the woman onto it.

Holly: When you said, "Something will come up out of the lake," I didn't have my eyes shut. It was just there.

Eric: It's really convincing and interesting that way. In the kind of psychotherapy we are all taught to do, you could spend weeks trying to identify the problem and its origins and searching into yourself. But you just *saw* it and then it's so convincing. What comes out is this marvelous dream, these very sympathetic feelings, your sense of yourself as a woman and person. And all of that appears not as a difficult matter of understanding, but as something you can start to use. It's so immediate that it's convincing.

It pops up. If you have the black box with the lid open, it is what comes out. It's not Pandora's box alone, full of problems, but rather the box with the solution and the solution to the problem comes out because the solution is down in the unknown problems. And it really is, too. Even though people give lip service to that, you can experience it.

FOLLOW-UP

In June of that year, I spoke with Melinda by phone. She told me that she was still with her partner, and that they bought a house together. She said that she was happy.

Developing Alternative Knowledge Through Imagery

As kingfishers catch fire, dragonflies draw flame;
As tumbled over rim in roundy wells
Stones ring; like each tucked string tells, each hung bell's
Bow swung finds tongue to fling out broad its name;
Each mortal thing does one thing and the same:
Deals out that being indoors each one dwells;
Selves—goes its self; *myself* it speaks and spells,
Crying *What I do is me: for that I came.*

—*Gerard Manley Hopkins (1995)*

The way in which a narrative of images can be constructed in therapeutic conversations will be shown again in these next several examples. While we know from individual experience the pains and triumphs of our "sense of self" and "life story," the ways of forming ourselves and our stories have always been more obscure, unseen.

It's been part of my intention to develop the connectedness of focused attention, visual imagery, communicative language, human relationship, and personal identity, and to show the seams of this connectedness in different lights. Seriously disordered lives, like those of people called schizophrenic, also are constructed from these fabrics.

Margaret Singer's (cited in Staff, 1979) work on conversation in families with young adults diagnosed schizophrenic substantiates the idea that "certain properties of verbal behaviors . . . manifest how people are able to focus their attention," and that both meaning and attention wander when language is less "visualizable," when it is less concrete, visual, and specific. She concludes that:

> *The correlation between the nonvisualizableness in the parents' conversation and the severity of dysfunction in the schizophrenic is quite high. Forcing use of more visual, concrete language is a prescription to be considered. (p. 2)*

Bateson's studies of schizophrenic conversation led him to notice that "in extreme cases there may be nothing left but a stolid acting out of the message, 'There is no relationship between us.' " The double bind is "summarized by saying that it is an experience of being punished precisely for being right in one's own view of the context." So, "the identified patient sacrifices himself to maintain the sacred illusion that what the parent says makes sense," and "the victims are faced with a trap, to avoid which would be to destroy the very nature of self" (cited in Haley, 1981, p. 30). We have seen this effect of misplaced loyalty on the self in many of the lives we've described and also in many difficulties of life both less and more perilous and punitive to persons than is schizophrenia.

To restore the sense of self requires works of attention, visualization, communication, and relationship. In these works, the freedom and expansiveness of meaning woven in the fabric of visual metaphor help us to develop alternative knowledge of life and of the self. A therapist, seeing her family problem as a tornado over the Great Plains, was filled with "exciting, risky emotions." She said, "Usually, when talking about my sister, I feel anxious and depressed, but talking like *this* I feel calm in the center of it." How the garments of the self are tailored, taken out, and refit to provide comfort and ease of movement in lived experience are addressed in these next four stories:

Tensegrity

R.C., a 50-year-old doctoral student, arrived in therapy with the goal of achieving "a better belief in myself." His dissertation concerned the relationship of architecture to human spirituality. When asked the color of the feeling of the project, he said, "It's magenta. A feeling of equidistance from God."

A number of uneven relationships in his life had left him with humbled emotions and uneasy notions of his place with others. Asked the color of self-confidence, he said, "Red–purple–orange, a reassuring force. Elongated, like redwood trees. That's the image I didn't know when I came in. I can't ignore this fact about me! The image makes me feel all right with myself. It's a positive view of myself." Asked, "If redwoods, then what about your dissertation?" he replied, "Then what is all the fuss? I feel rather positive about myself."

A hiker in the redwoods all of his life, he immediately strolled with himself: "The image of the redwood tree is a rich, symbolic image of the myself that's recognizable; that I can handle." Some months later, he noted, "The dissertation has become just a challenging little walk through the woods."

A therapist following this hiker first notices his goal, "better belief in myself," and the arena in which the goal is to be accomplished, the dissertation. The goal takes the place of the "symptom" in strategic therapy in providing a compass for the journey. The "feeling of equidistance," a nice spatial design, will resolve his feelings of shameful insufficiency. These feelings are given a place as well:

E.G.: What does this humbling tendency look like?
R.C.: Like a shrew.
E.G.: Where does it live?
R.C.: Between my shoulders on my back. (A *place of great tension in his body*.)
E.G.: What does its den look like?
R.C.: Dark, messy, smelly, and pungent.

E.G.:   Does it eat tension?

R.C.:   Yes. The tension in my neck lessens.

E.G.:   Can the shrew live in the cracks of the redwood? Suppose you make a cave for it with food and a paper nest? A wild beast in a domestic setting.

R.C.:   That's nice. The image helps the tension. It helps balance me.

E.G.:   Suppose you clean up the old nest?

R.C.:   It allows me to make a home.

The great, upright redwood and the busy shrew are symbiotes. Walking among the trees, we appreciate all the life they contain.

To add to this metaphor of enduring life, motion, and value, R.C. and I shared an article I found on "The Architecture of Life." There, Ingber (1998) discusses "tensegrity structures," architechtonic forms that self-assemble and form systems that stabilize themselves by balancing the forces of tension and compression. "Very simply, transmission of tension through a tensegrity array (distributes) forces to all interconnected elements and, at the same time, couples or tunes the whole system mechanically as one" (p. 56). Geodesic forms are pictured in scales from cell cytoskeletons to Fuller's huge, domed buildings.

Ingber cites evidence that modifying cell shape instructs cells to switch between genetic programs:

> The important principle here is the manner in which a structure shapes itself and holds its subcomponents together in three-dimensional space; this characteristic is what defines the way the structure as a whole will behave. (pp. 52, 56)

Discussion and imagining of the tensegrity space resolved one of R.C.'s painful headaches. "I'm not sure how I arrived at this, but it is working. It makes sense. I sense the beginning of health here. The way I'm growing now is the correct way. I feel righted. You're teaching me to recognize how my healing is going." Later on, R.C., some 200 pages into the text of his dissertation, noted, "I am righting myself. I am equal to other persons, not groveling to them."

Hard Reality

Toby, a married 30-year-old man, had became stuck in a low-level desk job after some years of playing tournament-level tennis. From his intelligent, psychologically minded mother and father, he had learned to call his life experience "anxiety and depersonalization/dissociation experiences and agorophobia." Migraine headaches completed his discomfort. Toby was encouraged to glance at himself in the rear-view mirror "to notice who you are looking at" in order to compete with anxiety while driving, and with migraines.

His tennis experiences were utilized throughout our 10 sessions together. Toby told me that "the will to win is in the gut," and that the feeling of intensity during play is the feeling of being oneself: "There's nothing like it. It happens automatically. The ball becomes the most interesting thing in the world." At our fourth meeting, he told me that he had signed up for USTA membership, "to play differently and to feel good about myself." Psychological abstraction had been a thief, stealing his sense of sensation, motion, exuberance; of himself. At our sixth meeting, Toby said, "My consciousness was different when playing tennis: I was awake! My body was excited in a good way."

By our third hour, Toby was experiencing little anxiety while driving: "I didn't think psychotherapy was supposed to work so fast. I'll have a little different experience (while driving) and then I'll glide right through it." The ability to focus, notice, glide to the ball, and follow through on a stroke are "unconscious learnings" Toby carried with him. Applying them to his problems allowed him to use his own experience to master the psychological assertiveness of others over his life. Toby described things this way at our sixth meeting:

> When I felt distracted, I looked in the mirror. It was fantastic! When I stop feeling like myself, the whole world around me is pressing down on me. I can't take the hard reality of the moment. After looking in the mirror at myself, I came into focus. The environment was not a threat.

Other discoveries followed:

Some of the thoughts I had about my body before, when I was anxious, were spurious and irrational. Some of the thoughts that were disturbing before can't exist anymore as a bother. They've evolved. Since I was 16, I've had anxiety inside my cranium. Now, I'm driving the car. I'm in control of my behavior. I'm amazing myself!

Now when I'm alone it's not a desperate feeling. I feel like I have another egg in my basket besides my wife: tennis and my wife. And my wife-egg is smaller now. I'm less dependent. I want to travel to a trade show on the East Coast, by myself. Tennis can help with flying.

Toby's remarks about therapy show the difference that appreciative attention to the virtues, skills, and style of the person can make and how we can learn from each other:

Psychotherapy is like pulling things from deep inside—like a rabbit out of a hat. I'm making these discoveries myself; you're like a reminder. I'm getting in touch with how I feel emotionally and physically and it worked very quickly. It felt like magic. I haven't had an anxious experience since then.

Looking to Shine

A Holocaust survivor's daughter, now in middle age, was about to take professional licensing exams in counseling for the first time. As a child in Israel, she had been ostracized by neighbors prejudiced against her family because of their past victimization by the Nazis. She feared that her fiancé's father, a well-known dentist, would pressure them to terminate their engagement if he found out about her family.

In our work together, she identified aqua as the feeling of competence, "brown–black goo" as the color of anxiety. When she moved the colors around, the goo broke into little globules. We conceived of this anxiety as the social feelings of others toward her. As she said about taking her deserved place in society, "You're not supposed to do that—to succeed. To be in that place means to be punished."

After our first meeting, she reported, "I practiced in the waiting room. It was easy to clean up the goo. It's paper. It's not real. I can tear it up."

Asked to scoop all of it up, she said, "There's a pocket of it near my ovary on the right side. It's amazing how much there is in it!" About 30 seconds of scooping cleaned it out. She was advised to blow air into it to eliminate bacteria.

Against her fear of being seen as "a pretender, a fraud," she was asked to wear the sky-blue color of her daughter's love for her as a veil. "Keep the veil" released strong emotions of relief and laughter.

In our third and final session, she said, "I'm excited, not afraid. I'm looking to shine!" Reporting that her body still felt too much adrenaline, she was asked to inform her body, and to unplug the electric current of fear. She then said, "I *truly* am excited and I know the vignettes. My body is quiet. I love it. I can feel my own body energy flowing. I'm relaxed, in touch with my body completely. It feels wonderful: doable!" She passed her exams on her first try.

To Write the Self Into Being

Ozma and I spent several years together, meeting every few weeks. Part of her story was told under "Knowledge Through Action"; another part is told here. Ozma claimed that she could never draw a picture or tell a story. One night though, she dreamed of telling me her *own* story:

> *It was complete. It was wonderful . . . a whole new knowing—this is what it's like to create a story—it created itself. I've never before told a story . . . It was not my history—I was suddenly privy to the meaning of me and I was telling it.*

In another dream, half a year later, she told her first story:

> *I was striding barefoot over the green hills of Africa. Where is the story? And out of the sky came a piece of paper with an image on it. It was so natural. No anxiety. I'm not outside the circle anymore. Just a small change where there was no change.*

Ozma told me a joke a couple of weeks later, saying, "I hope you recognize that I just told you a story." And, in the new year, "I have good news. I have my story started: 'She sat, as usual, on the front step, waiting for the earthquake.' Now that I can do it, what will I write?" She was encouraged to write, "How to Go About It," and did so:

> We're now going about converting the block to the writing. There had seemed to be no words for the feeling . . . they found their way to the paper. As soon as I have a pen and paper, I have feelings. It's done. It's happened.

Ozma read at the age of 2, "looking for meaning." She bought a pen and paper with her childhood allowance, but couldn't draw or write stories. All her adult life, she had found social ways of others to imitate, as she avoided institutionalization. Now, she said, "I'm discovering *my* customs, anthropologically." Our mutual anthropology became discussions held with a sheet of butcher paper on the floor between us and a box of crayons spilled out. We'd talk and Ozma would write words and make images in color on the paper. The project came to be called, "The Myth of Finding Out What Happened to Words." Ozma's insightful remarks are culled from several meetings:

> I had a wonderful experience of waking up with a story. In the barren space I might find something to say. I have a song, "I'm nobody's victim now." I'm dropping the dead language. The real growth happened because you let me do things my own way. It's a true thing that's happening.
>
> That original self of mine wanted to play. I want to play. That's all I'm here for. We're asking questions that are possible to answer! I've written something. Written something! I believed in being heard when I spoke and that enabled me to write. Brand new! It came out of our work. The play we do here is loosening things up.
>
> It's something now, to speak with my voice and now to put words to paper as they arise without forethought or purpose except to be purposeless. To write the self into being.

One day we drew a joke together and called it "The Bridge to Luxembourg." Ozma said, "That was kind of a weightless, weighty session." Soon after, she had a dream of "The Marvelous, Illuminated Menu," which we talked about while she drew it. Of this dream and drawing, she said:

> *This is all that I could want to say—all that I contain. This is com-*
> *pletely new. It's good enough. I love the feeling! Co-creating in this*
> *way seems to have been the only missing thing. It leads to myself, and*
> *to the beginning of naturalness, away from the lifelong self-conscious*
> *child, who was so stiff and afraid.*
>
> *The self is keening after finding out what to say. I wish to be part*
> *of a story. That's life! I saw it: in the story; in my body! There is, sort*
> *of, someone here.*

Ozma expresses best the sense that Jung (cited in Portman, 1952) stated this way: "From the psychological standpoint . . . I have called the mediating or 'uniting' symbol which necessarily proceeds from a great tension of opposites, 'the self' . . . an anthropomorphic image which we have merely named but not explained" (p. 111). The persons who have told their stories here stand for themselves, and our active contemplation of their lives and dreams allows us to share some of their emotion and struggle.

The question of how we can usefully think about these lived experiences and learn from them has accompanied this text, and is again engaged in the book's final chapter. What I have to say about therapy is heuristic: it ought to be tried on for size. Most of these considerations are gauged by appeals to one's own experience of life. Yet the work has several important antecedents in alchemy, yogic practices, and shamanism, and has affinities with several modern investigations into the relationships obtaining among brain functions, perception, language, imagery, and mathematics.

Chapter 5

The Structure of Healing

They should have apprehended the method of visualization and applied
the illimitable virtue thereof for exalting one's own condition.

—*W. Y. Evans-Wentz (1927)*

The *Tibetan Book of the Dead*, or *Bardo Thodol*, contains texts read to dying persons to guide them on through the terrors of death and rebirth, "the fearful ambush of the *bardo*." But the situations for which it prescribes forms of guided meditation are more general than that of dying. *Bardo* denotes an "intermediate" state, a state of consciousness and of uncertainty, of which six are named: the state of waking consciousness, the state of dream consciousness, the state of trance consciousness in meditation, the state of the experiencing of death, the state of consciousness of rebirth, and the state of the experiencing of reality. In these periods of transition, uncertainty, and, as we would say, anxiety, the person is counseled to be steadfast in face of the attraction and fear exercised by the images that "embody his or her own intellect." As with anxiety, this task becomes more difficult

242

the longer uncertainty obtains, and the images confronting the person become more horrific the longer the person fails to grasp his or her "present intellect, in real nature void, not formed into anything . . . the very reality," or, as we would say, the self.

The Buddhist view makes reality, self, and mind synonymous and, as in the *Bardo Thodol*, provides exercises and guidance in countering the fear and anxiety that bar one from the experience of seeing things truly. In her biography of Jung, Von Franz (1975) claims that his rediscovery of active imagination is a "return to the oldest known forms of meditation, as they existed before the subsequent development into yoga, Buddhist meditation, and Taoist alchemy." She thus ties yoga, alchemy, Tibetan Buddhist practice, and the devices of shamanism to their common use of visualization to allow liberation. She cites a Chinese Taoist text: "The wise man centers himself, concentrates and thus is able to rise to higher spheres and descend into the lower, and distinguish there the things which it would be proper to do."

This guidance about "what to do" in the changing situations of life is provided by the bonze to the dying Tibetan, or by the shaman to a client. Followers of Jung's work emphasize the function of the analyst in guiding active imagination so that one is able to experience the "transcendent function." R. F. C. Hull's (1971) bibliography of Jung's references to active imagination is useful for those interested in the correspondences, as is Von Franz's (Von Franz & Hillman, 1971) chapter in *Lectures on Jung's Typology*. Attaining to the "middle sphere" through active imagination is said to create the "transcendent function." Ego awareness is detached from identification with certain functions of experiencing and the person comes to resemble a Zen master: "At this moment one transmits, as it were, his feeling of life into an inner center, and the four functions remain only as instruments which can be used at will, taking them up and putting them down again."

I'll return to consider the sources of archetypal psychology in the next section, examining the concept of "archetype" and some of the associated therapeutic methods. Still, all psychotherapeutic methods have been in the public domain for thousands of years. The Buddha himself proclaimed that he had seen the ancient way, and followed it. There are as many ways of doing therapy as there are of experiencing life, and modern therapies use posture, art, imagination, relationship, attentional processes, and learning, as in bioenergetics, art therapy, guided fantasy, Gestalt therapy, hypnotherapy, and cognitive-behavioral therapy. In just this way, the yogic disciplines set out from the basic life experiences of vision, posture, sound, and pattern to develop their methods of visualization, mudra, mantra, and mandala.

Suffering and change are the problems to which yoga addresses its methods (the problems of "stress" and "growth," if we prefer a modern usage). These methods are experimental, and use both homology—the similarity of structure between patterns of events—and paradox—"an assertion seemingly contradictory . . . that yet may be true in fact"—to liberate persons from that suffering.

Homology is the basic process of representation itself, as when our words in the therapist's office are taken to represent patterns of our behavior toward our parents years ago. All ritual partakes of this sense that one set of things may represent another, or that thought may represent deeds. Mircea Eliade (1963), the historian of religions, cites homology as the principle of thought binding origin myths, healing practices of the shamans, and current forms of life in a society:

> This fact, that the cosmogonic myth can be applied on various planes of reference, seems to us especially significant. The man of the traditional societies feels the basic unity of all kinds of "deeds," "works" or "forms" whether they are biological, psychological or historical. An unsuccessful war can be homologized with a sickness, with a dark, discouraged heart, with a sterile woman, with a poet's lack of inspiration, as with any other critical existential situation in which man is driven to despair.

Still, there are methods that are more appropriate for one sort of situation than for another, or, more accurately, styles of working that utilize common principles in varying ways, according to the attributes of the patient and the customs of the times. Jung (1961) says, "In one analysis I can be heard talking the Adlerian dialect, in another, the Freudian." Von Franz (Von Franz & Hellman 1971) notes that intuitive types may do active imagination in clay, thinking types by dance, sensation types by writing weird fiction. In the fourth century B.C., Tantric Yoga was developed, parallel to the unfolding of gnosticism, hermetism, and alchemy, and specifically addressing itself to the men and women of Kali Yuga, the age of greatest darkness and degeneration according to Indian cosmologies. Eliade (1969) says:

> *The syndrome of Kali Yuga is marked by the fact that it is the only*
> *age in which property alone confers social rank, wealth becomes the*
> *only motive of the virtues, passion and lust the only bonds between*
> *the married, falsehood and deception the first condition of success in*
> *life, sexuality the sole means of enjoyment, while external, merely rit-*
> *ualistic religion is confused with spirituality. For several thousand*
> *years, be it understood, we have been living in Kali Yuga.*

The appropriate methodology for persons suffering in these ways begins directly with their bodily experience of life, utilizing the passions of sexuality in a yogic discipline, like tantric yoga. The materialism of the age, that "degeneration of symbolism" (Eliade, 1962) once expressed in the maxim, "If you can't eat it, screw it, or sell it, what is it?" is also met by special forms of yoga. Zimmer (1960) describes a process of meditation that begins with the observance of cult rituals—"offerings, whispered formulas, a swinging of lamps"—and concrete images of the deities, which are adorned with gifts. Little by little, "the whole outward ceremonial is repeated in a process of progressive visualization," and the rituals are replaced by inner processes:

> *Each day the rites become more intense; the inner process they are*
> *intended to provoke runs through the seven stages of the Yoga exer-*
> *cise, which is associated with the image of a god: from the contem-*
> *plation of the material image to the substitution of its inner*
> *likeness . . . then from an inner contemplation of this image in which*
> *contemplator and image exist separately to a union of the two*
> *(samadhi). . . .*

Paradoxically, this concentration on experience can lead one to liberation from the constraints of that experience, just as it is hoped that viewing the Glide Foundation films of every manner of sexual passion will free the viewer from hang-ups about sexual feeling and expression. The homology of mental and experiential structure is what chiefly interests us in this discussion, and specifically the place of imagery in representation of the world and in the adaptation of organisms to changing circumstances. But paradox is always at work also, in the reframing of experience and in the use of ritual to homologize current experience to the "sacred time" of myth, so that what Eliade (1958) calls the "rupture of the plane" of ordinary space, time, and paired, opposing concepts can occur.

Schwartzman (1982) even claims that "metaphor's basic characteristic is semantic paradox because the speaker or writer is in some sense *not* asserting the statement he or she makes" (p. 116). Emphasizing dissonances in family communication, he writes, "In this process, the response to paradoxical injunctions links the dissonance, becomes a metaphor for it, and is a social structural analogue for the creation of metaphor" (p. 118).

Within the structure of ritual healing, initiation, or meditation, paradoxical formulations of speech and relatedness, such as appear in the Zen traditions or, more recently, in the therapeutic work of Erickson (1980) and Haley (1963), lead to transcendence of the paired constructs that constrain understanding and living: "crazy" and "sane" may be transmuted to "crazy like a fox." Bateson (cited in Brand, 1974) nicely describes the positive experience of paradox:

> A paradox is a contradiction in which you take sides—both sides. Each half of the paradox proposes the other . . . If you sweat out one of these paradoxes you embark on a voyage which may include hallucinations and trance . . . But you come out knowing something you didn't know before, something about the nature of where you are in the universe.

The authority of these traditions—ascetic, mystical, or therapeutic—derives, says Eliade (1962), from "the direct, experimental knowledge of all that constitutes the bases and processes of the human body and the psychomental life." A parallel tradition with the yogic disciplines has been that of alchemy, elegantly researched and described in Eliade's (1962) *The Forge and the Crucible*. There he shows close connections between shamanism; the arts of song, dance, and poetry; and the art of the smith and the magician. The overlapping practices of these disciplines were handed down in initiation mysteries, the structure of which consists of the experience of suffering, death, and rebirth, leading to a transmutation of the person. The alchemical transmutation, the great work of the alchemists, can be seen as an initiation mystery in which they "projected onto matter the initiatory function of suffering."

As the texts cited by Eliade (1962), and by Jung (1968) in his *Psychology and Alchemy*, make clear, alchemists sought through relationship to matter to cause it to pass through four phases (black, white, yellow, and red) in order to transform it and themselves into the "philosopher's stone," that treasure that is as common as pebbles, but to which only the adept can find access. The water used in this process is, says Jung (Jung & Pauli, 1955), "the *deus ex machina* of alchemy, the wonderful solvent, the word *solutio* being used equally for a chemical solution and for the solution of a problem" (p. 37). The vessel of transformation is best seen as the self and, as the alchemist Zosimos (cited in Von Franz, 1975) said, "One the procedure, one the vessel, one the stone."

To relate with matter, the alchemists sought to use dreams, meditation, and fantasying, *phantasia vera et non phantastica*, that various authors cite as the same activity Jung rediscovered as active imagination. In alchemy, the practitioner guides matter into spirit, as the shaman—the guide, healer, psychopomp of traditional societies—guides souls. That the shaman is "the great specialist in the human soul" who alone "sees" it, for he knows its "form" and its "destiny" (Eliade, 1962), becomes important to this developing complex of yoga, alchemy, and shamanism in their relation to active imagination. The shaman suffers initiation, death, and rebirth in his own experience, not "symbolically." He "sees the forms of life," and thus can "demolish the barriers between dream and present reality" (Eliade, 1962) and reestablish the lost soul in the ritual space of the Great Time or the Dream Time.

The method used for these transcending maneuvers is, we have argued, homologous with that of visualization or active imagination. If it is so that a concentration on imagined experience can constrain, change, and transcend physical behavior patterns—and who has ever held otherwise?—then the question of the relationship of these thought forms to the active, lived experience of life and to the understanding of that life must be asked. Before considering current views of this relationship, we'll examine the Jungian view of "archetype" as displayed through active imagination.

Archetype and Image

We approach the id with analogies.

—*Sigmund Freud (1965)*

Image is psyche.

—*Carl Jung, (1968b, p. 75)*

Replication is a cardinal principle of the physical sciences, adored by psychologists, yet difficult to adhere to in experimental situations with people. In the canons of social science, criteria of replication are usually coupled with attempts at prediction, although it's been suggested by Orne (1962) that in research where "demand characteristics" are operative, *un*predictable or spontaneous subject responses can best fit a scientific model of psychology. Spontaneous subject reactions are especially telling, of course, when the data being considered are states of consciousness, rather than behaviors, since human experience is related—told—and verbal report is subject to suggestion and "demand" from the experimenter or observer. The many reports of spontaneously revealed experiences during therapy, in which subjects were unaware of a body of literature dealing with identical experiences and the therapist had no expectation of such outcomes, can be presented as unpredicted replications of important constancies of mind and emotion. The discovery of archetypal images in the course of his therapeutic work gave rise to Jung's view of the relation of images to what since has been called "the problem of mind."

An instance of the occurrence of an archetypal image in the course of psychotherapy will clarify what I mean. Ellen came to her session lonely and distraught after the collapse of an intimate relationship. Asked to speak of her emotion, she said she was fearful, and when asked, "What emotion would you feel if you were no longer fearful?" she said, "Sad." "And if no longer sad?" "Angry. But if I weren't angry, I'd be empty." When she pictured the lonely emptiness, Ellen imagined a long, dark tunnel. But, suddenly, at the depth of despair, she was confronted by the figure of a vibrant, wild, lovely woman. This figure, who appeared when "no one was there," guided her, gave her cheer and courage, fought for her, and gave her gifts of great value. One of the gifts was most remarkable. Ellen was given a "golden bough" whose fruit enabled her to enter "an inner world"—a vast desert with alien, masculine features, and huge rocks among which it was difficult to find a passage.

Now, *The Golden Bough*, Frazer's (1922) classic study, had sat unopened on my shelf for years. Ellen had never heard of the book; I had never read it. When I did, I found that the golden bough, which Frazer identifies as a type of mistletoe, was held to be able to "open all locks," and that Virgil had the hero, Aeneas, carry such a bough with him on his descent into the underworld as a living being. The fearful, narrow passageway and the labyrinthian or chthonic journeys are all, says Eliade (1962), patterns of initiation, which, we have seen, include the sequential suffering, death, and rebirth of the initiate.

As a process in living, such initiation may be guided by inner voices or visions, as in the shaman's work, or by outer guides, as when one is initiated into various clubs, societies, professions, and crafts. In therapy, the therapist is guide, but, as with all structures of healing, the guide may be carried as an internal image, either concurrent with the therapist's physical presence or at times when the patient is out of sight of the consulting room. Surely every practitioner has had people relate with some relief that they "thought of you when I got scared; of what you would say to me if you were here, and that helped pull me through." The archetype of healing, or initiation, exists through this relatedness of patient and therapist or novice and master. It does not reside in either one of them. As Jung (cited in Casey, 1974) said: "The fact is that the single archetypes are not isolated, but are in a state of contamination, of the most complete, mutual interpenetration and interfusion." Put another way, the image, or the single word that stands for it, obscures the relatedness that is the structure of the image. Eliade (1969) comments:

> *It is therefore the image as such, as a whole bundle of meanings, that is true and not any one of its meanings, nor one alone of its many frames of reference. To translate an image into a concrete terminology by restricting it to any one of its frames of reference is . . . to annul it as an instrument of cognition.*

Images are instruments of cognition, and are adequate both for dealing with problems of living and for understanding meanings, as "the concepts of complex psychology are, in essence, not intellectual formulations, but names for certain areas of experience" (Jung, 1959). These areas, the phenomena of human psychology, are best represented as events or interactions, not as entities.

To discuss these phenomena, one needs a language tied to relatedness and matrix. I'm arguing here that "dream language," or the archetypal structures developed though active imagining, provide proper understandings of human events, especially those we cannot speak about in the common language. Believing the strictures of the family therapists, systems theorists, or even psychoanalysts, who all remind us that individuals' lives are interdependent, we are left without terms that express this reality when we speak with each other.

Usually, the dilemma is resolved adequately by the use of anecdote, metaphor, or moral fable. This is apt, I think, for the picturing of relationships through imagery, and the consistent vocabulary provided by these images (the archetypal figures and the dramas of life) is a perfect representation or homolog of complex human experience. Dreams are what the Tibetans call *rang-snang* (Evans-Wentz, 1927), one's own thought forms or visions. This is true whether the dreams are spontaneous or brought forth spontaneously as imaginations in the therapist's office. Dreams provide understanding of what Wittgenstein (1958) calls "what has to be accepted, the given, the forms of life." That is, hearing and visualizing and experiencing an active imagination, one can understand forms of life and relationship. Speaking about the forms of life may be adequately accomplished by telling the dream (Greenleaf, 1973; Zucker, 1967).

Active imagination is thought of, in the Jungian notation, as a spontaneous amplification of archetypes into images. These images are conceived to be visual forms of the patterns of the organization of thought, "the typical modes of apprehension which . . . form an inner self-image, so to speak, of human instincts or of their structure" (Von Franz, 1975). Weaver (1973) writes: "Active imagination leads to the structure of the psyche . . . it is here one finds the basic struggles of mankind, the psychic growth and the forms upon which consciousness rests." Along with an experience of the interrelated forms of the archetypes, there comes change, for "we enter into the drama of the psyche itself by participating in what is psychically real: in what is capable of changing us in some basic way" (Casey, 1974).

Whether we emphasize the limitations of English or the ubiquity of visual thinking, dream language, couched in spatial terms like the common language and dramatically structured in visualized forms, provides proper and available understandings of human events, conceived as sets of functional relationships. Jung's concept of archetype was an attempt to represent this state of affairs, but there are, as well, several more recent formulations regarding the explanation of thought, action, and mind, which converge to support the ancient intuitions described earlier, as well as the modern uses of imagery in the psychotherapies. The dovetailing of modern understandings of hypnosis with those of imagery has been noted. To this we can add writings from the fields of epistemology, paleoneurology, the psychology of vision, comparative linguistics, and mathematics.

Images and the Structure of Thought

> We are rooted in reality and remain so, we reduplicate it in a certain
> way by representing it. . . . one therefore can recognize it if one sees
> it. . . . This knowing . . . is really no duplication of seeing, but rather
> "a knowing in and through the very act of seeing." . . . What one
> would like to say is, "Seeing by seeing."
>
> —L. Wittgenstein *(cited in Brand, 1979, pp. 255–256)*

I've emphasized that the basis of active imagining lies in action, not in explanation. If the terms "action" and "meaning" are separated, then one would say that understanding "follows" action or that insight is preceded by change. In another view, there is no such separation. Piaget (cited in Calvin, 1994) emphasized that "intelligence is the sophisticated groping that we use when not knowing what to *do*" (p. 101). Gardner's (1973) reading of the "structuralists" has it that "one's own knowledge of states of reality comes about through transforming them; thus, the very actions which constitute thought lead ultimately to knowledge of thought."

We are accustomed to thinking that the actions that constitute thought are primarily manipulations of "verbal concepts," the more so the more secondary process, rational, or abstract the thought required. But this assumption is increasingly difficult to maintain. Not only Piaget's decades of experimental work, but the currents of modern scientific, philosophical, and psychological thought run against it.

In Attneave's (1974) WPA presidential address, he raised the question, "How do you know?" arguing that it is a truism that knowing involves representation, and that representation of one system by another rests on some homolog between system parts and/or relations of parts. He asked in what way representing the world, or "knowing," is important for survival, and concluded that knowing how (rather than knowing why) is the biologically crucial component of knowing. Knowing how to do things, or where or what they are—what to eat, how to find water, how to mate—is the most useful knowledge, and the knower associates objects and processes in the world according to their relationships with each other and the integrative functions they serve in living.

Given this situation, what sort of representation is feasible? In what form is the information about relations processed? Attneave contrasts the representational system of language, in which relations are represented by categorical words, with an analog system, such as a map, for which relations among categories (rivers, roads, towns) are represented by relations on the surface of the map. Now, Attneave argues that many (although not all) psychological functions entail analog representation. He cited the representation of number as one such function, certain psychophysiological operations as others. Then he concentrated his attention on most important instance of analog representation: the system for representing physical space, imagined space as well as perceived space, since, as he noted, "The animal knows where the water hole is." He cited studies by Shepard (1978) that show that when a mental image is rotated, "the representation of the object is in fact going through all of the intermediate aspects in a continuous manner." These imaginary scenes and their active transforms enable persons to experiment with given courses of action before committing themselves to act. In this "work space," the associated strong emotions that accompany action may also be evoked and transformed, although Attneave does not make this explicit in his discussion.

Continuing from the analog nature of representation and its close ties with spatial perception and location, Attneave asks how the representational structures get their meaning. He notes that descriptions coded in words generate imagery, but goes on to say:

> There is another aspect of meaning that I think is even more essential. I can imagine going for a walk and encountering a dog, or a bird or a wildcat in the woods, but how the scenario progresses beyond that point is highly dependent on which one of the three I imagine

meeting. The rules of the game are by no means the same for dogs, birds and wildcats.

So, he argues, the utility of identifying situations and categories of objects lies in our access to their rules of interaction with us and with each other: their relationships. The connection of meanings with imagery and with rules of action is shown also by such phenomena as the reports of chess masters, who can reconstruct complete positions after cursory glances at the board. They do this by remembering functional relationships among the pieces—which piece guards which others, for instance— not by memorizing the place of each piece (or of its absence) on each of 64 squares. "In other words, the rules of the game turn out to be quite essential to the way the position is remembered and reconstructed." The philosophical activity initiated by Wittgenstein makes this relationship among meaning, rule, and the forms of life a touchstone of the nature of human thought, on the one hand, and of actions between persons in the world, on the other. That these "forms" are sensory and visual finds intense expression in passages on the "givenness" of experience:

> *Immediate experience, which has its meaning in itself, is to be accepted. It is a form of life. Even if we determine reality, even if we, in common actions, create something new, the fact that we do this or can do this is to be understood as a given form of life, and only as such. What is to be accepted, the given are—one could say—forms of life. It is only possible here to describe and to say, "such is human life."*
>
> *The face of others is also given to me immediately: their facial expression, their suffering, their anger, their mood, their friendliness, their gaze. . . . Are not goodness, cowardice, mildness, first and foremost given in the face itself? . . . Perhaps the ordinary givens, as given to me in primary forms of life, are colors, space, time, the faces of others, their ways of acting and other such givens. (Cited in Brand, 1979, pp. 262–265)*

In discussing "The Schreber Case" in Chapter 4, I showed some of the consequences of adopting Wittgenstein's epistemological position for the understanding of meanings in psychotherapy and for some of the standards of proof obtaining for inferences about causes and motives. For further confirmation of the origins of this epistemology, those without a taste for philosophy may look to the natural sciences.

H. J. Jerison (1976), writing on "Paleoneurology and the Evolution of Mind," deals with fossil evidence of the evolution of vertebrate nervous systems. He concentrates on the relationship between sensory-motor systems and the adaptive function of increasing encephalization. For the early hominids, wide-ranging nonarboreal primates, olfactory systems had been much reduced relative to those of such animals as wolves, who use scent to mark their territories. To develop adequate range markers, hominids required the use of auditory, visual, and vocal information. Humans could begin to develop language as a viable evolutionary direction. The conscious experience of the organism would result from a systematic neural integration of sensory information from the different modalities.

The neurophysiologist W.H. Calvin (1994), also writing about the emergence of intelligence in hominids, suggests that brain specialization involves a core facility common to language, the planning of hand movements, and music and dance. High intelligence in humans is achieved along with the ability to coordinate rapid, ballistic movements. The specialization has an evolutionary rationale:

> Omnivores have more basic moves in their general behavior (than herbivores) because their ancestors had to switch between many different food sources. They need more sensory templates too—mental images of things such as foods and predators for which they are "on the lookout." Their behavior emerges through the matching of these sensory templates to responsive movements. (p. 101)

Calvin finds that the language cortex also organizes "novel sequences of various kinds, both sensations and movements, for both the hands and the mouth" (p. 105). Play allows animals to try out novel combinations of search image and movement, for which uses may be found later on.

This analysis may seem to point to language as an integrative modality for understanding and communication among the early ancestors of men and women, but Jerison, as Calvin, scrutinizes the nature of language for its utility in providing a representation or model of essentially sensory events occurring during an animal's life. Language is seen to be a "sensory–perceptual development" whose basic use is in the construction of models of reality expressed as mental imagery. The communicative functions of language are seen as clearly secondary.

Jerison claims that if selection pressures had led to the development of language primarily for communication, "We would expect the evolutionary response to be the development of 'prewired' language systems with conventional sounds and symbols." These inflexible systems of fixed-action patterns are quite characteristic of bird intelligence, but quite uncharacteristic of mammalian intelligence. In fact, birds and mammals evolved quite separately from two different subclasses of reptiles. Of the birds, Jerison says: "Their behavior is tightly bound to specific stimuli by fixed action patterns of response, in contrast to an 'intelligence' system in which varied patterns of stimuli are transformed into invariant objects." True, Dr. Skinner's pigeons are intelligent, but of a different mind (and neural organization) from that of those humans to whom they have been compared. Modern Pavlovians, too, have noted this difference:

> *Traditional descriptions of conditioning as the acquired ability of one stimulus to evoke the original response of another because of their pairing are shown to be inadequate. . . . Instead, conditioning is now described as the learning of relations among events so as to allow the organism to represent its environment. (Rescorla, 1988, p. 151)*

In a wry reminder that learning itself is social, even between species, Bertrand Russell (cited in Calvin, 1994) once remarked:

> *Animals studied by Americans rush about frantically, with an incredible display of hustle and pep, and at last achieve the desired result by chance. Animals observed by Germans sit still and think, and at last evolve the solution out of their inner consciousness. (p. 101)*

The flexible patterns and modifiability of our language and sensory integrative systems are organized and represented as mental images, not as stimulus–response patterns without thought. Jerison's conclusions from the fossil record echo other of our major themes:

> *We need language more to tell stories than to direct actions. In the telling, we create mental images in our listeners that might normally*

be produced only by the memory of events. . . . .Mental images
should be as real as the immediately experienced real world.

Visual Thinking

How the world is experienced visually and reconstructed in imagery is
the subject of Rudolph Arnheim's (1969) *Visual Thinking*. He begins
with the observation that vision is an active, selective, and purposive
process that evolved as a biological aid for survival. To see is never to see
aimlessly, in the "blooming, buzzing confusion" attributed to infants.
Rather, it is, from the beginning, to see simple shapes, and hence to perform an abstraction. Releaser mechanisms, which integrate mother–child
behavior through the response of the organism to simple shapes and colors, are an early form of seeing, a spontaneous grasp of pattern and structure. The perception of shape is itself the grasping of generic, structural
features of the world. In this sense, concepts are percepts, perceptual
images, and thought is the handling of these images.

For thinking to be valid, images must be structurally similar to (iso-
morphic with) the features of the situation. But these features—"the primary physical facts from which the sense of sight takes off—are not a
bewildering spread of random samples, but highly consistent processes of
change." Concepts are, for Arnheim, like the Gestalt term *prag-
nanzstufen*, "phases of clear-cut structure within a sweep of continuous
transformation." Concept formation is then like the perception of structural simplicity, and this perception is one of relationships rather than of
absolute values and of genera rather than the experience of particulars.
Arnheim's biting description of the ways in which digital computers and
human beings solve analogy problems—a common test of intelligence—
elucidates this notion of concept.

Problem solving is the most important function of visual thinking.
Often a problem presents itself perceptually in the form of something
looking incomplete and the solution may be found when the situation
points to a completion. Will Attneave meet a dog or a wildcat in the
woods? What sort of tail is that near the oak tree? Or is it just a
shadow? Distortion in perception calls forth abstraction and the need
to do something to rectify the situation. Again, the situation represents
a pattern of forces seen as shape, form, and concept, and tied to some

goal image, under pressure of which the problem situation restructures itself perceptually: "Whew. Just a shadow of that limb of the tree. No need to run."

Now think again of dreams: Dreams give a picture of our own situation in life. The picture is related to symbols, taking symbol to mean, as Watzlawick, Beavin, and Jackson (1967) do, "the representation in real magnitudes of something that is essentially an abstract function, an aspect of a relationship." Dreams picture functional relationships. As Bateson (1972) quips:

> —*A dream is a metaphor or tangle of metaphors. Do you know what a metaphor is?*
> —*Yes. If I say you are like a pig, that is simile. But if I say you are a pig, that is metaphor*
> —*That's right. A metaphor compares things without spelling out the comparison.....The dream elaborates on the relationship, but does not identify the (original) things that are related.*

For most of these relationships, there are no useful near-forms in English, which is a language that treats primarily of entities and objects, not of relationships, at least in the common speech. In fact, Capra (1975), in *The Tao of Physics*, laments the inability of even a technical, scientific form of English to reflect the dynamic conditions of relativity, uncertainty, and particle formation that are currently understood as the nature of the physical universe. Einstein (cited in Miller, 1984), in "Physics and Reality," reminds us of this dilemma in representational thinking:

> *The whole of science is nothing more than a refinement of everyday thinking. It is for this reason that the critical thinking of the physicist cannot possibly be restricted to the examination of concepts of his own specific field. He cannot proceed without considering critically a much more difficult problem, the problem of analyzing the nature of everyday thinking. (p. 13)*

Jerison, Attneave, Calvin, and especially Arnheim, all place language in some relationship with the imagery that represents our reality to us. Bruner (1990) reminds us of the strong structural kinship between fictional and empirical narratives:

> *Given the specialization of ordinary languages in establishing*
> *binary contrasts, why do none of them impose a once-for-all, sharp*
> *grammatical or lexical distinction between true stories and imagina-*
> *tive ones? ... We know from studies of the autobiographical form*
> *particularly that fictional forms often provide the structural lines in*
> *terms of which "real lives" are organized. (p. 52)*

From the side of linguistics, Whorf (1956) presents a compelling position that ties language forms to the sort of actions people take and to
the concepts (in the form of visual metaphors) that inform these actions.
It's important to note that in his view, English and the other Standard
Average European languages objectify basic experience, "so that we can
hardly refer to the simplest nonspatial situation without consistent resort
to physical metaphors."

Whorf contrasts the situation in the Standard Average European languages with that in Hopi, where tensors convey distinctions of degree,
rate, constancy, repetition, increase of intensity, sequence, etc. Gardner's
(1973) reading of Piaget emphasizes that infants perceive the modal and
vectorial aspects of behavior (open–closed, force and direction, balance,
and so forth) and reproduce these "simple structures, even while eliminating aspects closer to the physical properties of the stimulus, but differ-
ing in dynamic quality." This squares quite well with Arnheim's position
regarding perception. Here perception is tied to action sequences as well,
and, through them, to the development of knowledge. But this knowledge, following Whorf, is limited in linguistic expression by the peculiar
structure of English and its ties to spatial metaphor. To speak of ourselves
in words requires, if we use English, expressing ourselves to one another
in spatial metaphor, the language mode of our dreams.

The relationship between mental images and visual perception was
investigated by Finke (1986) and his colleagues. They found that the two
share many of the same neural processes in the human visual system and
that the image, once formed, functions in some respects like the object
itself. Not only do mental spatial transformations of objects correspond
with those of real-world objects as Shepard (1978) found, but images
activate similar neural mechanisms at lower levels in the visual system.
Then, says Finke, the mental images, having acquired visual characteristics, may in turn modify perception.

This proposed equivalence between perception and imagination implies a second-order isomorphism (Shepard, 1978) between the functional relations among mental images and those among perceived objects. This isomorphism represents an analog rather than a logical process of thought:

> *These analog processes seem to be particularly effective in dealing with complex spatial structures and operations on such structures . . . without . . . taking the time, making the effort or running the risk of carrying the operations out in physical reality. (p. 135)*

Gilbert (1991) extends this analysis of images to a description of thinking in "How Mental Systems Believe": "As perception construes objects, so cognition construes ideas." In a discussion of the ideas of Descartes and Spinoza, he notes that in both perception and cognition, "the representation of an object or idea is *believed*—that is, empowered to guide behavior as if it were true—prior to a rational analysis of the representation's accuracy." He asserts that perception not only is a metaphor for cognition but that "the propositional system of representation that underlies cognition is an evolutionary outgrowth of . . . the imaginal system of representation that underlies perception" (p. 108). Cognition inherits the tendency of perceptual systems to immediately treat all representations as if they were true. Gilbert's conclusion ties this notion of imagistic thought to its transmission in social communication:

> *In other words, a newly evolved cognitive system might treat socially communicated propositions as if they were visually transmitted images, believing what it comprehends (Life is a bowl of cherries) just as immediately and thoroughly as it believes what it sees (This is a bowl of cherries). Perhaps it is not entirely absurd to think of human understanding as a sensory system that uses the propositional assertions of others as data—a kind of vicarious observation . . . (p. 116)*

If mental simulation helps in hunting (Calvin, 1994), social communication (Gilbert, 1991), creative thought (Shepard 1978), and sheer survival (Attneave, 1974), it must have application to psychotherapy. Taylor, Pham, Rivkin, & Armor (1998) begin their discussion of mental simulation, self-regulation, and coping in terms now familiar to readers who have traveled this far along with me:

*What do we mean by the imagination? On the one hand, the term
may be used very generally to refer to the ability to conjure up
images, stories and projections of things not currently present and the
use of those projections for entertaining the self, planning for the
future and performing other basic tasks of self-regulation.*

*On the other hand, the term imagination may be used quite specif-
ically to refer to the mental activities that people engage in when they
want to get from a current point in time and place to a subsequent
one, having accomplished something in between, such as going on a
trip or writing a paper. (p. 429)*

Mental simulations, although imaginary, are not typically magical.
Through their links to perception they tend to verisimilitude. As nine
empirical studies (cited in Taylor et al., 1998) demonstrate, people asked
to rate the likelihood of hypothetical events are more likely to believe
that those events will actually occur after mental simulation than after
other focused cognitive activities about these events. This vision of possible futures through mental simulation aids in the management of affective states and problem-solving planning: the tasks of self-regulation and
coping.

We know that expressing thoughts and feelings by talking or writing
about traumatic events can be beneficial, even that immune changes and
health-center visits parallel the emotional effects over time (Pennebaker,
cited in Taylor et al., 1998). We also know that mental simulations that
consist of painful ruminations about trauma and that characterize depression can interfere with self-regulation. Taylor and his associates add to
this the finding that a fantasy of success based solely on an image of some
desired end state also interferes with self-regulation and diminishes coping. A corruption of social constructivism that claims, like EST, that we
"create our own realities" leads to the notion, "Think and be rich," and
to its destructive twin, "How do you think you contributed toward causing your cancer?" Taylor and his associates put matters plainly:

*The sport psychology literature and the relapse-prevention litera-
ture illustrate a particular kind of mental simulation that has been
found to be effective in leading to behavior change. The critical component . . . is an emphasis on simulating the process needed for reaching a goal. (p. 431)*

The relationship between mental representation and the achievement of goals has, we've said, been thought to rest on conscious decision. Yet modern research implicates perception of the external world in forming those representations into schemata of goal-directed action. Experimental psychologists have only recently adopted the view that the entire process is nonconscious.

Nonconscious Representation

Assumptions upon which much contemporary psychological research rests are shown to be impossible. Moment-to-moment psychological life—evaluations, judgments, motivation, social interactions, emotions, and goal-oriented behavior—must occur through nonconscious means if they are to occur at all.

(J. A. Bargh & T. L. Chartrand, 1999, p. 462)

Bargh and Chartrand (1999) cite extensive modern research to argue that automatic social perception induces the idea of action in the same way that other features of the environment do. A direct and automatic route that excludes conscious thought goes from the external environment via perception to action.

> To produce the empirical evidence on which these claims rest, we ... have conducted ... experiments in which goals, evaluations, and perceptual constructs ... were primed in an unobtrusive manner. Through use of these priming manipulations, the mental representations were made active to later exert their influence without an act of will and without the participants' awareness of the influence. Yet in all of these studies, the effect was the same as when people are aware of and intend to engage in that process. (p. 476).

One example of this is the natural tendency of people to imitate others' moods. Social interaction is facilitated, and people like each other better, when they take on the other's postures and behaviors. Emotions, moods, and evaluations, heretofore treated as subjective judgments, are shown to operate along the nonconscious route, "serving a kind of natural signaling function about the overall safety or danger one is in at the moment"

(p. 474). Conscious judgments, made during longer periods of deliberation, are no different from nonconscious, immediate ones.

Goals, like other mental representations, can become automatically activated by environmental features. "The goal, once activated, should operate to produce the same effects as if it had been consciously chosen" (p. 469). The individual doing so is found to have no awareness of having pursued that goal. Bargh and Chartrand cite corroborating evidence from brain activation patterns to show that "once activated, a goal operates in the same way whether activated by will or by the environment" (p. 470). And, these nonconscious goals "not only produce higher performance, but manifest the same classic qualities of motivational states as has been documented for conscious, intentional goal pursuit in years of research" (p. 472).

What Bargh and Chartrand call "the acquisition of automaticity," Gollwitzer (1999) calls "simple plans," "intentions that specify the when, where and how of responses leading to goal attainment" (p. 494). He develops therapeutic practices to achieve such goals as eliminating procrastination and drug addiction, writing that these function by "passing the control of one's behavior on to the environment" (p. 495), thus facilitating the initiation of action:

> In everyday life, therefore, one can expect people who have formed implementation intentions to initiate the intended goal-directed response when the critical situation is encountered in the same manner as people start driving when the traffic light changes from red to green—no conscious intent to press the gas pedal is needed. (p. 498)

These "strong effects of simple plans," established in Gollwitzer's experiments, echo Erickson's inventive strategies to initiate action in clinical settings. Kirsch and Lynn's (1999) "Automaticity in Clinical Psychology" discusses the role of placebo effects, hypnotic and nonhypnotic suggestion, and automaticity of behavior in promoting the clinical use of expectancies for the nonconscious facilitation of positive change.

Several surprising experimental and meta-analytic studies are cited, supporting this familiar architecture of therapeutic effectiveness. In a section called, "Listening to Prozac but Hearing Placebo," Kirsch and Lynn find that the proportion of effect size of Prozac on depression is duplicated by placebo in the range of 75%. The effect of nonantidepressent drugs was as great as that of Prozac and, again, "an inactive placebo duplicated 76% of this effect. . . . Thus, only one in six patients showed long-term clinical improvement following medication, but would not have done so following placebo" (p. 506).

Kirsch and Lynn applaud the ethical nature of hypnotherapy, which, unlike placebos, does not require deception for its effect. Yet they cite some astonishingly effective placebo studies, including one in which false biofeedback indicating sexual arousal was given to sexually dysfunctional women as they watched erotic films: "(Palace) reported that false VBV feedback . . . increased actual VBV in 100% of sexually dysfunctional women, and the increase in actual response occurred within 30 seconds of the expectation of an increase" (p. 507).

To underline the role of social expectation and communication in hypnosis, they note that "any procedure in which the participant believes can be used to induce hypnosis."

> *Among the procedures that have been used to induce hypnosis are telling people to relax, telling them to become more alert, having them pedal on an exercise bicycle, instructing them to close their eyes, instructing them to keep their eyes open, flashing lights in their eyes, sounding gongs, applying pressure to their heads, and having them ingest placebo pills. (p. 507)*

Expectancy also influences suggestibility, and studies show that the correlation between expectancy change and behavior change is of the order of $r = .69$. In some samples, most subjects score in the high range of hypnotic scales, and none score in the low range. Expectancy involves both automaticity and nonconsciousness:

> *At the moment of activation, all behavior is initiated automatically, rather than by conscious intention. . . . it is not the experienced automaticity of ideomotor responses that is an illusion, but . . . the experience of volition that is claimed to characterize everyday behavior. (p. 508)*

There is strong evidence that even the effect of imagery depends on expectancies. In a test of ideomotor responsiveness, the correlation between imagery absorption and behavioral response was not significant, whereas that between belief in ideomotor response through imagination and behavior was $r = .64$.

The relational matrix, which entrains expectancies, positive goals, implementation intentions, and nonconscious natural processes, is constructed between therapists and patients in a narrative hypnotherapy. Kirsch and Lynn write that a hypnotic context enhances therapeutic outcomes:

> Although this may require little more than using the word "hypnosis" as a label for relaxation training and imaginal rehearsal, it can augment therapeutic expectancies and treatment outcome to a clinically significant degree. . . . Also, because response sets can be strengthened by repetition, imaginative and behavioral rehearsal . . . can help . . . rather than merely talking about what they might do. (pp. 511–512)

Imaginative rehearsal utilizes those mental images that accompany action and that, we have argued, form a consciousness of action, depicted in dreams and other storied forms of narrative.

Structure Abstracted

The "manifest" dream-picture is the dream itself, and contains the whole meaning of the dream.—*Carl Jung* (1968b)

The system is then its own best explanation and the study of its present organization the appropriate methodology.

—*P. Watzlawick, J. H. Beavin, & D. D. Jackson (1967)*

Given the complex, structural nature of human situations, and their representation as images, the question now arises as to whether there is a suitably abstract formalism that can enable us to represent to ourselves the representations. The attempt to evolve these formalisms resides in the several branches of mathematics. Typically, for psychologists, some sort of elementary mathematical statistics, highly useful for the description of populations of entities having equal valence and arranged in continuous distributions of certain types, is used.

Piaget (1968) has suggested that the concept of the mathematical group is more useful than that of typical statistics for the sort of developmental structures and operations that compel his interest. Piaget claims that the group concept is useful because, unlike usual forms of abstraction, which draw out properties from things—the more general the property, the more information lost through abstraction (cf. Chaitin, 1974)—the group property conserves information about systems. It is obtained through "reflective abstraction," a method that "does not derive properties from things, but from our ways of acting on things, the operations we perform on them; from the various fundamental ways of coordinating such acts or operations—'uniting,' 'ordering,' 'placing in one-to-one correspondence.' " The external structures of action are tied to the structure of mental operations. In fact, Piaget has claimed an isomorphism between the child's most primitive notions of time, causality, and number, derived from exploratory experiences, and the most sophisticated notions of time, causality, and number held by modern scientists.

The notion of the mathematical group is also utilized by Watzlawick, Weakland, and Fisch (1974) in their analysis of frames of reference and of the types of change that transcend a given frame or system. Their analysis in *Change* adds to the group concept Russell's "Theory of Logical Types," so that the framework of group theory, which allows the representation of change in invariant systems, is complemented by the theory of types, which discusses the relationships of member to class and the "peculiar metamorphosis which is in the nature of shifts from one logical level to the next higher."

Their inquiry into the effects of paradoxical communication on change is long-standing, and Russell's own writings deal directly with paradox and the reordering of categories of the understanding. The theory of logical types is also applied to instances of what the Jungians term "enantiadromia," the sudden conversion of something into its perceived opposite. This intertwining of opposites has interesting consequences for psychotherapy and suitably ancient roots, with homolog and paradox holding principal places as both the organizers of communicative structure and as the instruments of change. And, although Russell (cited in Cronen, Johnson, & Lannaman, 1982) called his ideas "not really a theory, but a stopgap" (p. 94), and later Bateson came to reject the idea that discrete levels of organization in meaning exist in a strict hierarchy, the inquiry persists as an investigation of reflexivity in systems of social meaning: "This reflexive relationship, extending over time between the products of human action and conceptions of who we are and what the social order might be, is at the heart of the human condition" (p. 110).

We wish to deal both with the question of how to represent structures of thought or action and with the sudden transforms characteristic of human change in action and understanding. We may take structure to mean, with Piaget (1968), "the set of possible states and transformations of which the system that actually obtains is a special case." Psychotherapy deals with the conditions for change in persons, usually indexed by emotional changes. It's a commonplace of our understandings that emotions are paired: joy and sorrow, terror and rage, romantic love and disgust, etc. It's also well known that emotions are subject to sudden change, as when a joke overturns anger (cf. Douglas, 1970). Moreover, the sudden changes of action—going on a binge or a fast, religious conversion, fighting or fleeing—both are evident in our lives and are endlessly puzzling.

A mathematical formalism, catastrophe theory, invented by René Thom and extensively applied by E. C. Zeeman (1976), depicts and maps exactly "those things that change suddenly, by fits and starts." Catastrophe theory is derived from topology, a mathematics dealing with the properties of surfaces in various dimensions, "a theory of pure form" (Thurston & Weeks, 1984, p. 108). Topology is cited by Piaget (1968) as one of the three parent structures of mathematics, and psychogenetically the earliest of the three to appear (the others are algebra and lattice or network structures). Topology appeals to us intuitively as a formalism for describing human events because (following our argument thus far) those events are best described with imagery. Intuitions about complex events, as Arnheim (1969) notes in his brilliant discussion of imageless thought, "more often than not require highly abstract configurations, represented by topological and often geometrical figures in mental space." In addition, as Zeeman (1976) emphasizes, the differential calculus that expresses Newtonian and Einsteinian theories of motion, gravitation, electromagnetism, and relativity is limited to phenomena for which change is smooth and continuous. Catastrophe theory describes phenomena that are discontinuous and divergent—the actions of disequilibrium modeled by the breakdown of smooth surfaces of equilibrium.

Thom has proved that for processes controlled by no more than four factors, there are just seven elementary catastrophes. Zeeman (1976) uses catastrophe theory to map such phenomena as aggression in dogs, cathartic release from self-pity, the buckling of an elastic beam, the propagation of nerve impulses, and the behavior and treatment of anorexia nervosa. In the last, the theory has the serendipitous effect of explaining patients' own descriptions of their experiences: "The seemingly incomprehensible terms in which some anorexics describe their illness turn out to be quite logical when viewed in the framework of the catastrophe surfaces." This sort of result would be hoped for if our association of image and experience has merit.

In addition, catastrophe theory has other now-familiar correlates: First, the attractor of a system, the factor that accounts for states of static equilibrium, when it is in dynamic equilibrium "consists of the entire stable cycle of states through which the system passes." So we have a term equivalent to Piaget's "structure." The neural mechanisms of the brain form a dynamic system, the equilibrium states of which can be represented by attractors, and Thom claims that all sudden jumps possible between the simplest attractors are described by elementary catastrophes. Zeeman holds that the model is most accurate in describing the limbic system (concerned with emotion and mood) rather than the more complex activities of the cortex. So the sort of emotional events that concern psychologists can be modeled in their sudden changes, and related to corresponding functions of the brain. Finally, "the model implies the possibility of divergence, so that a small perturbation in the initial state of the system can result in a large difference in the final state." The theory may thus require conditions that will map the family therapies, which, as Haley and Hoffman (1967) note, aim for just these "small perturbations" in complex systems of human interaction.

Other correspondences also come to mind: for example, the discontinuity found in dream sequences might be seen in the light of catastrophe theory as a visual model of the inaccessible region of a catastrophe, through which the sudden change occurs. The sudden appearance of (or access to) archetypal figures in consciousness is often seen to occur when situations of great conflict or paradox obtain and the subsequent change from despair to hope is very dramatic. Metacommunications (cf. Haley, 1963), statements in relationship that communicate about the relationship, provide a reframing, or sudden shift in logical type, that sets forth strong, sudden emotion and the images that we have come to call archetypal. The associated notions of rule, image, neural representation, archetype, percept, thought, and action, and their structural transforms through homolog and paradox, may find adequate abstract expression in the power and generality of Thom's mathematical language and maps.

However, "Topology cannot actually solve equations. What it provides is a mathematical vocabulary—adjectives and nouns—that allows a set of solutions to be discussed in a general way without actually being specified" (Thurston & Weeks, 1984, p. 108). Since Thom's work, the notions of chaos, nonlinear dynamics, and self-organizing systems have become general currency in the intellectual market. Barton (1994), echoing Varela, warns against facile comparisons of neuroscience and family therapy as sciences of self-organizing structures. He suggests that while nonlinear differential equations are useful in modeling neural systems, a systems dynamic approach better models social systems. Nonlinear attractors can model psychophysiological systems but require stable, clearly delineated cycles of behavior. As always with psychological variables, the absence of stable units of measurement obviates most sorts of sophisticated mathematics based on counting.

The value of ideas from mathematics taken as enactive metaphors and hints for practice, however, is undiminished. It is intriguing that nonlinear systems are both deterministic and unpredictable and that such systems are highly sensitive to initial conditions. The implication that study of each factor in isolation will not lead to knowledge of the system as a whole is liberating, for both thought and practice. Barton (1994) cites the characteristics of self-organization that apply to psychological systems:

> a) Multiple stable states that can change suddenly when a parameter value crosses a particular threshold. b) Cyclical state changes. c) The structural coupling of component processes. d) Temporal, spatial and behavioral organization. e) Localized instabilities that can lead one part of the system to organize itself differently from another part of the system. f) Entrainment: The ability of one unit to cause other units to oscillate at a harmonically related frequency. g) Behavior that can sometimes be modeled by a system of nonlinear equations. (p. 8)

A highly modern, abstract approach to psychological systems is proposed by Greeno and the Middle School Mathematics Through Applications Project Group (1998). Their concern is to develop a scientific understanding of activity through synthesizing dynamic-systems analyses and analyses of symbolic communication and reasoning, subsuming both the behaviorist and cognitive perspectives. They plan to employ behaviorism's emphasis on activity in environments, along with cognitivity's emphasis on the informational contents of activity, symbols, and meaning.

Their situative perspective differs from earlier projects in that they understand that human skills are aspects of a person's participation in social practices: "The situative perspective offers a more general framing (than behaviorist or cognitive analyses) in which significant aspects of activity evolve in processes of co-construction and negotiation between participants and other systems in situations" (p. 14). They suggest that developing their science in relation to the social practices of inquiry will evolve thought away from assessing whether or not propositions are true and toward whether their principles are useful assumptions for practice. They note the consistency of these views with those of Dewey and other American pragmatists. A description of the intellectual terms of their project will remind readers of the concerns of White and Epston (1992) in formulating narrative psychotherapy, and also of the appeal of mathematical metaphors to psychologists:

> *This would involve analyzing processes of communication and reasoning as trajectories of dynamic systems in state spaces of meaning and understanding. Attractors would correspond to patterns of social practice in inquiry, explanation and argumentation. . . . In this view, schemata of practices would be considered as attractors in the theoretical state space of interactions that people have with each other and with material, representational and conceptual systems in their physical and social environments. . . . Schemata of a practice also include trajectories of performing to accomplish various kinds of tasks, as well as trajectories of participating in discourse, such as patterns of turn-taking that take into account the participants' various positions of status in the social arrangement that prevails. . . . Schemata of discourse also include trajectories of referential meanings that the signifiers used in discourse are about . . . trajectories of representations of events . . . and trajectories of explanations . . . (p. 13)*

This notion of a ballistics of meaning, although it might tempt some thinkers to "go ballistic," has the same wistful appeal to psychologists as did Freud's "Project for a Scientific Psychology," along with the same dif-

ficulties discussed in Chapter 4 in "Understanding Human Action." Yet
the appeal of mathematics persists, as in Dart's depiction of the orthogonality of emotions. That she has scientific and mathematical training
doubles the problem of understanding back on itself, or, as Greeno and
associates (1998) say: "It leaves open the question of whether the fundamental principles that are understood by practitioners in the organization
of their activity are the same as the fundamental principles that are
needed for a systematic theory of activity. This is a profound epistemological question" (p. 13).

End Note

This discussion of using intellectual structures to organize a recognition
of images, and through them, of lives, reminds us again of the difference
between an abstracted contemplation and an activity of engagement. The
artist Wayne Thiebaud ("A Little Weirdness," 1996) thinks of viewing art
as a physical activity, a kind of exercise:

> It has to do with empathy, with our capacity as artists and as view-
> ers to transfer our feelings. As a viewer, you've got to participate bod-
> ily when you look at a painting. A painting is a physical metaphor, an
> extension of nerves, muscles, gestures, and to grasp it you've got to
> feel yourself in it.

Our discussion is reminiscent, too, of the tension between art creation
and art criticism. Critics of art are scorned by most artists. Their descriptive and theoretical writings are felt to hold little relationship to the per-
ceptive understanding, enjoyment, and contemplation of the works of
art that are the subject of the critical essay. Consider that art criticism
stands in relation to the work of art as theories of therapy do to the individual lives they purport to describe. You may encounter the same smug
and abstracted tone in narratives of case studies as you do in descriptions of painters' efforts and achievements. As Bruner (1986) noted,
"Arguments convince one of their truth; stories [and pictures] of their
lifelikeness" (p. 11).

I do not mean to complain overmuch about critics of painting or theorists of psychotherapy. What I hoped to show was how some considera-

tions important to imagining images provide a template for the psychotherapies, and a guide to creative thinking and action as well. The meeting place of these concerns is neither in the art gallery nor in the consulting room, but rather in the common experience of dreaming, with which we began. There, in a shifting and eccentric visual space, individual minds contrive narratives of stunning complexity, impact, and emotional valence. Dreams are close in form to both creative thought and interpersonal emotional drama, and so are close to the heart of the matter in thinking about psychotherapy and about the psyche, "something on the one hand *mathematically abstract* and on the other hand *fabulous and mythological*" (Portman, 1952, p. 110).

If we ask, "But which is it?" we are led to Wittgenstein's metaphor for his own activity of thought and speech: "A philosopher has to treat a question like an illness."

> *Here we run up against a marvellous and characteristic phenomenon in philosophical investigations: . . . (we) falsely expect an explanation; while a description is the solution of the difficulty; if we fit it correctly to our treatment. If we stay with it and do not try to proceed beyond it. . . . If after a description which is a solution one still looks for an explanation, one would get no further and would only again be led back to the description. "He who finds the road sign does not look for further instruction, but rather he simply goes." (Cited in Brand, 1979, pp. 174, 257)*

Before each of us goes his or her own way, here is a final thought—a myth about evil and its place among us:

The Curiosity of Pandora

> *Great Zeus . . . in his wrath over the theft of fire from the gods, said to Prometheus: You are wiser than all of us, you rejoice that you stole fire and deceived me. This will work harm to you and to men yet to be. For they will receive from me in retaliation an evil thing in which they will all rejoice, surrounding with love their own pain.*
> *At Zeus' bidding, the craftsman-god Hephaistos modeled an innocent maiden from the earth in the image of beautiful Aphrodite. This*

female figure, ancestress of all women, was called Pandora, "rich in gifts." All the gods and goddesses adorned her with their qualities. Zeus himself gave Pandora an insatiable curiosity. Then he gave her a sealed earthen jar with the warning never to open it.

Prometheus, the defier, knew not to accept gifts from the gods. But his brother, Epimetheus, could not resist when Hermes brought Pandora. So Pandora came to live among mortals.

It wasn't long before Pandora, overcome by curiosity, opened the jar, and out swarmed all the evils that had been shut up in it. Until then, they had been unknown to humans. She clapped the lid shut, just in time to keep Hope inside, but by then the earth was aswarm with numberless evils and their sorrows. With these too came sickness and death and humans were separated from the immortal gods.
(Zweig & Abrams, 1991, p. 166)

With this myth of curiosity, knowledge, power, desire, love, suffering, and hope, we taste the bread of the moral language of our broad culture, kneaded by the Greeks and Romans and baked by the Jews and the Christians. The poet Gerard Manley Hopkins (1995) adds water to refresh us at our meal and speed us along our way:

And, for all this, nature is never spent;
There lives the dearest freshness deep down things;
And though the last lights off the black west went
Oh, morning, at the brown brink eastwards, springs
Because the Holy Ghost over the bent
World broods with warm breast and with ah! bright wings.

Appendix: A Case of Incest

Transcript of the Session

Eric: Dr. C. has told me about some of the troubles you've been having in this life, and for a young person, it sounds like there have
been quite a few.

Isabel: Yeah.

Eric: And she tells me also that she spoke with you about learning
hypnosis and using it to make things better for you. Is that right?

Isabel: Yes.

Eric: I'm kind of glad that you agreed to do this, because there is a
room of all kinds of different people here—men and women,
younger ones, older ones—and I think it will give you more of a
notion of what folks in this part of the world are like. Can I ask
you a couple of questions before we go to the hypnosis? Have
you ever been hypnotized before? Can you tell me what the
worst thing is that you expect to happen?

Isabel: (*Long pause.*) The worst thing? I would get scared and would have another one.

Eric: Okay, and what's the best thing that you know could happen?

Isabel: That it will help me.

Eric: And when the hypnosis helps you, what changes am I going to notice in how you feel or how you act?

Isabel: A little less. . . . I don't know. . . . like now I am so scared of some sort of people. I hope it's going to help me relax more and avoid getting that tension. At least, I had another one this morning, so I hope it won't happen as often as it has been recently.

Eric: And that will happen when you feel less scared inside of certain people?

Isabel: Yes.

Eric: What will I be able to see when I see that you are less scared? How will you sit, how will you speak, where will you look? Can you show me what it's going to look like when you are less scared inside?

Isabel: Well, I am relaxed, and I don't . . .

Eric: Like. . . . yeah. Well, let me see, because I will have to know what we are looking for.

Isabel: I am relaxed. I am not worried. I don't have anything to worry about. I am not worried that I might collapse like what happened to me this morning.

Eric: Yes, that will be all behind you.

Isabel: Yes. I won't worry about anything.

Eric: Sort of like hair that was cut off years ago: You never think about it.

Isabel: Yes. I will just relax, I won't worry.

Eric: Okay, and when you relax, how will it look, so I'll know? Would your head lean back? And your hands would be how?

Isabel: I won't be cold.

Eric: You'll be warm in your hands?

Isabel: Yeah.

Eric: Okay. And that warmth, I guess, will come from the inside: It won't come from anybody holding your hand?

Isabel: No: inside.

Eric: Inside is the best, isn't it?

Isabel: Yeah.

Eric: Yeah. That's the best warmth, and you don't have to worry
            about it. So your head would be leaning back, or how would it
            be when you are real relaxed here? And then your hands would
            be comfortably how? Like that? And warmer from the inside.
            And what would I notice about your expression—your face, the
            way you show your feeling?

Isabel: I won't show any fear or anything. I would probably look satis-
            fied or relaxed, not always looking up with fear.

Eric: Yes, you won't look afraid. Can you show me what that satisfied
            look will look like? And that relaxed look, so I will know when
            I see it?

Isabel: Let's say I got an A.

Eric: That looks satisfied to me. That works. Is that a. . . . ?

Isabel: (*Laughs.*) Yeah, let's say I got an A in all my subjects.

Eric: Oh! That would be nice. Can I see the satisfaction of A–? How
            would that look? That would look almost as satisfied, but not
            quite.

Isabel: Yeah.

Eric: Like that. And if your hands were real warm and satisfied, where
            would they be right now? Where would you hold them?

Isabel: I can breathe freely here, and . . .

Eric: Yes, you can. And your hands would be comfortable, or you
            could scratch your head or whatever you would care to do with
            them.

Isabel: Yeah. I can breathe freely, and my muscles aren't, you know .
            I'll just be relaxed, and my muscles won't be. . . . , you know . . .

Eric: You won't be worried. You'll just be easy.

Isabel: Yeah, like that.

Eric: If while you were relaxed like this and you were breathing freely,
            if you felt sad, how would you look? Because you can be relaxed
            and sad—I guess you know that.

Isabel: Yeah.

Eric: That's a good sad face. And if you were feeling sort of silly, how
            would that look? Yeah, if you were just sort of having fun with a
            girlfriend or something.

Isabel: Silly.

Eric: Silly. That's close. And if you were feeling angry with somebody
            else, how would that look—if you were real relaxed and angry?

Isabel: Real relaxed and angry.

Eric: Yeah. It's a little difficult, but I know you can do it.

Isabel: Forget it.

Eric: Just like, "forget it?" I like that. Now suppose you had to be more forcefully angry. Oh that's very good! Can you do it toward me, please, so I can see it? That's sort of like disgusted and angry I think.

Isabel: Yeah.

Eric: Now suppose you are just flat-out angry. Your teacher said to you, "Well, you got an A on that last test, so we are going to give you five more papers to do this afternoon in order to see if you can get a C—something totally unfair. Oh, that's excellent! I like that one a lot. Now, if you can show me that feeling a little more intensely—if it were a serious thing. Okay, I like that one, and I very much like the one where you are just too disgusted. Now, see that you can breathe deeply now. That's better—not all the way there, but it's like a B, B+ breathing. By the time you leave here you will be breathing A, A+. I knew that would please you. (*Both laugh.*) Now among your arms and legs—two arms, two legs—and your fingers and toes, which is the warmest arm right now, and which are the warmest fingers?

Isabel: They are cold.

Eric: They are cold. Both equally cold, are they?

Isabel: No, the right one's colder.

Eric: Okay, so your left is a little warmer. Are your feet as cold as your hands?

Isabel: Kind of.

Eric: Kind of. Hmmm. How about your shoulders? Are they cold also?

Isabel: No.

Eric: Those are warm.

Isabel: I have pads.

Eric: Me too. You are right: They keep your shoulders warm. Men's clothes usually didn't have those, but now they do. It's nice sometimes to be able to feel that warmth.

Isabel: Yeah.

Eric: I've noticed that sometimes, though the warmth starts out under the shoulder pad, it kind of leaks down to my arm. Can you feel that, when the warmth leaks down a little further?

Isabel: Yeah.

Eric: Can you feel that on both arms: It gets a little warmer?

Isabel: Yes.

Eric: Good. You are very good at this. Now I just want you to let it leak all the way down into your wrists, and tell me when the warm feeling gets to your wrists, okay? Just take your time and breathe nice and easy. (*Pause.*) Okay. Now the difficult part is to let it kind of leak into your hands and fingers, and you can tell me when your hands and fingers feel warmer. Just take your time, and all you have to do is breathe and let it leak down.

Isabel: (*Pause.*) A little warmer.

Eric: Okay, and let them keep getting warmer, because as you breathe they will get warmer. Now if you want to make them really warm so they are completely comfortable, as you breathe feel something very strong—anger, disgust, happiness, pleasure, sadness, anything you want. (*Long pause.*) Is it getting warmer now? Okay. Now suppose you just lean back and take a deep breath and let that feeling settle down. That's excellent. That's very, very good. That's really right in the A range, and you can be happy with that A because you did something really difficult.

Now before you learn to relax more completely, there's one other thing I'd like you to do. I am going to choose one of your hands. I am going to point to one of your hands. Okay? When I point to one of your hands you will say, "Yes," because that will be the Yes hand. And when I point to the other hand you will say, "No." Now I know you are able to say "Yes," because I can tell by how you act and speak that you were brought up to be a good girl. So I know you will say "Yes" loudly and clearly when I point to the Yes hand. I also want you to say "No" just as loudly and clearly when I point to the No hand. Is that all right? Yes it is. So you decide inside yourself which hand is to be the Yes hand and which is to be the No, and don't tell me yet because I would like to be a little surprised. And tell me when you have decided. All set? When I point, I want you to say it loud enough to jar the ears of all the men in the room. And when you say "Yes," I'd like you to say it clearly enough to draw the attention of all the women in the room. Okay? Here we go.

Isabel: Yes.

Eric: And . . .

Isabel: No.

Eric: Okay, that's good—that's about a C, and if you don't mind, we'll practice again. But first take a deep breath, and we'll take our time this time. Okay? Now if you wouldn't mind, just look at me again. That's good. Okay, are you ready to try again? Now I know how difficult this is, and I want to make sure that you feel as warm and comfortable as you can before we practice a second time. So you tell me when you are ready.

Isabel: Okay.

Eric: All set? Okay, let's try it the same way. Here we go, and and I'd like to . . .

Isabel: Are you supposed to touch me?

Eric: No, I am not supposed to touch you, not unless you want that, and I don't want to.

Isabel: Yes.

Eric: And now . . .

Isabel: No.

Eric: That's very good. That's already a B, and that was an excellent question too. You know, I've noticed a lot of doctors go around touching their patients without ever asking their permission. Have you noticed that? You'll come in and you'll be examined, someone will roll up your socks, or tap your back, or listen to your ears or something. I think it's better if they ask permission, don't you? I don't think it's right to touch people without asking. People do that with kids too, have you noticed? Little kids. They'll go up and muss their hair and stuff. My son always hated that. He'd say, "Why do they do that, Dad?" I guess they think that if you are small, they can just muss with you any way they like, but I don't think that's right, do you? I guess it takes a while until kids, what they call in English, "reach their majority," when they become of a legal age when they get the right to have their way with people. I guess in California it's something like between 18 and 21 that that happens—when you don't have to answer to adults, because you're a grownup. It's a scary time, but it's a nice time. You get to say "Yes" and "No," and people have to listen.

          So I'd like you to breathe comfortably again, feel your hands getting nice and warm and strong, and when you're warm and when you're ready, we'll do it another time. See if you can also breathe with your stomach and chest, and that you really take in a good gulp of air. That's right. Just tell me when you are ready. We'll do this just this one more time. All right. And because you are going to have a tape recording of this, I'd like you to see if you can kind of jar the tape with your "Yes" and "No." So, one more loud sound? And this time let's see if you can kind of bounce the sound off the mirror back there, okay? Let's give it what in the theater they call projection, because that's why I've had you gather all that air in your chest. Now because this is the last time I'm going to give you this test, I'm going to do one more thing to make it a little more difficult. What I'm going to do is to stand up while I point without touching you. It will be a little more difficult, but I know, because you have practiced, that you can do it. Would that be all right with you? Okay, I'll still point with this finger—it's my favorite one.

Isabel: Yes!. . . . No. No!

Eric: Excellent! That's very, very good, Isabel. Now suppose you just lean back and close your eyes, and I'm just going to talk to you. And as I talk to you, I'd like you to feel pleased with your A+ performance. I'd like you to feel pleased in your mind, and I'd like you to feel comfortable in your body, and you may be as relaxed, as comfortable, as warm, as at peace, as safe as you may be. I'd like you to listen and enjoy my words and use the words that I speak that are useful to you. And the words that are not useful to you you can leave behind here when you go out into the world again.

I was thinking, when I spoke with Dr. C. about seeing you, that in a few years my son will be your age, and I was thinking about what happened to him when he was a child: the cuts and scrapes, the fearful things. I was thinking about how when he was real little he used to have a lot of earaches, and a couple of times he got real frightened by the bigger boys at school. Now that he is 14, he is not afraid of the big boys any more, but he is a little afraid of the big girls. I expect that when he gets to be 18, he will be less afraid of the big girls and less afraid of the big boys too. And I was thinking of all the trouble and trials that a baby goes through, and a kid as a toddler goes through, and a kid as a school kid goes through, and a kid as a 10-, 11-, 12-year-old goes through, and a kid as a teenager goes through. And I guess you've taken care of some kids, and you kind of know: They get scared, they get bullied, they get hurt. It's a damned hard thing growing up.

But I started to think about all those things he'd left behind in his childhood: all those earaches, and they stopped by the time he was 3; and nightmares he used to have, and those stopped by the time he was 10; and that kind of fear of other boys and that seems to have stopped by the time he was 14. And, of course, he had measles and chicken pox and all those childhood diseases. You know, as your body changes as you grow up, it leaves behind a lot of those old childhood diseases and illnesses. Your ear canal gets wide enough that infection doesn't easily grow within. Your coordination gets good enough that you don't easily stumble and fall when you walk. Very early on you leave behind wet diapers because your body learns to control what comes in and what goes out of it. You learn to eat and swallow and to excrete. And as a girl becoming a woman, you learn about the privacy and modesty of your body. When you are a baby, anyone can pick you up, turn you over, change your clothes, feed you or not feed you. But when you are a grown woman they can't do that any more. And in between being a baby and a young woman sometimes they do and sometimes they don't. But now, and from now on, it's up to you, and you can say "Yes" and you can say "No."

Before you came into this room and began to relax deeply and warmly inside, I was asking some of the doctors how long it takes to completely outgrow certain difficulties—morning difficulties, afternoon difficulties, evening difficulties—how long it takes for the emotional system to settle in and settle down. Dr. C. is an expert on children and teenagers. She told me that it takes 15 to 20 for the emotional system to settle down strongly, comfortably, confidently. I asked Dr. S. and Dr. Z. and Dr. M. how long it takes for a grown woman to outgrow seizures and leave them behind. They told me that often a grown woman outgrows seizures—but that they stay with her childhood as a memory.

I don't know how deeply you can relax, but I am convinced you can relax comfortably, safely, strongly, and deeply, even as I speak. And when you relax completely and deeply, you are going to notice a strange and interesting effect, and I am going to describe it to you, because this strange and interesting effect is what's meant by the word "hypnosis," and when you experience this strong, strange, and interesting effect, you will know that you have succeeded in being deeply hypnotized. And it's a strange effect, so I think I ought to describe it to you so you will recognize it when you begin to experience it, in just a few minutes. And, of course, whenever you are hypnotized, when you wish, and only when you wish, when you say Yes, and only when you mean Yes, and no other time, you can experience this strange, useful, and interesting state of mind, and I am going to tell it to you.

When you are deeply hypnotized, your mind becomes clear like a very large movie screen, and no matter what you see on that screen, your body remains relaxed, strong, and comfortable. Because after all, what you see on that screen is only pictures, and you can confidently look at almost any picture, and if you don't like what you see, you can slightly turn your head, and when you turn back, of course, there will be a different image on the screen. And I will tell you why this is particularly useful. At night—in sleep—the mind acts like a large motion picture screen, throwing up images that are pleasant or fearful, and in the dream a person is transfixed and cannot turn away. But in deep hypnosis, a person is free and she can turn away. She can watch the image, or she can say "No," and turn and not watch it. And when she turn back, the mind will have produced a different image. So whether the image is pleasant or horrible, she can look or not look.

The second advantage of hypnosis, which you are about to experience, is that you can see on the screen images of the past, the present, and in a shady, shadowy kind of way, images of the future. You can look forward and perhaps see a picture on the screen of your own face smiling. You may look forward to your next good friendship and see a picture on the screen of your face smiling. You may even see and look forward to becoming friendly with a boy, and you may see a picture of your face on the screen smiling, thinking of talking to him and laughing.

I'd like you to feel comfortably warm inside, and to help you to be hypnotized, I am going to count, the way hypnotists do, from 10 to 1, so that you can enjoy the feeling of being hypnotized and so that it can begin to help you to achieve the goals that you brought to this country and the goals that you brought to this city and the goals that you brought to this room. And after I count from 10 to 1, I'm going to count from 1 to 10. When I do, you'll find your eyes slowly open. You can look around without fear, in comfort, and see the men and women in this room. And later, when you walk about in this city, you can see the men and women of this city. And wherever you go in this country, you can see the men and women of this country. Ten, nine, eight. . . . You can breathe easy, deep, that's right. Seven, six, five, four, three, two, one. That's excellent, very excellent. That's very good indeed. Now a deep breath. One, two, three, four, five, six, seven, eight, nine, ten. (*Long pause.*) Would you like to stretch a little bit, because you have been sitting still?

Isabel: (*Pause. She stretches. Laughs.*) How do you do that? I saw some weird things, funny things.

Eric: Yes, you did. How do you feel now?

Isabel: I feel good. Now I can face my father!

References

Andersen, T. (Ed.). (1991). *The reflecting team: Dialogues and dialogues about the dialogues.* New York: Norton.

Arendt, H. (1959). *The human condition.* New York: Doubleday.

Arnheim, R. (1969). *Visual thinking.* Berkeley, CA: University of California Press.

Attneave, F. (1974). How do you know? *American Psychologist, 7,* 493–499.

Bandler, R., & Grinder, J. (1975). *Patterns of the hypnotic techniques of Milton. H. Erickson, M.D.* Cupertino, CA: Meta Publications.

Barber, T. X., & Spanos, N. P. (1974). Toward a convergence in hypnosis research. *American Psychologist, 7,* 500–511.

Bargh, J. A., & Chartrand, T. L. (1999). The unbearable automaticity of being. *American Psychologist, 54,* 462–479.

Barton, S. (1994). Chaos, self-organization and psychology. *American Psychologist, 49*(1). 5–14.

Bateson, G. (1972). *Steps to an ecology of mind.* New York: Ballantine.

Bettelheim, B. (1983). *Freud and man's soul.* New York: Knopf.

Blackman, H. A. (1995, December). In unpublished symposium at his retirement (radio broadcast, CNN).

Blakeslee, S. (1995, March 21). A new theory of consciousness. *New York Times.*

Boscolo, L., Cecchin, G., Hoffman, L., & Penn, P. (1987). *Milan systemic family therapy: Conversations in theory and practice.* New York: Basic Books.

Brand, G. (1979). *The central texts of Ludwig Wittgenstein* (R. E. Innis, trans.). Oxford: Blackwell.

Brand, S. (1974). *Cybernetic frontiers.* New York: Random House.

Bruner, J. (1986). *Actual minds, possible worlds.* Cambridge, MA: Harvard University Press.

Bruner, J. (1990). *Acts of meaning.* Cambridge, MA : Harvard University Press.

Calvin, W. H. (1994). The emergence of intelligence. *Scientific American, 10,* 101–107.

Capra, F. (1975). *The Tao of physics.* Berkeley, CA: Shambala.

Carroll, L. (1946). *Alice in Wonderland and through the looking glass.* New York: Grossett & Dunlap.

Casey, E. S. (1974). Toward an archetypal imagination. *Spring,* 1–33.

Chaitin, G. J. (1974). Randomness and mathematical proof. *Scientific American, 3,* 47–52.

Chang, C.-Y. (1969). *Original teachings of Ch'an Buddhism*. New York: Random House.

Cleary, T. (1993). *Zen antics: A hundred stories of enlightenment*. Boston: Shambala.

Cronen, V. E., Johnson, K. M., & Lannaman, J. W. (1982). Paradoxes, double binds and reflexive loops: An alternative theoretical perspective. *Family Process, 21*, 91–112.

Damon, W. (1999). The moral development of children. *Scientific American, 281*, 2, 72–78.

Douglas, M. (1970). *Natural symbols*. New York: Random House.

Draenos, S. (1982). The totalitarian theme in Horkheimer and Arendt. *Salamagundi, 56*, 155–170.

Ebbinghaus, H. (1913). *Memory*. New York: Columbia University Press.

Ehrlich, E., Flexner, S. B., Carruth, G., & Hawkins, J. M. (1980). *Oxford American dictionary*. New York: Oxford University Press.

Eliade, M. (1958). *Yoga*. New York: Harper & Row.

Eliade, M. (1962). *The forge and the crucible*. New York: Harper & Row.

Eliade, M. (1963). *Myth and reality*. New York: Harper & Row.

Eliade, M. (1964). *Shamanism: Archaic techniques of ecstasy* (W. Trask, trans.). Princeton, NJ: Princeton University Press.

Eliade, M. (1969). *Images and symbols*. New York: Sheed & Ward.

Eliot T. S. (1934). *The waste land and other poems*. New York: Harcourt, Brace & World.

Epstein, J. (1998, March 5). Prophet. *New York Review of Books*, pp. 10–13.

Erickson, M. H. (1964). An hypnotic technique and its rationale and field experiments. *American Journal of Clinical Hypnosis, 7*, 4–8.

Erickson, M. H. (1980). *Collected papers of Milton H. Erickson on hypnosis* (4 vols.). E. L. Rossi, (Ed.). New York: Irvington.

Erickson, M. H. (1983) *Healing in hypnosis: The seminars, workshops and lectures of Milton H. Erickson* (4 vols.). E. L. Rossi, M. O. Ryan, & F. A. Sharp (Eds.). New York: Irvington.

Erickson, M. H., & Kubie, L. S. (1939). Permanent relief of an obsessional phobia by means of communication with an unsuspected dual personality. *Psychoanalytic Quarterly, 8*, 471–509.

Erickson, M. H., & Rossi, E. L. (1979). *Hypnotherapy: An exploratory casebook*. New York: Irvington.

Erickson, M. H., & Rossi, E. L. (1981). *Experiencing hypnosis: Therapeutic approaches to altered states*. New York: Irvington.

Erickson, M. H., & Rossi, E. L. (1989). *The February man: Evolving consciousness and identity in hypnotherapy*. New York: Brunner/Mazel.

Errington, F. K., & Gewertz, D. (1990). *Cultural alternatives and a feminist anthropology*. Cambridge, England: Cambridge University Press.

Errington, F. K., & Gewertz, D. (1995). *Articulating change in the last unknown*. Boulder, CO: Westview.

Evans-Wentz, W. Y. (1927). *The Tibetan book of the dead*. London: Oxford University Press.

Ezrahi, Y. (1995). The theatrics and mechanics of action: The theater and the machine as political metaphors. *Social Research, 62* (2), 298 ff.

Feynman, R. (1965) *The character of physical law*. Cambridge, MA: MIT Press.

Finke, R. A. (1986). Mental imagery and the visual system. *Scientific American, 3*, 88–96.

Flew, A. (1954). Psychoanalytic explanations. In N. MacDonald (Ed.), *Philosophy and analysis*. Oxford: Blackwell.

Foucault, M. (1980). *Power/knowledge: Selected interviews and other writings*. New York: Pantheon.

Frazer, J. G. (1922). *The golden bough*. New York: Macmillan.

Freud, S. (1911/1959). Psychoanalytic notes upon an autobiographical account of a case of paranoia. *Collected papers*, vol. III, J. Strachey & A. Strachey, (trans.). New York: Basic Books.

Freud, S. (1913). On beginning the treatment. In A. Freud, A. Strachey, J. Strachey, & A. Tyson (trans. and Eds.) (1953–1974). *Standard edition of the complete psychological works of Sigmund Freud*, vol. 12 (pp. 134–136). New York: Macmillan.

Freud, S. (1930). *Civilization and its discontents*. J. Strachey (trans. and Ed.). New York: Cape & Smith.

Freud, S. (1935). *An autobiographical study*. New York: Norton

Freud, S. (1965) *New introductory lectures in psychoanalysis 31*, J. Strachey (trans. and Ed.). New York: Norton.

Furman, B., & Ahola, T. (1992). *Solution talk: Hosting therapeutic conversations*. New York: Norton.

Gardner, H. (1973). *The quest for mind*. New York: Knopf.

Gawande, A. (1998, September 21). The pain perplex. *New Yorker Magazine*, pp. 86–94.

Geertz, C. (1983). *Local knowledge*. New York: Basic Books.

Geertz, C. (1995). *After the fact: Two countries, four decades, one anthropologist*. Cambridge, MA: Harvard University.

Gentner, D., & Markman, A.B. (1997). Structure mapping in analogy and similarity. *American Psychologist, 52*, 45–56.

Gilbert, D. T. (1991) How mental systems believe. *American Psychologist, 53*, 429–439.

Ginott, H. (1965). *Between parent and child*. New York: Macmillan.

Goffman, E. (1967). *Interaction ritual: Essays on face-to-face behavior*. New York: Doubleday.

Goleman, D. (1991, October). Not-so-fleeting moods. *New York Times*, pp. D1, D7.

Gollwitzer, P. M. (1999). Implementation intentions: Strong effects of simple plans. *American Psychologist, 54*, 493–503.

Gone, J. P. (1998). So, are you a full blood? Sovereignty, status and the quest for an authentic Indian identity. Unpublished manuscript.

Gonsiorek, J., (Ed). (1995). *Breach of trust.* Thousand Oaks, CA: Sage.

Greenleaf, E. (1969a). Developmental-stage regression through hypnosis. *American Journal of Cinical Hypnosis, 12,* 20–36.

Greenleaf, E. (1969b). The Schreber case: Remarks on psychoanalytic explanation. *Psychotherapy: Theory, Research, Practice, 6,* 16–20.

Greenleaf, E. (1971). The red house: Hypnotherapy of hysterical blindness. *American Journal of Clinical Hypnosis, 13,* 155–161.

Greenleaf, E. (1973). Senoi dream groups. *Psychotherapy: Theory, Research, Practice, 10* (3), 218–222.

Greenleaf, E. (1974). Defining hypnosis during hypnotherapy. *International Journal of Clinical and Experimental Hypnosis, 22,* 120–130.

Greenleaf, E. (1975). The unconscious-mind mirror in active imagination. *Psychotherapy: Theory, Research, Practice, 12,* 202–206.

Greenleaf, E. (1978). Active imagining. In J. Singer & K. S. Pope (Eds.), *The power of human imagination: New methods in psychotherapy,* New York: Plenum.

Greenleaf, E. (1980). Senoi dream group therapy. In R. Herink (Ed.), *The psychotherapy handbook.* New York: New American Library.

Greenleaf, E. (1985). Conjoint hypnotherapy with an imagined co-therapist (pp. 507–514). In J. K. Zeig (Ed.), *Ericksonian psychotherapy, vol. III: Clinical applications.* New York: Brunner/Mazel.

Greenleaf, E. (1986). What to do when a patient falls asleep in hypnosis. In B. Zilbergeld, M. G. Edelstien, & D. L. Araoz (Eds.), *Hypnosis questions and answers.* New York: Norton.

Greenleaf, E. (1990) Suggestions to facilitate revivification. In D. C. Hammond (Ed.), *Handbook of hypnotic suggestions and metaphors.* New York: Norton.

Greenleaf, E. (1992, April). In the dream incubator of hypnotherapy. *i to i.*

Greenleaf, E. (1993). Case report: Isabel. *The Milton H. Erickson Foundation Newsletter, 13* (3).

Greenleaf, E. (1994a). Dreams: Strolling the royal road (videotape). Presented at the *Sixth International Congress on Ericksonian Approaches to Hypnosis and Psychotherapy.*

Greenleaf, E. (1994b). On the social nature of the unconscious mind: Pearson's brick, Wood's break and Greenleaf's blow, In S. R. Lankton & J. K. Zeig (Eds.), *Ericksonian monographs no. 10: Difficult contexts for therapy.* New York: Brunner/Mazel.

Greenleaf, E. (1994c). Solving the unknown problem (pp. 265–275). In M. F. Hoyt (Ed.), *Constructive therapies.* New York: Guilford.

Greenleaf, E. (1997). Locus and communication. *Journal of Systemic Therapies, 16* (2), 145–158.

Greenleaf, E. (2000). Transference/countertransference. In J. K. Zeig & B. B. Geary (Eds.), *Clinical handbook of Ericksonian hypnosis and psychotherapy.* Phoenix, AZ: Zeig, Tucker.

Greenleaf, E., & Dyckman, J. M. (1992). Review of repression and dissociation:

Implications for personality theory, psychopathology and health. *Imagination, Cognition and Personality, 2,* 106–114.

Greenleaf, E., & McCartney, L. R. (1975) Discussions with Irene: An unsuspected dual personality encountered while working with dream images. Unpublished manuscript.

Greeno, J. G., & Middle School Mathematics Through Applications Project Group (1998). The situativity of knowing, learning and research. *American Psychologist, 53*(1), 5–26.

Guggenbuhl-Craig, A. (1970). Must analysis fail through its destructive aspect? *Spring,* 133–145.

Haley, J. (1963). *Strategies of psychotherapy.* New York: Grune & Stratton.

Haley, J. (Ed.), (1967). *Selected papers of Milton Erickson, M.D.: Advanced techniques of hypnosis and therapy.* New York: Grune & Stratton.

Haley, J. (1973). *Uncommon therapy: The psychiatric techniques of Milton H. Erickson, M.D.* New York: Norton.

Haley, J. (1981). *Reflections on therapy and other essays.* Chevy Chase, MD: Family Therapy Institute of Washington, D.C.

Haley, J. (Ed.) (1985). *Conversations with Milton H. Erickson, M.D.* (3 vols.). New York: Triangle Press.

Haley, J. (1987). *Problem-solving therapy.* San Francisco: Jossey-Bass.

Haley, J. (1993). *Jay Haley on Milton H. Erickson.* New York: Brunner/Mazel.

Haley, J., & Hoffman, I. (1967). *Techniques of family therapy.* New York: Basic Books.

Havens, R. A. (Ed.) (1996). *The wisdom of Milton H. Erickson.* (2 vols.). New York: Irvington.

Hillman, J. (1973, 1974). Anima. (II) *Spring,* 113–147.

Hopkins, G. M. (1995). *Poems.* New York: Knopf.

Hull, R. F. C. (1971). Bibliographical notes on active imagination in the works of C. G. Jung. *Spring,* 115–120.

Ingber, D. E. (1998, January). The architecture of life. *Scientific American,* 48–57.

James, W. (1975) *Pragmatism.* Cambridge, MA: Harvard University Press.

Jerison, H. J. (1976). Paleoneurology and the evolution of mind. *Scientific American, 1,* 90–101

Jones, T., & Schmidt, H. (1960). *The fantasticks.* Milwaukee: Hal Leonard Publishing.

Jung, C. G. (1959). Four archetypes. In *Collected works, vol. 9,* pt. 1. Princeton NJ: Princeton University Press.

Jung, C. G. (1961). *Memories, dreams, reflections.* New York: Random House.

Jung, C. G. (1966). *The practice of psychotherapy.* Princeton N.J.: Princeton University Press.

Jung, C. G. (1968a). Alchemical studies. *Collected works, vol. 13.* Princeton, NJ.: Princeton University Press.

Jung, C. G. (1968b). Psychology and alchemy. Cited in Eliade, M. (1962), *The forge and the crucible.* New York: Harper & Row.

Jung, C. G., & Pauli, W. (1955). *The interpretation of nature and the psyche.* New York: Pantheon.

Keith, L. (1995, August). *Family Therapy News.*

Kettmann, S. (1992, May 24). Barry Bonds talk delights little leaguers. *San Francisco Chronicle.*

Kirsch, I., & Lynn, S. J. (1999). Automaticity in clinical psychology. *American Psychologist, 54,* 504–515.

Leary, D. E. (1995). Naming and knowing: Giving forms to things unknown. *Social Research, 62*(2), 267–298.

Lifton, R. J. (1969). *Death in life.* New York: Vintage Books.

"A little weirdness can help an artist gain cachet" (1996, August 23). *New York Times.*

"The long way round to Fermat" (1998). *San Francisco Chronicle.*

Madanes, C. (1990). *Sex, love and violence.* New York: Norton.

McIntosh, P. (1988) *White privilege and male privilege: A personal account.* Wellesley, MA: Wellesley College Press.

Meier, C. A. (1989). *Healing dream and ritual.* Switzerland: Daimon Verlag.

Millay, E. St. V. (1992). C. Folk (Ed.), *The harp-weaver and other poems.* New York: Harper Perennial.

Miller, A. I. (1984). *Imagery in scientific thought.* Cambridge, MA: MIT Press.

Miller, J. (1995, April 20). *New York Review of Books*

Morris, W. (Ed.) (1969). *American heritage dictionary of the English language.* New York: Houghton Mifflin.

Nagarjuna (1995). *The fundamental wisdom of the middle way.* J. L. Garfield (trans.). New York: Oxford University Press.

Nicklaus, J., & Bowden, K. (1974). *Golf my way.* New York: Simon & Schuster.

Odier, C. (1956). *Anxiety and magic thinking.* New York: International Universities Press.

Orne, M. (1962). On the social psychology of the psychological experiment: With particular reference to demand characteristics and their implications. *American Psychologist, 17,* 776–783.

Pearson, R. E. (1966). Communication and motivation. *American Journal of Hypnosis: Clinical, Experimental, Theoretical, 9* (1), 18–25.

Perls, F. (1969). *Gestalt therapy verbatim.* New York: Bantam.

Phillips, A. (1993). *On kissing, tickling and being bored.* Cambridge, MA: Harvard University Press.

Piaget, J. (1968). *Structuralism.* New York: Harper & Row.

Piaget, J. (1973). The affective unconscious and the cognitive unconscious. *Journal of the American Psychoanalytic Association. 2,* 250.

Portman, A. (1952). The significance of images in the living transformation of energy. *Eranos Yearbook.*

"Prokofiev" (1976, July 22). *San Francisco Chronicle.*

Rawson, H., & Miner, M. (Eds.) (1986). *The new international dictionary of quotations.* New York: Dutton.

Rescorla, R. A. (1988). Pavlovian conditioning: It's not what you think it is. *American Psychologist, 43* (3), 151–160.

Romanyshyn, R. (1977). Phenomenology and psychoanalysis. *Psychoanalytic Review, 64* (2), 215.

Rosen, S. (Ed.) (1982). *My voice will go with you: The teaching tales of Milton H. Erickson, M.D.* New York: Norton.

Rossi, E. L. (1996). *The symptom path to enlightenment.* Pacific Palisades, CA: Palisades Gateway.

Rossi, E. L., & Cheek, D.(1988). *Mind–body therapy: Methods of ideodynamic healing in hypnosis.* New York: Norton.

Schwartzman, J. (1982). Creativity, pathology and family structure: A cybernetic metaphor. *Family Process, 21,* 113–127.

Sechehaye, M. (1951). *Autobiography of a schizophrenic girl.* New York: Grune & Stratton.

Shepard, R. N. (1978). The mental image. *American Psychologist, 33* (2), 125–138.

Simonton, C. (1975). Belief systems and management of the emotional aspects of malignancy. *Transpersonal Psychology, 7,* 29–41.

Singer, J. L. (1974). *Imagery and daydream methods in psychotherapy and behavior modification.* New York: Academic.

Singer, J. L. (Ed.) (1990). *Repression and dissociation: Implications for personality theory, psychopathology and health.* Chicago: University of Chicago Press.

"The sky's the limit" (1997). *San Francisco Chronicle,* p. 69.

Staff (1979, September). MRI celebrates at conference. *MRI Newsletter,* 1–4.

Stafford, S. K. (1998). Unpublished manuscript.

Stanislavski, C. (1967/1926). *An actor prepares.* London: Penguin.

Stein, R. (1973). *Incest and human love.* New York: Third Press.

Stewart, J. B. (1997, November 24). Annals of crime: Professional courtesy. *New Yorker Magazine,* 90–103.

Stewart, K. (1951). Dream theory in Malaya. *Complex, 6,* 21–34.

Sullivan, H. S. (1954a). *Conceptions of modern psychiatry.* New York: Norton.

Sullivan, H. S. (1954b). *The psychiatric interview.* New York: Norton.

Sullivan, H. S. (1956). *Clinical studies in psychiatry.* New York: Norton.

Swedenborg, S. W. (1975) *The inner guide to the archetypes.* Unpublished manuscript.

Tavris, C. (1998). The paradox of gender. Review of *The two sexes: Growing up apart, coming together. Scientific American, 279* (4), 126–138.

Taylor, S. E., Pham, L. B., Rivkin, I. D., & Armor, D. A. (1998). Harnessing the imagination: Mental simulation, self-regulation and coping. *American Psychologist, 53* (4), 429–439.

Thurston, W. P., & Weeks, J. R. (1984, July). The mathematics of three-dimensional manifolds. *Scientific American,* 108–120.

Von Franz, M.-L. (1975). *C. G. Jung: His myth in our time.* New York: Putnam's.

Von Franz, M.-L., & Hillman, J. (1971). *Lectures on Jung's typology*. Zurich: Springer.

Watkins, M. (1974). The waking dream in European psychotherapy *Spring*, 33–58.

Watzlawick, P., Beavin, J. H., & Jackson, D. D. (1967). *Pragmatics of human communication*. New York: Norton.

Watzlawick, P., Weakland, J. H., & Fisch, R. (1974). *Change: Principles of problem formation and problem resolution*. New York: Norton.

Weaver, R. (1973). *The old wise woman: A study of active imagination*. New York: Putnam's.

White, M. (1998). *Remembering, definitional ceremony and rich description*. Adelaide, Australia: Dulwich Centre Publications.

White, M., & Epston, D. (1990). *Narrative means to therapeutic ends*. New York: Norton.

White, M., & Epston, D. (1992). *Experience, contradiction, narrative and imagination: Selected papers of David Epston and Michael White, 1989–91*. Adelaide, Australia: Dulwich Centre Publications.

Whorf, R. L. (1956). *Language, thought and reality: Selected writings*. Cambridge, MA: MIT Press.

Winch, P. (1958). *The idea of a social science*. London: Routledge & Kegan Paul.

Winnicott, D. W. (1965). *The maturational processes and the facilitating environment*. London: Hogarth.

Wittgenstein, L. (1958). *The "blue" and "brown" books*. New York: Harper & Row.

Zeeman, E. C. (1976). Catastrophe theory. *Scientific American, 3*, 65–83.

Zeig, J. K. (Ed.) (1982). *Ericksonian approaches to hypnosis and psychotherapy*. New York: Brunner/Mazel.

Zimmer, H. (1960). On the significance of the Indian Tantric Yoga. *Papers from the Eranos Yearbooks, 4*, 3–58.

Zucker, H. (1967). *Problems of psychotherapy*. New York: Free Press.

Zweig, C., & Abrams, J. (Eds.) (1991). *Meeting the shadow: The hidden power of the dark side of human nature*. New York: Putnam's.

Index

Jones, T., 115

Jung, C. G., 6, 10, 35, 43, 59–60, 97, 169, 196, 241, 243, 244, 247, 248, 249, 251, 264

Jungian psychotherapy, 20

Kali Yuga, 244–245

Keith, L., 43

Kekule, August, 18

Kettman, S., 134

"Kill the Children" case, 93–95

Kirsch, I., 262–264

"Knife in the Heart, A" therapy sessions, 111–113

Knowledge through action, 209–215

Kuhn, Thomas, 180, 181

"Lady of the Lake, The" class, 216–233

Language

images and the structure of thought and, 252–258

metaphorical, 43–44, 57–67, 246

sensory-perceptive vs. communicative function of, 254–256

of therapeutic communications, 43–44, 74–76, 109

See also Narrative of images

Lannaman, J. W., 265

"Leaning Forward" intervention, 94–95

Learning, ways of, 41–42

"Learning-to-live" therapy, 94

Leary, D. E., 180, 181

Lectures on Jung's Typology, 243

"Lethality and Legality" intervention, 94

Locke, J., xvii

Locus:

cooperative conversations and, 85–87

externalizing conversations and, 200

meaning and, 87–89

misplaced, and relational solutions, 89–109

structure and, 88–89

struggle over, 85

Logical types, Theory of, 265

Lynn, S. J., 262–264

Maccoby, Eleanor, 91

Madanes, Chloe, 90

Mathematical group, 264–266

Mathematics, 17–18, 264–270

McCartney, L. R., 20–36

McGwire, Mark, 17

McIntosh, P., 91

Meaning:

authoritative, 87

ballistics of, 269–270

connection with imagery and action, 251–256

dream, dream action and, 13–16

locus and, 87–88

in situative therapy, 193

Meier, C. A., 1

Meissner, Reinhold, 181

Melzack, 196

Mental simulation, 259–260

Mesmer, Franz, 39–40

Metacommunications, 267

Metaphorical communication, 43–44, 57–67, 246

See also Narrative of images

Middle School Mathematics Through Applications Project Group, 268–269